INSIGHT GUIDE

ALASKA

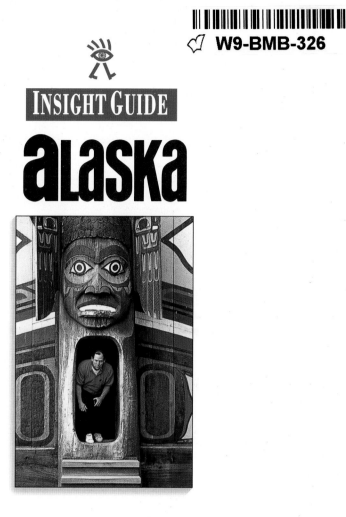

DISCOVERY CHANNEL

APA PUBLICATIONS

Part of the Langenscheidt Publishing Group

ABOUT THIS BOOK

Editorial
Project Editor
Pam Barrett
Editorial Director
Brian Bell

Distribution

UK & Ireland
GeoCenter International Ltd
The Viables Centre, Harrow Way
Basingstoke, Hants RG22 4BJ
Fax: (44) 1256 817988

United States
Langenscheidt Publishers, Inc.
46–35 54th Road, Maspeth, NY 11378
Fax: (1) 718 784-0640

Canada
Thomas Allen & Son Ltd
390 Steelcase Road East
Markham, Ontario L3R 1G2
Fax: (1) 905 475-6747

Australia
Universal Press
1 Waterloo Road
Macquarie Park, NSW 2113
Fax: (61) 2 9888-9074

New Zealand
Hema Maps New Zealand Ltd (HNZ)
Unit D, 24 Ra ORA Drive
East Tamaki, Auckland
Fax: (64) 9 273-6479

Worldwide
**Apa Publications GmbH & Co.
Verlag KG (Singapore branch)**
38 Joo Koon Road, Singapore 628990
Tel: (65) 865-1600. Fax: (65) 861-6438

Printing

Insight Print Services (Pte) Ltd
38 Joo Koon Road, Singapore 628990
Tel: (65) 865-1600. Fax: (65) 861-6438

©2001 Apa Publications GmbH & Co.
Verlag KG (Singapore branch)
All Rights Reserved
First Edition 1985
Fifth Edition 1998, revised 1999
Reprinted 2000, 2001

CONTACTING THE EDITORS
We would appreciate it if readers
would alert us to errors or out-
dated information by writing to:
**Insight Guides, P.O. Box 7910,
London SE1 1WE, England.
Fax: (44) 20 7403-0290.
insight@apaguide.demon.co.uk**

This guidebook combines the interests and enthusiasms of two of the world's best known information providers: Insight Guides, whose titles have set the standard for visual travel guides since 1970, and Discovery Channel, the world's premier source of non-fiction television programming.

The editors of Insight Guides provide both practical advice and general understanding about a destination's history, culture, institutions and people. Discovery Channel and its popular website, www.discovery.com, help millions of viewers explore their world from the comfort of their own home and also encourage them to explore it first-hand.

Like all Insight Guides, this book is the work of many hands. Alaska is too vast and too diverse for any one person to know every aspect of it, but the team of expert writers and photographers assembled here bring to bear a formidable expertise.

How to use this book
The book is structured to convey an understanding of Alaska's people and culture, and guides readers through its destinations.:

◆ To understand Alaska today, you need to know something about its past. Therefore, the first section of the guide covers the state's history and varied cultures in lively, informative essays.

EXPLORE YOUR WORLD
Discovery CHANNEL

◆ The main Places section provides a complete run-down of all the places worth seeing. The main sites of interest are coordinated by number with full-color maps.

◆ The Travel Tips listings section provides information on travel, outdoor activities, specialist tour operators, hotels, restaurants and festivals. Information may be located quickly by using the index printed on the back cover flap – and the flaps themselves are designed to serve as bookmarks.

The contributors

This new edition was edited by **Pam Barrett** and builds on the original edition produced by **Janie Freeburg** and **Diana Ackland**, under the editorial direction of **Brian Bell**.

The editors sought out writers with the ideal combination of affection for, and detachment from, their specialist subject.

Bill Bjork and **Debby Drong-Bjork**, who wrote the chapters on Fairbanks and the Interior, are native Minnesotans who have both worked as teachers in a remote Athabascan village; **Mike Miller**, who contributed his inside knowledge of Juneau, Misty Fjords National Monument and the Panhandle communities, is a member of the State House of Representatives; **Jeff Brady**, who wrote the Skagway chapter, is the editor and publisher of the *Skagway News*. **Kris Capps**, who here writes about Alaska's Native villages and artifacts, is a resident of Denali National Park.

Among those who have written about Alaska's national parks are **Leslie Barber**, a member of the Citizens' Advisory Commission on Public Lands; **Rick McIntyre**, a naturalist and park ranger at Denali; **Bill Sherwonit**, who spent many summers at Wrangell-St Elias, and **Diane Brady**, a commercial pilot for an air taxi service.

Other contributors to the guide included **Chris Blackburn**, **Chris Carson**, **Kathy Hunter**, **Katy Korbel**, **Kyle Lochalsh**, **Gloria Maschmeyer** and **Mark Skok**.

This edition was ably updated by **Natalie Phillips**, a journalist who covers resource issues for the *Anchorage Daily News*, who also overhauled the Travel Tips section.

Among the many talented photographers who have contributed to this edition of the book are **Brian** and **Cherry Alexander**, **Bill Sherwonit**, **Jeff Shultz** and **Harry Walker**. Picture research was by **Hilary Genin**.

Map Legend

‒‒ ‐‐	International Boundary
‐‐‐‐	State Boundary
⊖	Border Crossing
•‐•‐	National Park/ Nature Reserve
‐‐‐‐	Ferry Route
✈	Airport
🚌	Bus Station
P	Parking
ℹ	Tourist Information
✉	Post Office
✝ ☩ ♂	Church/Ruins
♦ ♂	Castle/Ruins
∴	Archaeological Site
∩	Cave
★	Place of Interest

The main places of interest in the Places section are coordinated by number (e.g. ❶) with a full-color map, and a symbol at the top of every right-hand page tells you where to find the map.

CONTENTS

Maps

Glacial splendor

Travel Tips

THE LAST FRONTIER

It is often said that there are no more frontiers to explore.

Alaska is the great exception

Alaska: the Great Land, the Last Frontier – more than 580,000 sq. miles (1½ million sq. km) that taunted early explorers and still defies modern-day researchers, while exerting a fascination which attracts more and more travelers looking for something which a conventional vacation cannot give them. The hint of urban sophistication in Anchorage and Juneau rapidly gives way to the frontier, where outdoor survival skills are among the most useful attributes a resident can possess.

Alaska has lush rain-drenched forests and barren windswept tundras. There are lofty mountains, still-active volcanoes, and spectacular glaciers, as well as three million lakes and endless swamps. Along with a handful of modern high-rise buildings there are countless one-room log cabins. Within hours of dining sumptuously in a first-class restaurant it is possible to tread on ground that has never known a human footprint: ground belonging to the grizzly bear and the wolf and shared only reluctantly with human beings.

This varied land is best viewed from a light plane or surveyed from a canoe; it cannot be seen properly from a car (although increasing numbers of people are experiencing parts of the state by traveling the highways), and it would take forever to cover on foot. Alaska is an outdoor world, a wilderness, a land of many faces, few of which can be explored by moving from hotel to hotel.

The Alaskan experience includes the sheer wonder of finding what hides beyond the horizon or over the next ridge. No one person has ever seen it all; no one person ever will. Therein lies the essence of Alaska. Something new, something different and something very rare always waits around the next bend in the river or twist in the trail. Only those who have looked upon Alaska, however briefly, can appreciate its fierce and unforgiving majesty. ❑

PRECEDING PAGES: Mount Brooks; a living glacier at Tracy Arm; Prince of Wales Island; a summer hiker in Gates of the Arctic National Park.
LEFT: releasing a radio-tagged eagle.

NDARY LINE ON CHILKOOT PASS

Decisive Dates

EARLY ALASKANS

30–10,000BC

Migration of tribes from Asia across a land bridge which then linked Siberia and Alaska.

10,000BC

The Aleuts settled in the Aleutian Islands. The name Alaska came from their word "Alaxsxag" meaning "the object toward which the action of the sea is directed." Other tribes dispersed throughout North and South America but the Aleuts, the

A CHILCAT MAN.
From a Drawing by Mrs. Willard.
The buckskin suit is trimmed with fur and quills. The narrow snow-shoe is used in hunting and running, and the broad one in packing.

Eskimos (Inupiats and Yup'iks) and the Indians, which included the Athabascans and the coastal Tlingits and Haidas, settled in Alaska.

THE RUSSIAN INVASION

1741 First Russian ships arrive. Vitus Bering turned back and died before he could reach home, but Alexei Chirikof landed on Prince William Island. The fur trade was established, and the Natives forced to hunt on the Russians' behalf.

1778 Captain James Cook visited the Aleutian Islands. His visit was brief but prompted English interest in the fur trade.

1784 Grigor Ivanovich Shelikof arrived on Kodiak Island. He enslaved and ill treated the Natives,

then set up the first permanent Russian settlement on Three Saints Bay where he built a school and introduced the Russian Orthodox religion.

1790 Alexander Baranof took over the fur enterprise. He treated the Natives more humanely than his precessors had, and moved the Russian colony to the site of the present city of Kodiak.

1802 The Tlingits razed to the ground the Russian town of Mikhailovsk, built near the site of present-day Sitka on land they had sold to Baranof.

1799 The Russian-American Company was formed.

1812 Russia reached a settlement with America over hunting rights in Alaska.

1833 The British Hudson's Bay Company established a fur-trading outpost in Alaska.

Mid-19th century Russian power diminished. British and Americans undermined the fur monopoly and the Tlingits waged guerrilla war.

1866 A Western Union expedition under William H. Dall produced the first scientific studies of Alaska and the first map of the Yukon River.

AMERICA TAKES OVER

1867 US Congress, at the instigation of Secretary of State William Seward, bought Alaska from the Russians for $7.2 million.

1870s–80s Fish canneries established around Nushagak Bay to exploit the huge runs of salmon. In the Aleutians fur seals and otters were slaughtered ruthlessly. Whalers pursued their quarries to the high Arctic.

THE GOLD RUSH

1880 Gold was discovered at Silver Bow Basin, and the town of Juneau was founded.

1882 The Treadwell Mine, across the Gastineau Channel from Juneau, flourished and the town of Douglas grew up.

1896 Gold was discovered in the Klondike, a tributary of the Yukon, and the easiest route to it was by ship to Skagway. The White Pass and Chilkoot Trail to the gold fields were tackled by thousands and Skagway became a thriving center.

1899 Gold was discovered at Nome in the far northwest and many prospectors who had been unsuccessful in the Yukon moved west to try again.

1902 Felix Pedro struck gold in the Tanana Hills.

1903 The town of Fairbanks, near the strike, was founded on the site of a trading post set up by entrepreneur E.T. Barnette and named for a senator who had given him financial support.

early-1900s Prospectors flocked to Alaska from all over North America and Europe.

1910 Kennicott, the riches copper mine in the world, started operations in the Wrangell-St Elias mountains.

WORLD WAR II

1942 The Alaska Highway (the Alcan) was constructed in under nine months as both a means of defense and an overland supply route to America's Russian allies, after sea routes were cut off following the Japanese attack on Pearl Harbor. The Japanese landed on the islands of Kiska and Attu. The villagers were interned in Japan for the remainder of the war. Aleuts living in the Pribilofs and Aleutian Islands' villages were evacuated.

1964 The Good Friday earthquake hit South Central Alaska. Over 100 people were killed, mostly by tidal waves. Valdez, Seward, Cordova and Kodiak suffered the worst effects.

1968 Oil discovered at Prudhoe Bay.

1971 The Alaska Native Claims Settlement Act gave Natives title to 44 million acres (18 million hectares) of land, and $963 million, distributed among specially formed Native corporations.

1971–77 The construction of the trans-Alaska pipeline to Valdez created thousands of jobs and transformed Anchorage and Fairbanks into bright, modern cities.

1977 The trans-Alaska pipeline was completed. Oil

DOG-DRIVING NEAR THE VESOLIA SOPKA.

1943 After a two-week battle the Americans retook Attu in May. In July the Americans bombed Kiska and the Japanese retreated on transport ships under cover of fog.

STATEHOOD AND OIL

1957 Oil is discovered at the Swanson River on the Kenai Peninsula.

1959 Alaska became the 49th US state in January, a few months before Hawaii joined the Union.

PRECEDING PAGES: boundary line on the Chilkoot Pass.

ABOVE LEFT: traditional Native footwear.

ABOVE: an early dog-sled team.

began to flow and the state economy boomed, with most communities benefitting from oil revenue.

1976 The Alaska Permanent Fund was created to ensure long-term benefits from oil revenues.

1989 The *Exxon Valdez* tanker spilled 11 million gallons (42 million liters) of oil into Prince William Sound. A huge clean-up operation was launched.

1990s The ecosystem of Prince William Sound recovered, although long-term effects are not fully known. Decline in production at Prudhoe Bay led to lay-offs and the realization that the oil would not last for ever. Low-impact ecotourism flourished, with a consensus by government, industry and residents that Alaska's beauty and resources must be preserved for future generations.

THE FIRST ALASKANS

Alaska was inhabited for thousands of years by a variety of native groups, each with their own culture and language

Despite its rugged appearance, Alaska is a young country, geologically speaking. Composed of fragments of the earth's crust that rafted from the Pacific area on the backs of crustal plates and then "docked" together, the entire region is still in the process of coming together.

Its youth and place on the globe are responsible for much of Alaska's diversity. America's largest state has arctic tundra, 5,000 glaciers, icefields, four mountain ranges, broad valleys, immense forests, active volcanoes, 12 major river systems, three million lakes and countless islands.

Alaska covers more than twice the land area of its closest competitor, Texas, and it has 33,900 miles (54,500 km) of sea coast – 50 percent more than the contiguous United States. With all this land mass, it's not surprising that Alaska has six distinct geographic areas.

Arctic Alaska stretches north from the southern edge of the Brooks Range to the Arctic Ocean. It contains huge stretches of tundra that flower spectacularly in the night-less summer. Average mid-summer temperature is 40°F (4°C), while the mid-winter temperatures reach -17°F (-26°C). The area's minimal rainfall of 5 inches (13 cm) a year qualifies it as a desert.

Southeast Alaska (also known as the Panhandle) is a narrow, 400-mile (640-km) strip of land sandwiched between the Pacific Ocean and Canada, and cut off from the rest of Alaska by the towering St Elias range. The Southeast is covered by huge forests nurtured by the region's mild climate: readings of 60° or 70°F (15° or 21°C) are not uncommon in the summer, and in the winter the mercury does not often dip below -10°F (-12°C).

Southcentral Alaska lies along the Gulf of Alaska. A region of mountains, fjords and lakes, it includes Prince William Sound, the Kenai Peninsula, Cook Inlet and Kodiak Island, as well as the fertile Matanuska Valley. Temperatures vary from -20°F (-29°C) in winter to 60°F (15°C) in the summer.

Southwest Alaska is the home of the Aleutian Islands, which stretch 200 miles (320 km) west into the Bering Sea. A warm current from Japan meets the icy northern air over the Aleutians, creating the rain and fog that enshroud them. Temperatures on the islands range from 0°F (-17°C) in winter to 50–60°F (10–15°C) in summer.

Alaska's Interior is a broad lowland cradled between the Brooks and Alaska mountain ranges. Within the Interior are the mighty Yukon, Tanana and Kuskokwim rivers. In some areas, birch and spruce thrive; others support only vast reaches of tundra. Temperatures here can drop to below -50°F (-45°C) in winter and climb to 70–80°F (21–26°C) in the summer.

Western Alaska and the Bering Sea coast stretch from the Arctic Circle down to Bristol Bay. Much of the land is treeless tundra underlain with permafrost; the Yukon and Kuskokwim rivers flow through this harsh land on the final leg of their journey to the sea. Temperatures in this region range from 0°F (-17°C) in the winter (with frigid wind-chill factors) to 60°F (15°C) in the summer.

MAJESTIC MCKINLEY

The highest mountain in North America is Alaska's Mount McKinley (also known as Denali) at 20,320 feet (6,195 meters).

The Alaska Natives

Who were the people who first thrived in such an unforgiving environment? Anthropologists believe the ancestors of the Alaska Natives migrated in three waves over a land bridge which joined Siberia and Alaska thousands of years ago.

When Europeans first encountered Alaska Natives in the early 18th century, there were dozens of tribes and language groups throughout the region, from the Inupiat Eskimos in the Arctic region to the Tlingits in the Southeast. Today, these early Alaskans are divided into

---

LEFT: a true Alaska Native.

several main groups: the southeastern Coastal Indians (the Tlingits and Haidas), the Athabascans (also Indians), the Aleuts, and the two groups of Eskimos: Inupiat and Yup'ik.

The Coastal Indians

These were probably in the first wave of immigrants to cross the land bridge although many of them initially settled in Canada. Of this group the Tlingits were the most numerous; they claimed most of the coastal Panhandle, leaving only a small southern portion to the less populous Haidas. (In the late 1800s they were joined by the Tsimshian, Coastal Indians who emigrated from Canada to Annette Island off the southeastern coast.)

The Tlingits were excellent navigators, and were known to travel more than 1,000 miles (1,600 km) south to trade with Native peoples in the Pacific Northwest. The standard of currency was "blanket value," based on blankets made of cedar bark, dog and goat hair.

The Coastal Indians had great respect for the natural world, which provided them with all they needed. They believed that fish and animals gave themselves willingly to humans, and strove to acknowledge and honor that sacrifice. A bear killed for meat might be brought to the

habitans des îles Aléoutiennes.

Coastal Culture

The mild climate and plentiful resources of the Panhandle allowed the Coastal Indians to develop a rich culture. They had leisure time to devote to social pastimes, travel and trade. They enjoyed ceremony and drama, and the traditional recitation of family histories and bloodlines kept an accurate account of the generations. The painted designs developed by the Coastal tribes feature fish and animals, often in bold patterns of black and red. They decorated their crafted goods: domestic utensils, clothing, masks, canoes, ritual objects and the characteristic totems that marked family residences.

house, greeted with a welcome speech and placed in a seat of honor for a day or two. The bones of a consumed salmon were always returned to the river where it had been caught, to allow for reincarnation. Great care was taken to return all the bones, or else the fish would return deformed.

The Coastal Indians lived in a capitalist society that allowed private ownership. Each household owned economic goods, such as weapons, utensils and clothing, anything they had made themselves, while the clan owned religious titles and objects – for example, the right to perform a certain dance or practice a profession such as seal hunting.

In the social organization of the Tlingits and Haidas, status was determined by wealth. To maintain position, a person of power demonstrated wealth by giving a ceremonial potlatch when he would give away, destroy or invite guests to consume all his food and possessions. Those who received goods at one potlatch had to reciprocate and better their host in the future. Another important feature of the potlatch was the recitation of family histories and bloodlines.

The Athabascans

The Athabascan Indians of Alaska's harsh Interior were hunters and inland fishermen. Most

tant, and the Athabascans designed extremely efficient snowshoes made of birch.

Some Athabascan groups inhabited permanent winter villages and summer fishing camps. Most bands consisted of a few nuclear families, and had limited internal organization. Leadership was acquired by great warriors or hunters.

Athabascans also gave potlatches for a variety of reasons: to mark a death, to celebrate a child's first successful hunt, as a prelude to marriage. Those who aspired to leadership were expected to host especially memorable potlatches, at which the would-be leader would give away all his possessions then prove his

lived in small nomadic bands along the region's rivers. They traveled for days without food and existed in temperatures of -50°F (-45°C) or less without shelter or fire. Endurance and physical strength were prized; game was often run down on foot over difficult terrain.

Athabascans hunted salmon, rabbits, caribou and bear with the help of snares, clubs, and bows and arrows. But despite their inventive hunting methods periods of famine were not uncommon. Because they were semi-nomadic and hunted on foot, footwear was very impor-

LEFT: Natives from the Aleutian Islands.
ABOVE: young women in their best furs.

prowess by providing for himself and his family for an entire year without outside help.

The Athabascans used birch from the vast Interior forests to make canoes, containers, sleds and even cradles. Clothing was of animal hides, decorated with porcupine quills colored with plant dyes.

The Aleuts

This group settled the windswept islands of the Aleutian chain some 10,000 years ago. Although their location allowed them to harvest the sea's bounty, they also had to contend with unpredictable weather, as well as earthquakes.

Aleut fishing technology included fish spears,

weirs, nets, hooks and lines. Various darts and nets were used to obtain sea lions and sea otters. Whales were usually killed with a poisoned, stone-bladed lance. The job of women and children was to gather shellfish along the beaches at low tide.

Aleut society was divided into three categories: honorables (usually respected whalers), common people and slaves. At death the body of an honorable was mummified, and sometimes slaves were killed in honor of the deceased. The one- and two-man skin boats

NAMING ALASKA

"Alaska" comes from the Aleut "Alaxsxag," which means "the object toward which the action of the sea is directed."

Because of a ready supply of grass in the summer, Aleut women became skillful at basketry – their baskets were so closely woven that they could even hold water. Mats and some kinds of clothing were also made in this way.

The Eskimos

Eskimos, the Native group most familiar to non-Alaskans, were originally divided into two sub-groups. The Inupiat Eskimos settled in Alaska's Arctic region, while the Yup'ik lived in the west. For both groups, but for the Inupiat on the harsh Arctic

used by the Aleuts were called "bidarkas" by the Russians. Because of their dependence on the sea, Aleuts seldom went over a mile inland, but they did develop a clever method of transportation over snow. Their skis were made by drying hair-seal skins over wooden frames. When the traveler went uphill the hair would dig into the snow and act as a brake; on the downhill journey the hair would lie flat to provide speed.

In winter Aleuts wore hoodless, knee-length parkas; in colder weather they added knee-length skin boots. Waterproof overgarments made from the intestines of sea lions were also worn, and this material was also fitted over the tops of their skin boats to keep the hunters dry.

coast especially, life was a constant struggle against hunger and the cold. Seasonal food was stored against future shortage and for the long dark winter; and even though his own family might be wanting, a hunter always divided a fresh kill evenly throughout the community. Status within a village was determined by hunting ability.

Eskimo village sites were chosen for availability of food sources. The Arctic coast people depended on seal, walrus and whale, while the inland Eskimos lived on a diet of caribou, birds and other small game animals. Eggs were gathered, and berries, roots and wild greens were eaten fresh, or preserved in skin containers.

The Eskimos used boats called *umiaks* to hunt larger sea animals. They also used smaller, one-man craft, called kayaks, from which come the modern boats of the same name. Both were made of a frame of wood covered with skins or hides. Sleds and dog teams were used for winter travel, and during the summer dogs were used as pack animals.

Women were skilled in basketry and sewing. They stitched and fitted waterproof garments made of animal intestine and fish skins. The Eskimos' everyday clothing of trousers, boots and coats were sewn from skins and fur, sometimes in complex geometric designs. The coats, be found in tourist shops today and is appreciated by contemporary cooks both for its beauty and its utility.

European contact

By the time the first Europeans arrived, in the 18th century, these Alaska Native groups had inhabited their respective homelands for hundreds of generations. Their lives were harsh and often difficult, but they had refined methods for hunting, for clothing themselves, and for living in harmony with the animals and environment that supported them. Then came the Russians, and everything changed. ❑

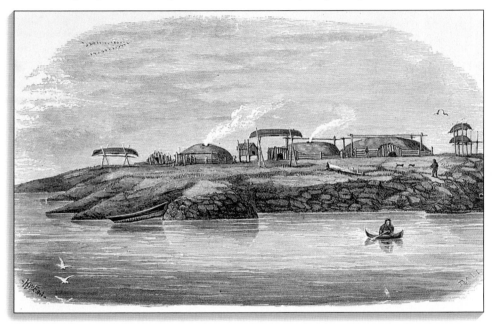

which were called parkas, featured an attached hood and ruff.

Eskimos are renowned for their fine carving, especially their small ivory pieces. In early times household utensils and weapons were beautifully ornamented. Using wood, bone, baleen (bony plates that line the mouths of baleen whales), walrus ivory and fossil mammoth tusks, Eskimos crafted dishes and knives, oil lamps, small sculptures and game pieces, and goggles to protect their eyes from the glare of snow and ice. The *ulu*, or woman's knife, can

LEFT: a *kayak* made of animal hide.
ABOVE: a Native village in the 18th century.

HARDY ANCESTORS

A recent archeological find at Barrow uncovered five members of an Eskimo (Inupiat) family in their wood and sod house. The family apparently had been crushed to death hundreds of years ago by an enormous piece of ice that must have rafted in from a stormy sea.

Autopsies performed on the bodies revealed the effects of seasonal starvation and the soot that accumulated in the dwellings were noticeable. One of the five, a 42-year-old woman, had survived bacterial pneumonia, an infection of the heart valves, arthritis, trichinosis and blood poisoning. She had also recently given birth.

THE RUSSIAN INVASION

The discovery that Alaska was rich in furs brought Russian traders here,
and changed the lives of the Native people for ever

The story of Russia's invasion of the land long inhabited by Alaska Natives begins in 1741, when two tiny vessels, the *St Peter* and the *St Paul*, captained respectively by a Dane, Vitus Bering, and a Russian, Alexei Chirikof, set sail from Russia.

The ships, two-masted crafts only 80 ft (24 meters) long, left the Siberian port of Petropavlovsk in June 1741. Six days later they lost sight of each other in a thick fog. Both commanders continued to sail east.

On July 15, Chirikof sighted land – probably the west side of Prince of Wales Island in Southeast Alaska. He sent a group of men ashore in a long boat. When the first group failed to return, he sent a second. Eerily, that group also vanished. Chirikof pulled anchor and moved on.

In the meantime, Bering and the crew of the *St Peter* sighted a towering peak on the Alaska mainland – Mount St Elias, which at 18,000 ft (5,500 meters) is second only to Mount McKinley in height. Turning westward, Bering anchored his vessel off Kayak Island while crew members went ashore to explore and find water. Georg Wilhelm Steller, the ship's naturalist, hiked briskly along the island, taking notes on plants and wildlife. Here he first recorded for science the striking blue-and-black jay which bears his name. Bering was anxious to return to Russia before bad weather came, and so turned westward, leaving the magnificent country behind him unexplored.

Chirikof and the *St Paul* returned to Siberia in October with news of the land they had found. But Bering's concern over bad weather had proved prophetic: his ship was battered by relentless storms, and in November he and his crew were forced to land on one of Russia's uninhabited Commander Islands. Bering, ill with scurvy, died on the island, and soon thereafter high winds dashed the *St Peter* to pieces. The stranded crew wintered on the island; when the weather improved the 46 survivors managed to build a crude 40-ft (12-meter) boat from the wreckage of the *St Peter* and set sail for Petropavlovsk in August 1742.

Bering's crew returned safely to Russia with sea otter pelts – soon judged to be the finest fur in the world. Spurred by the riches represented by the fur-bearing marine life and mammals

Russia threw itself wholeheartedly into setting up hunting and trading outposts.

Native contact

For the Native populations of Alaska, the coming of the Russians was an unprecedented disaster. Rather than hunting the marine life for themselves, the Russians forced the Aleut people to do the work for them. As word spread of the riches in furs to be had, competition among Russian companies increased and treatment of the Aleuts deteriorated even further, as they were forced into slavery.

Catherine the Great, who became Czarina in 1763, proclaimed goodwill toward the Aleuts

---

LEFT: Grigor Ivanovich Shelikof.
ABOVE RIGHT: the Natives were not always welcoming.

and urged her subjects to treat them fairly. But Catherine was thousands of miles away, and the hunters' all-consuming quest for furs made them disregard Aleut welfare. Hostages were taken, families split up, individuals forced to leave their villages and settle elsewhere. The Aleuts revolted that year, and won some victories, but the Russians retaliated, killing many and destroying their boats and hunting gear, leaving them with no means of survival.

Eighty percent of the Aleut population was destroyed by violence and European diseases, against which they had no defenses, during the first two generations of Russian contact.

SHELIKOF'S REVENGE

A contemporary report says that "Shelikohov (sic) loaded two bidarkas with his people ... and murdered about 500 ... If we count those who ran in fear to their bidarkas ... and drowned each other the number will exceed 500. Many were taken as prisoners of war. By order of Mr Shelikohov, the men were led to the tundra and speared, the remaining women and children, about 600 altogether, he took to the harbor and kept for three weeks. The husbands who succeeded in escaping began to come. Shelikohov returned their wives to them, but retained one child from each family as hostage."

Other Europeans

About this time, the British were continuing their search for the Northwest Passage, the fabled water route between the Atlantic and the Pacific. Captain James Cook sailed north from Vancouver Island to the Aleutians in 1778. The Russians tried to impress him with the extent of their control over the region, but Cook saw how tenuous was the position of this ragtag group of hunters and traders stationed 3,000 miles from their homeland.

Although Cook died in Hawaii after visiting Alaska, his crew continued on to Canton, China, where they sold for outlandishly high prices sea otter pelts they had obtained in Alaska. Britain became interested. Cook's expedition spurred the English to increase their sailings along the northwest coast, and they were followed by the Spanish, who were already well established on the coast of California.

Gaining a foothold

The Russians were determined to dig in and keep Alaska's fur wealth for themselves. One particularly determined individual, Grigor Ivanovich Shelikof, arrived in Three Saints Bay on Kodiak Island in 1784 with two ships, the *Three Saints* and the *St Simon*. The indigenous Koniag, wary of the foreigners, harassed the Russian party, and Shelikof responded with appalling violence, killing hundreds and taking hostages to enforce the obedience of the rest.

Having established his authority on Kodiak Island, Shelikof founded the first permanent Russian settlement in Alaska on the island's Three Saints Bay, built a school to teach the Natives to read and write Russian, and introduced the Russian Orthodox religion.

In 1790 Shelikof, back in Russia, hired Alexander Baranof to manage his Alaskan fur enterprise. Baranof moved the colony to the northeast end of Kodiak Island, where timber was available: the site is now the city of Kodiak. Russian members of the colony took Koniag wives and started families whose names continue today: Panamaroff, Petrikoff, Kvasnikoff. Baranof himself proved brilliant at managing the Russians who were the permanent hunting contingent on Kodiak Island. He also set up comparatively humane ground rules for interaction with the Koniag Natives.

In 1795 Baranof, concerned by the sight of non-Russian Europeans trading with Natives in southeast Alaska, established Mikhailovsk 6 miles (10 km) north of present-day Sitka. He bought the land from the Tlingits, but in 1802, while Baranof was away, Tlingits from a neighboring settlement, perhaps ruing their decision to allow the strangers onto their territory, attacked and destroyed Mikhailovsk. Baranof returned with a Russian warship and razed the Tlingit village. He then built the settlement of New Archangel, which became the capital of Russian America.

Meanwhile, as Baranof secured the Russians' physical presence in Alaska, the Shelikof family continued to work back in Russia to win a

Russians never fully colonized Alaska; for the most part they clung to the coast, shunning the rugged inland. And by the 1830s, the Russian monopoly on trade in the region was weakening. The Hudson's Bay Company, formed by the British in 1821, set up a post on the southern edge of Russian America in 1833. The English firm, more organized and better run than the Russian, began siphoning off trade.

Colonial powers

The Americans were also becoming a force. Baranof began to depend heavily on American supply ships, since they came much more fre-

monopoly on Alaska's fur trade. In 1799, Shelikof's son-in-law, Nikolay Petrovich Rezanov, had acquired a monopoly on the American fur trade from Czar Paul I. Rezanov then formed the Russian-American Company. As part of the deal, the Czar expected the company to establish new settlements in Alaska and carry out an expanded colonization program.

By 1804 Alexander Baranof, now manager of the Russian-American Company, had consolidated the company's hold on fur trade activities in the Americas. But despite all these efforts, the

LEFT: Captain James Cook.
ABOVE: New Archangel.

quently than Russian ones. In addition, Americans could sell furs in the Canton market, which was closed to the Russians.

The downside of the American presence was that American hunters and trappers encroached on territory the Russians considered theirs. In 1812 a settlement was reached giving the Russians exclusive rights to the fur trade above 55°N latitude, the Americans to that below. The agreement soon went by the wayside, however, and with Baranof's retirement in 1818 the Russian hold on Alaska was further weakened.

When the Russian-American Company's charter was renewed in 1821, it stipulated that the chief managers from then on be naval offi-

cers. Unfortunately, most naval officers did not have any experience in the fur trade, so the company suffered under a string of incompetent, albeit sometimes well-meaning, "governors."

The second charter also tried to cut off all contact with foreigners, especially the competitive Americans. But this strategy backfired, since the Russian colony had become used to relying on American supply ships, and America had become a valued customer for furs. Eventually the Russian-American Company entered into an agreement with the Hudson's Bay Company, which gave the British rights to sail through Russian territory.

Although the mid-1800s were not a good time for the Russians in Alaska, for those coastal Alaska Natives who had survived contact – primarily the Aleuts, Koniags and Tlingits – conditions improved.

The Tlingits were never conquered, and continued to wage guerrilla warfare on the Russians into the 1850s. The Aleuts, many of whom had been removed from their home islands and sent as far south as California to hunt sea otter for the Russians, continued to decline in population during the 1840s. For them, the naval officers of the Russian-American Company were a blessing: they established schools and hospitals for the Aleuts, and gave them jobs. Russian Orthodox clergy moved into the Aleutian Islands; Father Ivan Veniaminof, famous throughout Russian America, lived among them and developed an Aleut dictionary and grammar. Slowly, the Aleut population began to increase.

But by the 1860s the Russians were seriously considering ridding themselves of Russian America. Zealous overhunting had severely reduced the fur-bearing animal population, and competition from the British and Americans exacerbated the situation. This, combined with the difficulties of supplying and protecting such a distant colony, brought about a distinct waning of interest.

A Russian emissary approached the US Secretary of State William Henry Seward about a possible sale, and in 1867 the US Congress, at Seward's urging, agreed to buy Russian America for $7.2 million – which was just under 2 cents an acre. ❑

LEFT: William Seward (seated) and the Alaska purchase.

A NEW AMERICAN TERRITORY

America's new possession was regarded as a wild land, producing nothing but furs,

until the discovery of gold made the world sit up and take notice

America wasn't sure what, exactly, it had bought when it purchased Alaska. Vast regions remained unexplored. The interior had been little touched by the Russians, who had stayed in the coastal areas. In 1865, Western Union had decided to lay a telegraph line across Alaska to Bering Strait where it would connect with an Asian line. Robert Kennicott, part of a Western Union surveying effort, had led his crew to Nulato on the banks of the Yukon. He died the following year and William H. Dall took charge of scientific affairs. The Western Union expedition conducted the first scientific studies of the region and produced the first map of the entire Yukon River.

That same year (1866), workers finally succeeded in laying an Atlantic undersea telegraph cable, and the Alaskan overland project was abandoned. Dall returned to Alaska many times, recording and naming many geographical features. A breed of sheep and a type of porpoise bear his name.

The Alaska Commercial Company also contributed to the growing exploration of Alaska in the last decades of the 1800s, building trading posts along the Interior's many rivers. Small parties of trappers and traders entered the Interior, and, though the federal government provided little money to explore the region, Army officers would occasionally do a little reconnaissance on their own.

In a four-month journey, Lt Frederick Schwatka and his party rafted the Yukon from Lake Lindeman in Canada to Saint Michael near the river's mouth on the Bering Sea. Lt Henry T. Allen made an even more remarkable journey. In 1885 Allen and four others left the Gulf of Alaska, followed the Copper River, crossed a mountain range and traveled down the Tanana River to the Yukon, portaged to the Kanuti and then the Koyukuk rivers. Allen went up the Koyukuk, then back down to the Yukon, crossed over to Unalakleet on the coast, and

then made his way to Saint Michael, exploring about 1,500 miles (2,400 km) of Interior Alaska.

But whether the United States knew what it had or not, the territory still needed to be governed. Unfortunately, back in Washington, DC, legislators had their hands full with post-Civil War reconstruction issues, and little time to ded-

icate to Alaska. As a result, a US Army officer, General Jefferson C. Davis, was put in charge.

Gold

It was the discovery of gold in the Yukon in 1896 that finally made the United States (and the rest of the world) sit up and take notice of America's northern possession. A wave of fortune hunters clamored for passage to the Klondike. The Klondike was in Yukon Territory, Canada, not Alaska (as many would-be miners believed), but the easiest route was by ship to Skagway, in Southeast Alaska. Once in Skagway, miners had their choice of two brutal passes across the mountains to the Yukon gold

LEFT: US Secretary of State William Seward.
ABOVE RIGHT: an early supply tent.

fields: White Pass, also called Dead Horse Trail, because it was littered with corpses of pack animals, or the Chilkoot Trail, an old Native route.

Alaska, in fact, had plenty of gold of its own, and many who didn't make their fortunes in the Klondike strike came back to look for it. An earlier strike had established Juneau in Southeast Alaska, and gold was found in Nome in 1899. A combination of fortune and misfortune led to a gold strike and the birth of Fairbanks in the early 1900s. For several years a prospector called Felix Pedro had been searching in the Tanana Hills of the Interior, for a gold-rich creek he had stumbled upon years earlier but had been

forced to abandon. As the summer of 1901 drew to a close, Pedro was about to embark with his partner on a 165-mile (265-km) walk to Circle City for supplies. It was then that he met up with E.T. Barnette, who had been forced to disembark from the steamer *Lavelle Young* (*see* box below) with his entire load of supplies – some of which he was happy to sell to Pedro.

It was a match made in heaven: Pedro and his partner were delighted to be saved the long walk to Circle City, and Barnette was equally delighted to see his first customers walking out of the wilderness. Replenished with supplies, Pedro continued his search in the area, and

BARNETTE'S GAMBLE

E.T. Barnette had been trying to get thousands of dollars' worth of supplies up the Tanana River to Tanana Crossing, a point on the proposed Valdez-to-Eagle trade route. He convinced the captain of the steamer *Lavelle Young* to take him, his wife, his partner and the supplies to where the Chena River entered the Tanana. The captain agreed to take Barnette farther if he could work the *Lavelle Young* through the shallow river channel, but if not the party would be put ashore. The channel proved impassable, and that was how Barnette ended up on a slough off the main Tanana River.

finally struck gold in July 1902. Shortly afterwards Barnette's outpost was transformed into a booming town. Named Fairbanks in honor of a US senator, the settlement grew as more miners and new businesses arrived. Public services, libraries and hospitals all eased the early days in Fairbanks. The town had shanties on the fringes, but the center offered many of the conveniences of the rest of the USA. Traffic came and went on the river, and an overland route to Valdez cut days off a trip to the Lower 48.

Eventually the Tanana Mining District became a huge gold producer, and the precious metal acted as a powerful magnet for Americans and Europeans alike.

Of course, not everyone in Alaska was a gold miner. Many more found ways to profit from the gold rushes without actually panning for the metal themselves. At Ruby Creek, for example, a strike in 1907, and a more substantial one in 1910, brought the predictable rush of miners to the area and the town of Ruby was born. Newcomers arrived, some by small riverboats, others on large paddlewheelers. The steamers required large quantities of wood to keep them moving, and residents along the river

TALL TALES

Rumors of salmon so large you could cross streams on their backs drew fishermen to Alaska from far and wide.

larly copper. In 1910, the richest copper mine in the world started operation at Kennicott in the Wrangell-St Elias Mountains. The mine extracted more than 591,535 tons of copper ore from the earth, and in its heyday employed over 800 workers.

The more traditional ways of life – fishing, in particular – also provided a livelihood for many Alaskans, particularly after canning was introduced. In 1878 businessmen built the first two canneries at Klawock and Sitka. In 1883 the Arctic Pack Company established a

banks supplemented their trapping and fishing by maintaining profitable wood lots.

Ruby grew from a tent city in 1911 to a bustling river port. With running water in summer, a theater, shops and cafés, it sought to provide all the amenities of its rival, Fairbanks. By 1917, at the height of the rush, creeks south of Ruby had yielded $875,000 worth of gold.

Other ways of life

There were other precious and semi-precious metals to be mined in Alaska as well, particu-

cannery at Nushagak Bay, where they were able to exploit the immense runs of salmon. Two years later the Alaska Packing Company opened a cannery across the bay, and by 1908, 10 canneries ringed Nushagak Bay. Kodiak's first canneries were built in the late 1800s, when word of phenomenal fish runs became widespread.

By the turn of the century, commercial fishing was gaining a foothold in the Aleutian Islands. Packing houses salted cod and herring, and salmon canneries were opened.

Another traditional occupation, whaling, continued, with no regard for overhunting. Bowhead whales, the awesome behemoths of northern seas, attracted a parade of whale

LEFT: trudging up the Chilkoot Pass.
ABOVE: reindeer-drawn mail sled.

hunters to the high Arctic. Following routes they had used since the end of the Pleistocene Age, the bowheads migrated twice yearly through the Bering Strait on their run from the southwestern Bering Sea to summer feeding areas in the Beaufort Sea. Weighing a ton per foot and reaching lengths of 60 ft (20 meters), bowheads filter food through large plates of baleen and carry huge quantities of oil in their tissue. Sadly, whalers seeking the oil pursued the bowhead to the edge of extinction, but in recent decades their numbers have rebounded to the point that Native whale hunters are able to harvest many each year without affecting the population.

The American fishing, canning and whaling operations, as well as walrus hunting, were as unchecked as the Russians' hunting. The Aleuts soon suffered severe problems due to the depletion of the fur seals and sea otters which they needed for survival. As well as requiring the flesh for food, they also used the skins to cover their boats, without which they couldn't hunt. The Americans also expanded into Interior and Arctic Alaska, exploiting the fur-bearers, fish and other game on which Natives depended.

World War II

On June 3, 1942, the Japanese launched an air attack on Dutch Harbor, a US naval base on Unalaska. US forces managed to hold off the planes, and the base survived this attack, and a second one, with minor damage. But on June 7 the Japanese landed on the islands of Kiska and Attu, where they overwhelmed Attu villagers. The villagers were taken to Japan and interned for the rest of the war. Aleuts from the Pribilofs and Aleutian villages were evacuated by the United States to Southeast Alaska.

In fall 1942, the US Navy began constructing a base on Adak, and on May 11, 1943, American troops landed on Attu, determined to retake the island. The bloody battle wore on for more than two weeks. The Japanese, who had no hope of rescue because their fleet of transport submarines had been turned back by US destroyers, fought to the last man. The end finally came on May 29 when the Americans repelled a banzai charge. Some Japanese remained in hiding on the small island (only 35 miles long and 15 miles wide/56 km by 24 km) for up to three months after their defeat. When discovered, they killed themselves rather than surrender.

The taking of Attu was the second bloodiest battle of the Pacific theater; only Iwo Jima was more costly in terms of human lives.

The US then turned its attention to the other occupied island, Kiska. From June through August, tons of bombs were dropped on the tiny island. But the Japanese, under cover of thick Aleutian fog, escaped via transport ships. After the war, the Native Attuans who had survived internment in Japan were resettled to Atka by the federal government, which considered their home villages too remote to defend.

World War II affected Alaska in unexpected ways. One was the construction of the Alaska–Canada Military Highway (Alcan), which was completed at great speed in 1942 to form an overland supply route to America's Russian allies on the other side of the Bering Strait. Running from Great Falls, Montana, to Fairbanks, the road was the first stable link between Alaska and the Lower 48.

The construction of military bases also contributed to the population growth of some Alaskan cities. Anchorage almost doubled in size, from 4,200 people in 1940 to 8,000 in 1945. And two other catalysts of change were just around the corner: statehood and oil. ❏

ABOVE LEFT: gold prospectors.
RIGHT: a turn-of-the-century "sourdough" on parade.

STATEHOOD TO THE 21ST CENTURY

*Alaska has come a long way since it first became part of the United States,
and its setbacks have provided lessons for the future*

After its purchase by the US in 1867 Alaska was governed at different times by the US Army, the US Treasury Department and the US Navy. Finally, in 1884, the federal government declared the territory the District of Alaska, and a civil government was appointed by President Chester Arthur.

By the turn of the century, a movement pushing for Alaska statehood had begun. But in the Lower 48, legislators were worried that Alaska's population was too sparse, its location too distant and isolated, and its economy too unstable for the territory to be a worthwhile addition to the United States.

World War II and the Japanese invasion of Attu and Kiska highlighted Alaska's strategic importance, and the issue of statehood was taken more seriously. But it was the discovery of oil at Swanson River on the Kenai Peninsula in 1957 that really dispelled the image of Alaska as a weak, dependent region, and on January 3, 1959, Alaska became a state. Juneau, the territorial capital, continued as state capital. William A. Egan was sworn in as the first governor.

Disaster

It was not long before the young state underwent its first trial. On March 27, 1964, the Good Friday earthquake struck Southcentral Alaska, churning the earth for four minutes. At an estimated 8.7 on the Richter scale, the Good Friday quake is one of the most powerful ever recorded, killing 103 people. Most of them were drowned by the tidal waves (tsunamis) that tore apart the towns of Valdez and Chenega.

Throughout the Prince William Sound region towns and ports were destroyed, land uplifted or shoved downward, islands tilted. The uplift destroyed salmon streams, as the fish could no longer negotiate waterfalls and other barriers to reach their spawning grounds. Ports at Valdez and Cordova were beyond repair – what land and mud slides didn't claim, ensuing fires did.

At Valdez, an Alaska Steamship Company ship was lifted by a huge wave over the docks and out to sea. Amazingly, most hands survived. Witnesses on shore swore that at one point they could see daylight all the way under the ship. There were very few witnesses, however, because most of those who had been waiting on

the dockside to greet the ship were swept to their deaths.

At Turnagain Arm, off the Kenai Peninsula, the incoming water destroyed trees and caused cabins to sink into the mud. In Anchorage, huge chunks of road asphalt piled on top of each other like shingles. At Seldovia, near the junction of Kachemak Bay and Cook Inlet, fish processing facilities and an active fishing fleet were laid waste, along with Seldovia's harbor.

On Kodiak, a tidal wave wiped out the villages of Afognak, Old Harbor and Kaguyak, and damaged other communities. Seward, a thriving port town at the southern terminus of the Alaska Central Railroad, also lost its harbor.

LEFT: tanker maneuvers in Prince William Sound.
ABOVE RIGHT: Native Alaskan bark house.

Oil and land

Despite the extent of the catastrophe, Alaskans rebuilt many of the devastated communities. Four years later, the state experienced a different sort of upheaval. In the mid-1960s Alaska Natives had begun participating in state and local government and flexing their electoral muscles. More than 200 years after the arrival of the first Europeans, Natives from all ethnic groups united to claim title to the lands wrested from them. The government responded slowly until, in 1968, the Atlantic-Richfield Company discovered oil at Prudhoe Bay, and catapulted the issue of land ownership into the headlines.

was new urgency for an agreement, and in 1971 the Alaska Native Claims Settlement Act was signed, under which the Natives relinquished aboriginal claims to their lands. In return they received title to 44 million acres of land and were paid $963 million. The land and money were divided among regional, urban and village corporations. Some have handled their funds wisely; others have not, leaving some Natives land-rich and cash-poor.

The settlement compensated Natives for the invasion of their lands. It also opened the way for all Alaskans to profit from the state's tremendous natural resource, oil.

Prudhoe Bay is on Alaska's Arctic coast. Drilling at such a remote location would be difficult enough – but transporting the resulting crude to refineries in the Lower 48 seemed almost impossible. The best solution seemed to be to build a pipeline to carry the oil across Alaska to the port of Valdez (rebuilt a few miles from the ruins of the previous town). At Valdez the oil would be loaded onto tanker ships and sent by water to the Lower 48. The plan was approved – but a permit to construct the pipeline, which would cross lands involved in the Native land claims dispute, could not be granted until the Native claims had been settled.

With major petro dollars on the line, there

YOUNG AT HEART

Alaska is the place for young people. Many of them have moved here from outside, probably because the state attracts those who both like and can cope with an active and not always easy life. According to the 1998 census the average age was 32.4. Although the population is increasing rapidly, there are still only just over 600,000 permanent residents – very low compared with most other states in the union. Most of them live in urban areas, and more than half live in and around Anchorage. According to the same census, Alaska Natives make up 15.6 percent of the population.

The pipeline

After the Claims Settlement Act was signed, it still remained to build a pipeline stretching from Arctic Alaska to Valdez. Between the two points were three mountain ranges, active fault lines, miles and miles of unstable *muskeg* (boggy ground underlain with permafrost) and the migration paths of caribou and moose. The pipeline was designed with all these factors in mind. To counteract the unstable ground and allow animal crossings, half the 800-mile (1,285-km) pipeline is elevated on

COUNTING THE MINUTES

The first oil took 38 days, 12 hours and 54 minutes to travel through the pipeline.

The Alaska Permanent Fund

During the years of pipeline construction, Anchorage and Fairbanks blossomed into bright modern cities. As the oil bonanza took shape, per capita incomes rose throughout the state, with virtually every community benefitting. State leaders were determined that this boom would not end like the fur and gold booms – in an economic bust as soon as the resource had disappeared. This time Alaskans would consider the future.

To this end, the Alaska Permanent Fund was

supports. The supports hold the pipe – and its cargo of hot oil – high enough to keep it from melting the permafrost and destroying the natural terrain. To help the pipeline survive an earthquake, it was laid out in a zigzag pattern, so that it would roll with the earth instead of breaking up.

The first oil arrived at Valdez on July 28, 1977. The total cost of the pipeline and related projects, including the tanker terminal at Valdez, 12 pumping stations and the Yukon River Bridge, was $8 billion.

LEFT: Anchorage after the 1964 earthquake.
ABOVE: the latest in pipeline technology.

created in 1976. Into the fund is deposited 25 percent of all mineral lease proceeds. Income from the fund is divided in three ways: it pays annual dividends to all residents who apply and qualify; it adds money to the principal account to hedge against inflation; and it provides funds for state legislature use.

The fund is the largest pool of public money in the United States, and a top lender to the government. It is estimated that, by the year 2000, the fund should produce more revenue than the Prudhoe Bay oil fields, where production is already diminishing. Prudhoe Bay oil may dry up early in the 21st century, but the fund should continue to benefit the state for a while.

Tourism and the environment

In the second half of the 20th century, Alaska discovered another important source of revenue. Tourism got started after World War II when men stationed in the region returned home praising its natural splendor. The Alcan Highway, built during the war, and the Alaska Marine Highway System, completed in 1963, made the state more accessible than before.

Tourism is now big business in Alaska: over 1.3 million people visit the state every year. Once there, they flock to the top attractions, Denali National Park, Katmai, Glacier Bay and the Kenai Peninsula. Wildlife-watching is a

main attraction, although only a small proportion of visitors take to the wilderness.

With tourism more and more vital to the state's economy, environmentalism has also risen in importance (*see* page 43). Alaskans are working to balance the needs of their remarkable land with the needs of its residents. Much is already well protected – the Alaska National Interest Lands Conservation Act (ANILCA) of 1980 added 53.7 million acres (22 million hectares) to the national wildlife refuge system, parts of 25 rivers to the national wild and scenic rivers system, 3.3 million acres (1.3 million hectares) to national forest lands, and 43.6 million acres (17.5 million hectares) to national

park land. As a result of the lands act, Alaska now contains two-thirds of all American national parklands.

The oil spill

Nothing better illustrates Alaska's struggle to protect the environment and to benefit from the state's natural resources, than the *Exxon Valdez* disaster. The tanker ran aground on March 24, 1989 in Prince William Sound, releasing 11 million gallons (42 million liters) of crude oil into the water. The oil eventually spread along 1,100 miles (1,760 km) of formerly pristine shoreline.

It was an ecological disaster of unprecedented proportions. According to the US Fish and Wildlife Service, at least 300,000 sea birds, 2,000 otters and countless other marine animals died as a result of the spill. Exxon spent $2 billion on clean-up in the first year alone.

During the summer of 1989, 12,000 workers descended on the soiled shores of the sound. They bulldozed blackened beaches, sucked up petroleum blobs with vacuum devices, blasted sand with hot water, polished rocks by hand, raked up oily seaweed, and sprayed fertilizer to aid the growth of oil-eating microbes.

For Alaska's tourism industry, the spill strained an already uneasy relationship with the state's petroleum interests. Not only did it generate horrendous international publicity but the influx of clean-up workers filled to capacity virtually every hotel and campsite in the Valdez area – which was bad news for the tourist industry, but very good for Valdez' economy.

Exxon, working with state and federal agencies, continued its clean-up efforts into the early 1990s. In some areas, such as Smith Island, which was an oil-soaked wasteland directly after the spill, winter storms did more to wash the shore clean than any human efforts.

Government studies show the oil and the cleaning process itself caused long-term harm to the ecology of the Sound, interfering with the reproduction of birds and animals in ways that still aren't fully understood. Some fishermen, particularly those dependent on shellfish, worry about hard-to-measure impacts on their catch.

Prince William Sound seems to have bounced back, but scientists still dispute the extent of the recovery and Alaskans are working hard to ensure their state is not put to the test again. ❑

Above Left: cleaning up after the oil spill.

Economy & ecology

Almost every dollar that flows through Alaska's economy originates from its land or water. The oil and mining industries extract vast wealth from under the ground, fishermen harvest much of the nation's seafood from the water, and loggers and tourism operators exploit the landscape itself. Other industries and government pass those dollars from hand to hand, but natural resources are the real reason the economy, and the people it employs, are here at all.

Oil is by far the largest of Alaska's industries, but fishing is second and employs more people. Tourism also is a large employer. The logging industry is shrinking under the pressure of new environmental concerns. Government employs more people than any other industry, and it is largely funded by oil.

It's not surprising that most Alaskans strongly support more resource development. Every new oil field discovered on the North Slope creates jobs and new government revenues that affect every citizen. When the salmon season is good, coastal towns thrive. And the flow of summer visitors employs thousands.

But many Alaskans also advocate environmental protection, and not only because they tend to be young and to spend time outdoors enjoying the beauty of the place. Fishermen know that oil spills damage the waters from which they draw their livelihood. Tourism operators know their clients aren't interested in visiting areas that have been clear-cut for logging. Both industries trade on the ability of Alaska's name to symbolize the purity of unfettered wilderness all over the world.

When, in 1989, the tanker *Exxon Valdez* spilled 11 million gallons (42 million liters) of crude oil in Prince William Sound, both industries worked as hard to clean up the image of their products as Exxon did to scrape the oil off the shore (see page 42). A decade later, industry is doing fine,and visitors to the Sound still see abundant wildlife.

Large-scale logging has altered the environment in ways that affect other industries. On Prince of Wales Island logging roads open up miles of backcountry, but much of the area opened by these roads has been denuded of the towering old-growth Douglas fir and western hemlock that make the area so attractive. Besides the vistas, fishermen

worry about logging near streams reducing the productivity of salmon spawning.

Yet tourism and fishing can harm the environment as well. In Glacier Bay National Park, environmental groups have sued the National Park Service to stop it granting more permits for cruiseships to enter the bay, contending that they are scaring away the humpback whales. There are questions, too, about noisy helicopter sightseeing in wilderness areas, a proposal for a new road in Denali National Park, and the pressures of ever more visitors brought by "industrial tourism."

As for fishing, environmentalists blame large-scale factory trawlers operating in the Bering Sea

for reducing marine mammal populations by taking too many fish from the food chain. Congress recently approved new laws to reduce the huge ships' massive waste of "bycatch," or unwanted fish species that end up in their nets by chance.

Government plays the key role in these issues. Alaska's resource storehouse is vast, covering 365 million acres (148 million hectares), a land mass roughly similar to the size of France, Spain, Germany and the United Kingdom combined, of which a fraction of 1 percent is privately owned. The federal government controls more than half, and the state government about a third.

Only with their permission can the wealth be drilled, netted, cut or displayed for the benefit of the people who live here ❑.

ABOVE RIGHT: the Prudhoe Bay Refinery.

VISITING ALASKA'S NATIVES

Learning about Alaskan Native cultures is a valuable experience,
but the people must not be treated as a tourist attraction

Many Native Alaskans still live a subsistence lifestyle that depends upon collecting meat and fish during the abundant summer months and preparing it for storage to sustain them over the long winter. In the southern part of the state, Natives depend upon deer, salmon and other food from the sea. In the Interior, the Athabascans fish on the rivers and hunt caribou and waterfowl. Further north, Eskimos hunt whale and seals. Most villages are located in remote areas without roads to connect them with cities and luxuries such as large well-stocked grocery stores. Until recently, about the only outsiders who spent any time in villages were friends, relatives, health care workers or teachers. Now the list is growing.

Villages welcome visitors

An international fascination with indigenous people has spread to Alaska, and village residents from Saxman Native Village in Southeast Alaska to Gambell on St Lawrence Island in the Bering Strait are cautiously opening their doors to visitors. Visiting an Alaska Native village can be a great adventure for people who are both flexible and open-minded. Organized tours are now offered in at least a dozen villages throughout Alaska and by the year 2000, as many as 30 villages may offer such tours.

In these encounters, both the visitors and the visited learn from each other. Visitors learn how Natives live in various parts of the state and along the way they discard stereotypes about igloos, wardrobes of animal skins and rubbing noses. "Visitors come with an expectation that they're going to go back in time," says the Alaska Native Tourism Council, an organization formed in 1992 to promote rural tourism and help Native groups who operate tours. "They find out that visually it's very familiar in terms of clothing – people wearing Nike tennis

shoes – but the culture and life of the people hasn't changed a lot. Value systems are still deeply rooted in the past and in their culture."

For their part, Natives learn to share their love for the land and a desire to preserve their way of life and the teachings of their ancestors. In recent years, as more and more young people

leave villages for life in the cities, Natives have worked to keep their culture and their language alive. Tourism now provides an impetus for them to do so. Young Natives learn the dances and stories of old, passing them on to their own children and to the rest of the world.

Changes afoot

The 20th century has brought numerous changes to Alaska's Native communities. Thirteen regional, four urban and 200 Native village corporations were formed to manage money and land received from the government as a result of the 1971 Alaska Native Claims Settlement Act. The measure approved the

PRECEDING PAGES: ready for après-ski; Yup'ik Natives ice fishing.

LEFT: a Nulato boy.

ABOVE RIGHT: residents of a Yup'ik village.

transfer of 44 million acres and $963 million to corporations in exchange for giving up their aboriginal rights to the land.

Some of these corporations have been phenomenally successful, parlaying the oil, mineral and other natural resource wealth of their lands into large annual dividends for members. Others have not done as well. Some made bad investments and others were tainted by corruption.

Although snow-machines are largely replacing dog sleds as a means of winter travel and boats with motors replace the skin boats that their ancestors used for fishing and hunting, Natives still follow traditional ways. Now, however, they must have money to buy gasoline for their snow-machines and bullets for their guns. Their subsistence way of life requires modern tools and they meld the old with the new.

a little easier. Under her fur parka, an Eskimo woman may be wearing a dress bought through a mail-order catalog. Her whaler husband and friends track movements of their prey with a short wave radio, and when the meat is consumed raw, as in the old days, they wash it down with canned fizzy drinks.

Needs must

For many remote communities, welcoming tourists is a step prompted by an increasingly gloomy economic outlook. "While there is a growing demand for a cash economy in the village, paying jobs are on the decline," says Larry

It's a delicate balance. Natives struggle to keep their own culture intact as they embrace the conveniences of modern society. Essentially they have a foot in both worlds.

The modern world, which lures away younger Natives, has also brought its share of ills to Native communities and many struggle to overcome high rates of alcoholism and suicide. A number of villages have voted to stay dry, with no alcohol allowed.

Yet modern conveniences have also made life

Schafer, who helped begin a tourist program in the Interior village of Huslia. For years the Federal Bureau of Land Management hired young villagers to fight summer forest fires, but a series of rainy seasons put a damper on that. To employ the young people, the village decided to try tourism. It wasn't an easy decision: the 250 residents took seven years to achieve unanimous agreement. The first season, only a dozen people visited; the second, over 20 arrived, and now numbers are growing every year.

Tips for travelers

One of the biggest hurdles for some villagers to overcome has been the fear of losing their privacy. Indeed, outsiders who show up unescorted in some villages still receive a chilly reception. Allowing a stranger into their village is like a North American family inviting an unknown person into their home.

Whether you are visiting as part of an organized tour or on your own, remember that what happens in Native villages is real life, not a tourist attraction. Even on tours, day-to-day community life sometimes takes precedence over visitors' needs.

Read up on the people and their culture and learn as much as you can about Native values before you reach a village. Many books are

304, Anchorage, AK 99510, tel: 274-5400 will give you details.

Show your respect for Native culture by the way you behave during your visit. Don't pepper villagers with lots of personal questions. Observe for a while first, then ask a question respectfully. You will probably get an answer. Be prepared to fend for yourself. Accommodations and amenities are limited and sometimes conditions can be primitive. Don't expect room service and don't count on sticking to a strict time schedule.

Your reward will be a rare insight into the world of the Alaska Natives. ❑

available about Native groups in Alaska and can be found at most libraries.

In some villages, interaction between visitors and residents is controlled and limited, with visitors escorted. Many isolated communities want to break into the tourism business slowly and tailored tours accommodate that need.

Contact the village council before you show up, to make sure that residents are happy to see visitors, or find a tour operator that includes Native villages on its itineraries. The Alaska Native Tourism Council, 1577 C Street, No.

LEFT: Aniak children pose for the camera.
ABOVE: Yup'ik dance ceremony.

RESPECT THE RULES

Some residents worry about tourists walking into their houses unannounced, as if they were strolling into a Disneyland attraction, or indiscriminately snapping photographs. It is common courtesy to ask before taking photographs of people. Some villages, such as Gambell, prefer that you ask before taking any pictures at all. And the travel brochure publicizing Arctic Village specifically prohibits video cameras.

"We ask visitors to respect villagers' privacy," says Audrey Ranstead, who takes groups to a fish camp on the Yukon. "We set ground rules before we get there, and people respect that."

ALASKAN RESIDENTS

Alaska's largely youthful population is hard to categorize, but most people share an aptitude for enjoyment and for coping with difficult situations

Alaskans are a very special breed of people, accustomed to the cold and to the long hours of winter darkness, and resourceful enough to cope stoically with most things that climate and geography demand of them. And it's not just a case of putting up with hard conditions because they have no choice: some 25 percent of Alaska's population has moved to the state within the past five years.

Defining a "typical" Alaskan

Before Alyson Rigby Ronningen, who grew up in England, traveled to Alaska for the first time, she thought she had a pretty clear idea of what Alaskans were like: "They all wore flannel shirts, had big bushy beards, and they owned guns and big dogs," she recalled.

Alyson eventually married an Alaskan and moved to the Far North. Once there, she looked around at her Fairbanks neighbors, confirmed her suspicions, and smugly told a friend, "I was right."

But Alyson was not a "typical" visitor, or even a run-of-the-mill new Alaskan. She spent her first winter living in a wall tent with her husband and new baby. While her husband worked as a carpenter nearby, she used a tiny wood stove for both warmth and cooking. Temperatures plummeted as low as -30° or -40°F (-34° to -40°C) but Alyson stayed toasty by baking on her trusty wood stove, and she didn't seem to mind at all.

Even some seasoned Alaskans would be horrified at spending a winter under those conditions, but Alyson fitted in with what many believe to be an unspoken code of the north: be independent and self-sufficient.

In that way she was a "typical" Alaskan, yet it is difficult to generalize about what is typical, because it depends so much on where you live and what your circumstances are. Alaska is so huge and the various parts of the state are so dif-

ferent from each other that the residents are bound to differ widely as well.

Anchored down in Anchorage

The hub of the state is its largest (although not its capital) city, Anchorage. Rural Alaskans often joke that Anchorage is only 20 minutes

from Alaska. That may well be true, but many urban Alaskans make the best possible use of those 20 minutes.

In a state where the average age is 32, Anchorage (with 42 percent of the population) is a city of young professionals, including active sports lovers, such as rock climbers, mountain bikers, whitewater kayakers and runners. Many people bring their outdoor toys to work with them, and at the end of the day, they head for the hills, the biking trails or the rivers. In summer time they don't have to worry about running out of daylight, either, because it never gets dark.

People in Anchorage also spend a lot of time getting out of town. Lake Hood, a floatplane

PRECEDING PAGES: gold miner's cabin in the Wrangells.
LEFT: selling Tlingit jewelry in Sitka.
ABOVE RIGHT: a very young Alaskan resident.

base in the city, is the largest and busiest such base in the world, with as many as 800 take-offs and landings recorded on a peak summer day. Where do they all go? Just peek out of a plane window as you fly into Anchorage and you will see hundreds of little getaway cabins tucked into the surrounding wilderness and the more remote areas.

John Power, long-time Alaskan resident, but a new urban dweller, thought about getting one of these cabins when he first moved to Anchorage, but instead bought a 30-ft (9-meter) sailboat, which he keeps in Prince William Sound, and uses whenever he can.

about the plumbing freezing or the heat being on when I was gone."

He misses his reliable little wood stove most of all. "I used to like getting up in the morning, building my fire and cooking pancakes in the kitchen with the wood stove roaring away," he said nostalgically.

There are several thousand Fairbanks residents who still embrace the wood-stove-no-running-water lifestyle with enthusiasm. These people usually fill 5-gallon (22-liter) water jugs at the laundromats in town, or at their places of employment. Showers are available at the laundromats as well.

No water, no problem

Power, a 39-year-old geophysicist with the Alaska Volcano Observatory, moved to Anchorage from Fairbanks, where for many years he had lived in a little cabin with no running water and, like Alyson, just a wood stove for heating. This may seem extraordinary to people used to modern comforts, but not to John.

"I liked it," he says. "I liked living in a place where I didn't really have any neighbors. I liked not having to worry about it when I left in winter, which I frequently did when I was traveling. It was inexpensive. I first got into that lifestyle when I was a student and I never really changed. I didn't have to worry about house-sitters, or

When winter settles in and the mercury begins to drop, conversation generally revolves around the weather, particularly the frigid temperatures. Eventually, someone will complain about water pipes freezing and bursting, and those who have no running water try not to look too self-satisfied as they silently assure themselves that they have chosen the right lifestyle.

In communities along the Alaska coast, life revolves not only around the weather, but more importantly around the fishing season. Extra-Tuf rubber boots and heavy-duty raingear are the fashion *du jour*. This is especially true in Kodiak, where fishing is not a summer activity, but a year-round economic necessity.

Since many students and some teachers fish, the school calendar is based on fishing openings and closures. When the fishing is poor, the whole town suffers. If people can't pay tradesmen's bills, businesses can't pay theirs either, and the economy of the whole community is in trouble. The population of Kodiak, like that of other fishing communities, swells in the summer when people arrive to fish, then contracts when they leave again at the end of the season.

The Russian community

Some Alaskans are visitors who came here long ago and stayed on, overcoming hardship and secution by the Orthodox Church, the government, and later the Stalinist purges, they call themselves "the Old Believers."

Today they work in local businesses, or operate companies of their own, and manage their own fishing fleet. But their lives revolve around their religious beliefs. The study of holy books is mandatory during periods of fasting before Christmas and Lent. They wear traditional clothes: the women and girls always cover their heads with scarves, and men dress conservatively, often sporting close-trimmed beards.

Yet they are no less Alaskan than the man who lives in the bush and calls the Lower 48

skepticism. Typical among them are the descendants of Russian immigrants in the Kenai Peninsula, Kodiak and Sitka. The first Russians came to Alaska in the late 18th century (*see* page 27) and established communities first in Kodiak, then in present-day Sitka, which became the headquarters of the fur trading Russian-American Company. Both towns retain strong Russian influences, but it is on the Kenai Peninsula that a strict Russian Orthodox community still survives, based around their "Island of Faith" near Anchor Point. Survivors of per-

LEFT: snowshoeing at the Fur Rondy.
ABOVE: the start of Seward's marathon race.

states "America," as if he inhabited a separate country; or the Anchorage college graduate, rushing from his downtown office to the mountain tops at weekends. In Alaska, everyone is free to be who they want to be, to start from scratch, to reinvent themselves, to become just another "typical" Alaskan.

Bush pilots

Life in Alaska can be tough, and it has always attracted people who are not easily daunted. Among the most intrepid of Alaskans are the bush pilots. Their history begins in the 1920s, when Alaska and the airplane became partners in a relationship best described as complicated bliss. Despite an obvious need, Alaska wasn't equipped for airplanes. There were lots of places to go, but there was no place to land once you got there. This created a special breed of flyer: the bush pilot.

Being a bush pilot in the early years sounds exciting but it definitely lacked glamor. Alaska's first taste of aviation was courtesy of James V. Martin, who had contracted with three businessmen to fly an airplane over Fairbanks in honor of the 4th of July in 1913. Undeterred by difficulties, he loaded his disassembled airplane on a steamship and sailed it to Skagway. There he transferred it to the White Pass and Yukon

son lifted this same plane from the ground in Fairbanks on July 3, 1923. This was the initial appearance of the man considered the foremost bush pilot of his era.

Where to land?

For Alaska's early bush pilots, the size of their territory was summed up in the distances between cities, and only four really mattered in 1923: Juneau, Fairbanks, Nome and Anchorage. From Juneau to Anchorage it's about 600 miles (965 km); Anchorage to Fairbanks, 275 miles (440 km); and Fairbanks to Nome, 450 miles (720 km). These were the business centers of

Railroad for the 125-mile (200-km) trip to Whitehorse, Yukon Territory, in Canada.

Finally, Martin loaded his plane on a sternwheeler and steamed 800 miles (1,300 km) down the Yukon River, then 100 miles (160 km) up the Tanana and Chena rivers to Fairbanks. After the boxes arrived in Fairbanks, Martin reassembled the plane. It flew in exhibition for 11 minutes, was taken apart and carted out of the territory.

After World War I, surplus "Curtiss Jennies" were readily available for about $600. Inevitably some of them found their way to Alaska. The first was *Polar Bear*, flown from New York in 1922. A year later Carl Ben Eiel-

BUSH BABIES

"Bush" was not originally an American term. It was the name that Australian visitors at the turn of the century gave to Alaska's boondocks, thinking that it was as appropriate here as in their own outback. It may not be a very complimentary term, but it stuck. Later, a pilot who flew anywhere away from the periphery of a town or village became known as a bush pilot. And that meant most of the early aviators.

But remember, if you hear urban Alaskans referring to the "outside," they don't mean the rural areas, they mean anywhere outside Alaska – usually the rest of the United States.

Alaska, and in order to make a living a pilot had to fly between them regularly. This created a few problems.

The old Jennies cruised at about 85 mph (135 kph) and carried only four hours' worth of fuel. The only non-stop, city-to-city trip possible was between Anchorage and Fairbanks. This meant the baggage compartment on longer flights was filled with fuel cans. Halfway between stops a pilot landed wherever he could, poured in fuel, and took off again.

Finding a place to land was the hard part. A pilot needed a long gravel bar on a river, or a stretch of level ground. Yet fields didn't exist in

didn't know if his engine would stay warm enough to run. At -65°F (-52°C) he flew 350 miles (560 km) with the cylinder head temperature at 100°F (37°C). Normally it's twice that.

Winter stopovers were a real joy. As soon as the propeller stopped, a pilot drained the oil and carefully set it aside. He covered the engine with an insulated blanket, tied his plane down to withstand winds of up to 90 mph (145 kph) and then looked to his own comforts.

In the wild, pilots had to fend for themselves. Most carried a wealth of gear, including a tanned caribou hide. For sleeping in the cold there is no warmer ground cloth available.

many places because Alaska had never been plowed. The land was natural, and nature rarely creates straight lines. In later years planes were equipped with floats for water landings.

Winter weather

Winter made landings easier. Rivers and lakes froze, snow filled the bumps on the ground, and pilots put skis on their craft. Alaska's winters, however, brought a host of other problems to pilots of open-cockpit biplanes. Veteran pilot Noel Wien once took off when it was so cold he

Left: a landing on Kodiak Island.
Above: meeting the mail plane in Chefornak.

Each of the early aviators would have the best sleeping bag he could find, two tents – one slightly smaller so it could be set up inside the other – and a stove of some sort for heating food, water and oil. The oil which had been drained from the plane on landing would be warmed almost to boiling and poured into the frozen engine prior to starting in the morning.

Harrowing moments

Weather conditions have often placed pilots in unusual roles. Steve Mills was forced down by a blizzard while flying an appendicitis victim from Bethel to Anchorage in March 1937. He nursed the woman all night in sub-zero temperatures until the weather cleared. Katherine Clark was born in the back seat of Jim Dodson's Stinson in 1938. Jim's reward for expert one-handed flying and one-handed midwifery was to be chosen as the baby's godfather.

Noel Wien describes his worst flight as plagued not by weather but by problem cargo. He was carrying a 9-lb (4-kg) poke of gold to Fairbanks for a miner. En route, the leather sack slipped off the board under his feet where he had stowed it; Wien was not sure whether or not it had dropped through a

> **PIONEERS' MEMORIAL**
> Memorials to Will Rogers and Wiley Post, two early bush pilots who crashed in 1935, can be seen at the crash site south of Barrow.

hole in the fabric. As it happened, the poke had lodged under the cockpit deck. Had it fallen out of the plane in flight, Wien Air Alaska may not have become one of the major air carriers in Alaska, which it was for several years.

Rescues and heroes

Cargo and passengers paid the bills, but the spectacular rescues – almost always voluntary – made the bush-pilot legends. In 1955 Don Sheldon, one of Alaska's last flying legends, made what was probably the most harrowing rescue ever attempted. An eight-man Army scout team from Fort Richardson, attempting to chart the Susitna River, was defeated by treach-

erous Devil's Canyon. Sheldon flew over the proposed route after the team had been gone for two days. First he found pieces of their wrecked boat in the river below the canyon, then he spotted seven men clinging to a tiny ledge just above the roaring water. Upstream was a fairly straight part of the canyon and Sheldon carefully guided his plane down through the tricky air currents.

Upon landing, he immediately found himself going backward at 30 mph (48 kmph) as the river swept the plane downstream. He kept the power on to slow his backward run and allow him to steer. He eased over the bank, and one man jumped aboard for the first trip.

Sheldon made three more trips into the canyon, taking out two men each time. Later he found the eighth man 18 miles (30 km) downstream. Don Sheldon received the standard accolade – a Certificate of Achievement.

That was bush flying. The hazards were many, the pay uncertain, the hours absurd and the conditions unique. Yet from this beginning came the Alaska-based air carriers operating today. Slowly but surely the planes have evolved, making it possible for passengers to fly in first-class comfort and luxury. The plane is warm, it flies above most of the weather, and sophisticated electronics guide it almost effortlessly to its destination. It's a far cry from the good old days of the Alaskan bush pilot, but even if conditions are easier, the pilots still have to turn out in all weathers and people still rely on them to turn up in emergencies, and to deliver the mail if not – they hope – the babies.

A trapper's life

Life in the Alaskan bush can be exhilarating but it is very hard and often tedious. Trapping is one of the hardest, least profitable professions there is, and one that has changed little over the years, but there are those who love the life. One change, which has made life easier, is that many trappers now use snow-machines instead of the traditional dog sleds. This has its disadvantages, of course: after all, dogs don't break down, as machines do, and a trapper now always needs to carry survival gear and showshoes for walking home when the engine inexplicably dies.

Two sisters, Julie and Miki Collins, living in the bush and still working in the traditional ways are typical of some who have stuck to the dog sleds, and their story paints a picture of a hard but rewarding way of life.

A trapper must be able to control a sled drawn by a dozen huskies, capable of doing some 60 miles (100 km) a day on a good trail, in temperatures dipping as low as -50°F (-45°C). Many things can go wrong on a trip: a sled could clump a sapling in its careening descent of a slope; there could be a dog fight, or a threat from runaway dogs; a last-minute repair job might be needed, or a sloppily loaded sled could buck burlap sacks of frozen fish from the canvas tarp. The towline can disconnect from the sled, sending the dogs flying in formation without their driver. And sometimes a one-ton bull moose can challenge the team's right to use the trail.

A trapper must remain constantly alert for unseen dangers: thin ice, deadly water hidden under deep snow, irritable moose, open creeks, or a fresh tree blown down across the trail, all hazards which usually crop up suddenly and without warning.

There's always something to watch out for, and the trapper must work in close unison with the team. The dogs are guided verbally, with commands to tell a leader which trail to take, to order slack dogs to speed up, or to encourage the team as a whole when they begin to tire. By watching ears, eye contacts and attitudes, an experienced trapper can determine whether the dogs scent a moose or an animal in a trap ahead, if they want to fight or balk, if they're happy, discouraged, or tired. Sensitive observation and interpretation of this subtle language enables a trapper to keep the dogs at peak performance.

The seasons are very important in the remote Alaskan bush – for those working with machines as much as for those still using dog teams. In the summer, many trappers concentrate on fishing and cultivating vegetables and fruit for the rest of the year. Long hours may be spent picking berries for fresh fruit and jam. The fish nets must be run daily and the dogs fed with cooked whitefish and rice. Any extra fish are cut and dried for next winter.

In the slow summer months, too, trappers

LEFT: a dog team in a snowstorm.
RIGHT: a trapper's hard life.

> ### FUR TRADE
>
> Handmade items are often not paid for in money: a fur hat may be traded for essential winter equipment.

may build dog houses and dog sleds, sew sled bags, dog booties and harnesses. Some trappers, like the two sisters, also tan and sew furs from the winter's catch, making hats and mitts to sell for extra cash. Summer is also the time when machines are serviced, so that there won't be too many engine problems when the trapping season starts again.

When the fall arrives there are cranberries to be picked and root vegetables to be harvested and stored. And when the annual fish run begins, whitefish are netted and frozen whole

for the dogs' food. With winter comes the trapping season, and the truly hard work: snowshoeing through deep snow; skiing miles to set trails; and cutting cord after cord of firewood. By late winter trappers are tired of constant work in bitter weather, and in need of a brief vacation.

So it goes. The yearly cycle of putting food up in summer and fall, and trapping and woodcutting in winter and spring. The weekly cycle, measured by the mail plane and the trapline rounds, and the daily cycle of mushing dogs, maintaining equipment and feeding fires. It's a hard life, but for many, it's a happy and fulfilling one. ❏

LIFE IN WINTER

Sled dog racing, skiing, and aurora watching all help
Alaskans get through the long, cold winters

Winter is Alaska's longest season, and its quietest – at least from a tourism perspective. The majority of visitors explore the state between the end of May and the beginning of September, when daylight hours are long and temperatures warm – though in some parts of the state, warm may mean only 50 or 60°F (10 or 15°C).

By mid-September, most tourists have gone south with the waterfowl and locals have begun preparing for the winter, which in most of the state will last seven or eight months. Yet Alaska is not a frozen wasteland, and unlike bears, its human residents do not go into hibernation.

As would be expected, Alaska's Interior and Arctic regions experience the most severe and prolonged winter conditions. Barrow, the nation's northernmost outpost, averages subzero temperatures from December through March. Temperatures bottom out in February, which has average daily lows of -25° F (-32°C) and highs of -12° F (-24°C). But Barrow isn't just frigid in winter – it's also very dark. The long winter night begins at noon on November 18 and lasts through January 24 – that's 67 days from sunset until the next sunrise.

Winter in Anchorage

By comparison, Anchorage is downright bright and balmy. The city's shortest day (the winter solstice, December 21) has 5 hours and 28 minutes of daylight, plus a couple of hours of twilight. Its coldest month, December, has average daily highs and lows of 20° and 6°F respectively (-7 and -15°C). Even more moderate conditions are experienced in Southeast Alaska. Ketchikan, near the Panhandle's southern tip, has 7 hours, 6 minutes of daylight on the winter solstice and even its coldest month, January, averages above-freezing temperatures of 34 °F (1°C).

PRECEDING PAGES: a proud pilot and a tricky journey; high noon in Fairbanks in winter.
LEFT: well-insulated cabin.
ABOVE RIGHT: dressed up for the Anchorage Miners' and Trappers' Ball.

For further evidence of Alaska's winter extremes, consider that the state's record snowfall for one season is 974.5 inches (24.75 meters), at Thompson Pass (near Valdez) during the winter of 1952–53. The one-day record, also at Thompson Pass, is 62 inches (1.6 meters) in December 1955. Barrow holds the state

record for the least snowfall in a season: 3 inches (7.5 cm), in 1935–36.

Not only do darkness and cold tend to keep Alaskans indoors much of the winter, they also produce a variety of malaises, from cabin fever to seasonal affective disorder (appropriately shortened to SAD). To combat winter woes and help the longest season pass more quickly, residents around the state participate in a variety of activities and special events – some strenuous and skillful, others just plain fun.

Alaska's winter sport

Among the most popular cures for seasonal blues is sled dog racing, designated Alaska's official winter sport. And the best known of the mushing events is the Iditarod Trail Sled Dog Race, also known as "The Last Great Race."

The Iditarod is officially billed as a 1,049-mile (1,690-km) race but in reality mushers and dogs travel well over 1,100 miles (1,770 km). The race commemorates a frantic dash in 1925 to get diphtheria vaccine to Nome, which was on the verge of an epidemic. The trail follows an historic freight-and-mail route established during the gold rush era of the early 1900s. It traverses two mountain ranges, runs along the Yukon River for about 150 miles (240 km) and crosses the pack ice of Norton Sound. From its

The mushers, of course, are the glamor figures in sled dog racing and the top contenders are household names throughout Alaska and, increasingly, in much of the Lower 48. But many would agree that the dogs are the true heroes, the athletic stars, of this and other mushing events. They're specially bred, raised, trained and conditioned to race.

Speed and stamina

While the Iditarod is unquestionably Alaska's best-known sled dog race, dozens – perhaps hundreds – of other competitions are staged around the state. Another major long-distance

ceremonial start in Anchorage – traditionally, the first Saturday in March – until the final musher has reached the finish line in Nome, the Iditarod is given center stage throughout Alaska.

A contest in which men and women compete as equals – four titles have been won by Susan Butcher – the Iditarod not only pits competitors against each other, but also against the wilderness and Alaska's brutal winter weather. But most importantly, the Iditarod celebrates Alaska's frontier past and the adventurous spirit in us all. The first Iditarod took place in 1967, as a two-day event that covered 50 miles (80 km). Six years later the inaugural race from Anchorage to Nome was run.

WINNING WAYS

If you hear anyone in Alaska talking about the mother and father of the Iditarod, they're referring to historian Dorothy Page and musher Joe Redington, who conceived and organized the event more than 30 years ago.

The winner of the first full-length Anchorage to Nome Iditarod in 1973, Dick Wilmarth, finished the race in just over 20 days and earned $12,000. But speeds and rewards both increased over the next two decades or so. Doug Swingley, the 1995 winner, set a record-breaking time of 9 days, 2 hours, and his prize money was $50,000 plus a new truck.

event is the 1,000-mile (1,600-km) Yukon Quest, staged each February between Fairbanks and Whitehorse, in Canada's Yukon Territory.

At the other end of the mushing spectrum are the so-called "speed races," or sprints. People of all abilities and ages compete in limited-class races (most are divided into three-, five-, six- or eight-dog categories), while more serious speed mushers often "graduate" to the unlimited open-class events, which offer greater financial awards and prestige – and greater challenges.

The two most prestigious speed races are the North American Open, a three-day event staged each March in Fairbanks, and the Fur Ren-

100 to 300 miles (160 to 480 km). A growing number of Alaskans also run dog teams purely for recreation and several companies in the state's Southcentral and Interior regions now offer sled dog rides that range from a few hours to over a week.

Iron dogs

While some Alaskans choose to explore the winter landscape behind a team of sled dogs, many others prefer "iron dogs." Snow-mobiles, also locally known as snow-machines and sno-gos, have replaced sled dogs as the primary means of winter transportation in most of rural

dezvous World Championship, another three-day affair (teams run 25 miles/40 km each day), and the main attraction of Anchorage's mid-February winter festival. While Iditarod champions such as Butcher and Swingley have achieved far greater acclaim outside Alaska, several of the premier speed racers – George Attla, Charlie Champaine and Roxy Wright-Champaine among them – are every bit as famous within the state.

In addition to the well-known titles there is a range of middle-distance races, ranging from

Alaska, where roads are minimal. Though commonly used by bush residents for work, or simply "getting from here to there," snow-machines are also popular for recreation and racing in both urban and rural Alaska.

The most challenging snow-mobile race by far is the Gold Rush Classic, a long-distance event along the Iditarod Trail between Nome and Big Lake (in the Susitna Valley). Another intriguing race is the Arctic Man Ski & Sno-Go Classic, which is staged annually in the Hoodoo Mountains near Paxson.

It's something of a rarity to see skiers and snow-machiners enjoying each other's company in the backcountry. Some recreational

LEFT: on the Iditarod Trail.
ABOVE: sleds are for shopping as well as competing.

areas popular with both user groups – for instance Chugach State Park in the mountains just east of Anchorage, Hatcher Pass in the Talkeetna Mountains and Turnagain Pass on the Kenai Peninsula – have designated snowmobile corridors, to minimize conflicts.

Nordic and alpine skiing

Skiing is especially popular in and around the main towns. Anchorage has one of the nation's premier cross-country ski-trail systems: more than 100 miles (160 km) of trails wind through a variety of terrain, with opportunities for both traditional diagonal striders and skate skiers.

three most popular Nordic retreats are Hatcher Pass Lodge, in the Talkeetna Mountains; Sheep Mountain Lodge along the Glenn Highway; and Denali View Chalet – also known as Sepp Weber's Cabin, after its builder and owner – in the Alaska Range foothills. Each of the lodges offers groomed trails, wood-fired saunas, heated rooms, home-cooked meals and other amenities. Both Hatcher Pass and Sheep Mountain are accessible by road, while Denali View is about 2 miles (3.5 km) from the nearest road.

Though not known as a mecca for alpine skiers, Alaska nonetheless offers a wide variety of downhill ski areas. They range from

The city's best-known Nordic center, at Kincaid Park, has hosted several national championship races, as well as the Olympic Trials. For those who want backcountry solitude, Chugach State Park – Anchorage's "backyard wilderness" – has dozens of valleys and ridges to explore. Several well-used trailheads are within a half-hour's drive of downtown. Other popular Nordic backcountry destinations within a half-day's drive of Anchorage include the Talkeetna Mountains, Chugach National Forest on the Kenai Peninsula, and the Peters Hills, foothills of the Alaska Range.

While most of Alaska's lodges shut down for winter, a few cater to cross-country skiers. The

Alyeska's world-class facility in Girdwood, about 40 miles (65 km) south of Anchorage, to the single-run volunteer operation at Salmonberry Hill outside Valdez.

Probably the most unusual of Alaska's eight downhill sites (which include three in the Anchorage area, two near Fairbanks and one on Douglas Island, 12 miles/20 km from Juneau) is the Eyak Ski Area, near the coastal community of Cordova. The tiny, single-seat Prince lift here used to operate at Sun Valley until it was replaced in 1969 by a triple-seat chair. Eventually the lift made its way north to Cordova, where it has been in operation every winter since 1974.

The northern lights

A less strenuous activity than skiing, snow-mobiling or mushing is sky gazing, or aurora watching. Alaska is the best place in the USA to view the aurora borealis, or northern lights. Literally meaning "dawn of the north," this is a solar-powered light show that occurs in the earth's upper atmosphere when charged particles from the sun collide with gas molecules.

The northern lights occur most intensely in an oval band that stretches across Alaska (as

WHAT'S ON

For more information on winter festivals and special events, contact the Alaska Division of Tourism, P.O. Box 110801, Juneau, 99811, tel: 465-2010.

pale yellowish green – the most common shade – to red, blue and purplish-red. Northern lights often begin as long, uniform bands, stretching from horizon to horizon, but may develop vertical bars or rays, that give the appearance of waving curtains. Some people claim they can not only see the aurora but can hear it as well. Scientists at the University of Alaska-Fairbanks, who have been studying the northern lights for years, are interested in such reports, but have yet to confirm them.

well as Canada, Greenland, Iceland, Norway and Siberia). All the state, except parts of the southwest and the Aleutian Chain, are within the "auroral zone," with the best light shows visible north of the Alaska Range. One of the best views to be had is in Fairbanks, which has recently begun calling itself an "auroral desti-nation," in an attempt to lure winter visitors.

The aurora occurs throughout the year, but can only be seen when the sky is really dark. In Alaska that means from fall through spring, with peak viewing in winter. Colors vary from

LEFT: winter skiers near Nome.
ABOVE: the northern lights above Fairbanks.

Festivals

Not even auroras, sled dog rides and ski resorts are enough to get Alaskans through the long winter, so many communities host festivals to chase away winter doldrums. In December, there's the Barrow Christmas Games, followed in January by Kodiak's Russian New Year and Masquerade Ball celebration.

Things really begin to pick up in February, with the Anchorage Fur Rendezvous, the Wrangell Tent City Winter Festival, Cordova Ice Worm Festival and Valdez International Ice Climbing Festival. March brings the North Pole Winter Carnival and the Bering Sea Ice Golf Classic tournament in Nome. ❑

A WEALTH OF WILDFLOWERS

The flowering season in Alaska is relatively short, but it brings a profusion of brightly colored blossoms from the high tundra to the highway edge

When a tiny purple flower pokes out of the melting snow, Alaskans know spring has arrived. The pasque flower, or spring crocus, is the first of a colorful floral palate that will paint Alaska in the weeks that follow. The color cavalcade begins in late May, but some places won't see a blossom until mid-June or later. Then, as days lengthen, wildflowers reach for the sun from the most unlikely places – the crevice of a rock, the top of a ridge, alongside rushing streams, on top of coarse, dry gravel bars, or in the middle of the tundra.

SHORT AND SWEET

The growing season is short, but critical, since flowering plants provide nutrients for the many animals that feed on them. Ground squirrels, marmots and other rodents start munching as soon as flowers start blooming, and a bad year for flora is a bad one for dependent fauna, too. Plants of the same species may bloom as much as six weeks apart, depending on their location. Flowers on south-facing slopes receive more sunlight, so they are most likely to bloom before similar plants on cooler, north-facing slopes.

BLANKETS OF COLOR

At mid-summer, whole fields and hillsides of bushy, bright pink fireweed saturate many parts of Alaska. Fireweed blooms from the bottom of the stem to the top, and Alaskans say that when the top flower finally blooms, it means that summer is almost over. It isn't unusual for dwarf fireweed, also known as river beauty, to completely cover gravel bars along glacial streams.

△ **BEARBERRIES**
Bearberries grow close to the ground in rocky alpine areas and on the tundra, covering the ground like a carpet with course, leathery leaves and black berries. At lower elevations, berries are bright red. The fruits are juicy but have very little flavor and are not prized, although Eskimos will pick them in poor berry seasons and mix them with more tasty blueberries.

▷ **FIREWEED**
Growing as high as 5 ft (1.5 meters) tall, fireweed can turn a hillside into a blaze of bright pink or purple. This plant, probably the most commonly seen in Alaska, gets its name not from its color, but from its ability to renew itself rapidly after a fire, as its deep roots manage to escape the conflagration.

◁ **PASQUE FLOWERS**
Purple pasque flowers, a species of anemone, are often the first wildflowers to emerge through melting snow. Their name is derived from "Pasch," which comes from both the Latin and Greek terms for Easter.

◁ COTTON GRASS

Cotton grass grows along lakes and ditches, and in any wet, peaty soil. Like an exploded Q-Tip, the ball of cotton sits atop a stiff stem. The lower stems and roots of tall cotton grass are edible. Despite the name, this isn't a grass, but is related to the sedge.

▽ ARCTIC POPPIES

These delicate lemon-yellow colored flowers cover the tundra or grow in any sandy soil – sometimes right along the roadsides – from mid-June to late July. The inner temperature of this Arctic flower may be 18°F (10°C) warmer than the air outside.

◁ FORGET-ME-NOT

The forget-me-not is the Alaska state flower. This lovely blue perennial blooms in late May to June. The leaves are slightly bristly and the flowers, which grow in coiled springs, are only about 1/4-inch (7 mm) across. In many parts of Europe the forget-me-not has been seen as an emblem of love and remembrance since the middle ages – hence its name.

▽ LOW BUSH CRANBERRIES

Look out for these glossy dark red berries after the first sharp frost of winter. They nestle close to the ground, the warmest and least windy zone available to them, and remain on the plant throughout the winter.

AN EXPLOSION OF COLOR

Above the treeline lies the tundra, a lumpy carpet of bushes, grasses and flowers. Soil is scarce here and flowers cling to the edges of rocky slopes or windswept meadows. They hug the ground, offering surprisingly brilliant bursts of color. Many have developed unusual adaptations that allow them to survive wind and often brutal temperatures.

The woolly lousewort, a delicate pink Arctic flower, has white hairs on its leaves to keep it warm when it blooms early in the season. The Arctic poppy has a flower shaped like a radar antenna, tracking the motion of the sun and reflecting its heat onto the seeds.

Many plants have pre-formed buds which take shape at the end of each growing season. When spring comes the following year, the buds are ready to open. The tundra's growing season is so short that plants need all these adaptations to increase their growing time.

The northern anemone *(above)* is one of the earliest wildflowers to bloom, often right after snow melts. The flowers measure a mere 1 inch (25 mm) in diameter.

Once temperatures drop, blueberries and cranberries ripen and the tundra is ready for harvest. Soapberries, scattered on gravel bars, in woods or on mountain slopes, are a favorite part of the bear's diet, because of their high fat content.

WILDLIFE

Alaska's wildlife is protected by the national parks system

to ensure that it is still there for future generations

Some people think of Alaska as a wasteland permanently covered with snow and ice. In fact, it is a world teeming with wildlife. For many people, the most exciting part of an Alaskan adventure is discovering the birds and mammals of the state.

Birds

More than 400 different species of birds have been officially documented in Alaska. With few exceptions, these species inhabit the state only during spring and summer and then migrate south. They come north to take advantage of the eruption of life which occurs on the tundra each spring, when a multi-colored explosion of flowers covers the ground. The tundra offers an almost unlimited banquet of foodstuffs – plants, insects and small animals – for birds attempting to raise their hungry young.

The Arctic tern is the world's record holder for migration distances. These gull-like birds breed and nest on the shores of Alaskan tundra ponds. In late summer, the terns and their young start a migration which will eventually take them all the way to the Antarctic. Summer is just beginning in the Southern Hemisphere as the terns arrive. The round-trip flight from Alaska to the Antarctic and back is approximately 25,000 miles (40,000 km).

Other long-distance commuters include the American golden plover, the surfbird, the long-tailed jaeger and the Arctic warbler. Some plovers winter on the Hawaiian Islands while others migrate to Argentina. Tierra del Fuego, at the tip of South America, is the winter home of the surfbird. The jaeger spends its winters on the open ocean in the central Pacific or near Japan. The Arctic warbler resides in southern Asia during winter months.

Alaska's state bird, the willow ptarmigan, was chosen by a vote of the state's school children. Along with its close relatives, the rock ptarmigan and the white-tailed ptarmigan, the

willow ptarmigan lives in Alaska year round. A ptarmigan is brown in summer and white during winter, changing its coloration to blend with the surroundings. During extremely cold winter weather, ptarmigans keep warm by burrowing into snow drifts. The males fiercely defend nesting females: one male was actually seen

attacking a grizzly bear which had stumbled on his mate's nest. The ptarmigan is usually to be found on high ground: look for them in willow thickets and on the open tundra.

Eagle habitat

Alaska is the stronghold of the bald eagle. More of them live in Alaska than in the other 49 states combined. White heads, white tails and 8-ft (2.4-meter) wing-spans make them easily identifiable, even at a great distance. They are most often seen where fish are common, especially along the coastal areas of Southeast Alaska.

The best place to see bald eagles is near Haines, during October and November. The

LEFT: flowers in the high tundra.
ABOVE RIGHT: a mature bald eagle.

Chilkat River, just north of town, attracts thousands of Bald eagles, which feed on the dead or spent salmon. A single tree may contain dozens of roosting eagles – an extraordinary sight. Because fish are available throughout the winter in coastal areas, these bald eagles have no need to migrate from Alaska. You can visit the American Bald Eagle Foundation in Haines (*see* page 115) for attractive displays and useful information about the birds.

Golden eagles, the darker cousins of the bald eagle, are normally found in tundra and mountainous areas. They hunt rodents, such as the Arctic ground squirrel, rather than fish. The

for their highly developed powers of navigation), cormorants and puffins live along the coastlines.

Most of the national parks, national forests, national wildlife refuges, state parks and many communities have developed bird checklists, which they offer free to visitors.

Mammals

The premier wildlife area in Alaska is Denali National Park. Grizzlies, moose, Dall sheep, caribou, red foxes, snowshoe hares, beavers, Arctic ground squirrels, and hoary marmots are seen by almost everyone who visits Denali. The

Polychrome Pass area of Denali National Park is an excellent place to watch for golden eagles.

Alaska's birds can be seen and studied by anyone possessing time, patience and a pair of binoculars. While near tundra ponds, look for loons, grebes, geese, ducks, yellowlegs, phalaropes and sandpipers. On the tundra, watch for long-tailed jaegers, golden plovers, whimbrels, snow buntings, wheatears, sparrows and water pipits. Owls, woodpeckers, gray jays and chickadees are common in forested areas, as are goshawks, the large, handsome birds of prey which swoop down through the trees and catch their prey completely unawares. Gulls, terns, murrelets, auklets, shearwaters (known

park's shuttle bus system is designed to maximize wildlife sightings. Because the buses cause comparatively little disturbance, many animals, including grizzlies, can be photographed within 100 yards (90 meters) of the road .

If you are lucky, you may also spot wolves in Denali, although these creatures – which are mostly gray in color, and nearly always to be found traveling in packs – are not fond of human company and you are more likely to hear them than to see them (*see* page 235 for more information on these fascinating and much-maligned animals).

Denali and the other great Alaskan national parks are textbook examples of what national parks were meant to be. Each of these areas protects an entire ecosystem in a condition nearly identical to its original state. The population levels of wildlife such as Dall sheep, moose and caribou are controlled not by human intervention, but by the area's natural predators, the grizzly bears and wolves. The vegetation, prey species and predators interact in the same way their ancestors did thousands of years ago. If you are lucky enough to see a grizzly dig out a ground squirrel from its burrow or a wolf pack chase a caribou herd, you will be witnessing a scene which could have taken place during the last Ice Age.

the peak season for salmon spawning (*see* the chapter on Katmai, page 218, and the information panel on page 215). The McNeil River State Game Sanctuary (just outside the park) provides the ultimate bear-watching experience, but you literally have to enter a lottery to get in.

Much of Kodiak Island is home to a particularly large variety of brown bear, a huge mammal that captures the imagination of most would-be and genuine hunters. Native to the island group, these bears stick primarily to the interior highlands except during the salmon run. While salmon is their preferred food, the bears also eat carrion and, being omnivores, balance

Alaska's bears

Katmai National Park is the place for brown bears. At one time, grizzlies and browns were considered different species but most experts now believe they are the same animal (*Ursus arctos*). The brown bears in Katmai National Park and other coastal areas live where large numbers of salmon are available. Partly because of the almost unlimited supply of salmon, these bears can grow to weights of up to 1,700 lbs (770 kg). The best place to see them is at Brooks Camp, in Katmai, and the best time is in July,

LEFT: parakeet auklets; a hoary marmot.
ABOVE: a grizzly in Denali Park.

STREAMS OF SALMON

The lives of brown bears and salmon are inextricably linked, since salmon are the bears' favorite food. The fish come in five varieties – sockeye, king, chum, silver and pink – and are as popular with fishermen as with bears. Understandably so, since their flesh has so much more flavor than the farmed variety so often found in supermarkets. Witnessing a salmon run (from July to mid-September), when thousands of the fish cram the streams and leap the waterfalls, as they swim upstream to spawn, is a wonderful experience. Watching the bears who come to prey on them is unforgettable.

their diet with grass and berries. Black bears also inhabit Kodiak Island. Confusingly, black bears are often brown in color, and the best way to distinguish between the two species is by looking for the hump which the brown variety has at the back of its neck.

Polar bears live along the northern and northwestern coasts of the state. They are the largest land carnivores in the world, with some of the older males weighing over 1,500 lbs (680 kg). They live on the ice floes of the Arctic Ocean and can swim long distances in the frigid ocean waters without difficulty. A number have been spotted 50 miles (80 km) from the nearest ice or

land, but these nomads, which survive on a diet of seals and other marine mammals, are very seldom seen by travelers to Alaska.

Deer and oxen

It is sometimes said that a camel is a horse designed by a committee, and much the same could be said of the moose: its legs are too long and its nose is too big. But if you watch these lumbering creatures running or swimming you will realize that nature got it right after all. The best places to see them are in Denali Park and at the Kenai National Wildlife Refuge. The Athabascan Indians once relied on the moose for their survival, eating the meat and using the

skins for clothing, blankets and boat making. The animals are still hunted extensively during the season by Alaskans and visitors.

Denali is, again, the best place to be if you want to see caribou, of which there are estimated to be well over half a million in the state. Like other varieties of deer, caribou are herbivores and will eat the available grasses and berries as they travel the very long distances between their calving grounds and their overwintering areas.

Reindeer are the domesticated version of caribou. The first ones were introduced into Alaska in 1892 as a dependable source of food and clothing. Today, there are approximately 30,000 reindeer in Alaska. The largest herd lives near Kotzebue on the Seward Peninsula. A small herd can be viewed at the Reindeer Research Station in Cantwell, south of the entrance to Denali National Park.

Sitka black-tail deer are distributed throughout the Southeast: these small, rusty-brown animals (their coats turn gray in the winter) are most likely to be seen in Misty Fjords National Monument and on Kodiak Island. Other island residents are the Roosevelt elk, mountain goats, and numerous smaller mammals.

Also on Nunivak is grazing for what is perhaps the most extraordinary native animal: the musk ox, a stout, shaggy, creature which appears to be the result of an amorous encounter between a prehistoric ox and a mountain sheep. Musk oxen are few and far between, and shy in the wild, but they are preserved in research stations, particularly in the Large Animal Research Facility which is part of the University of Alaska-Fairbanks.

Sea creatures

Alaska is rich in marine life: humpback, killer and minke whales can all be seen in Glacier Bay National Park, although belugas, the small, white whales once plentiful in Cook Inlet, are now disappearing.

Bearded seals and walrus are found near Kotzebue, and harbor seals and sea lions are frequently sighted in the Gulf of Alaska and Prince William Sound. In fact, Alaska's coasts, like its inland areas, offer opportunities for wildlife watching which are difficult to match. ❏

LEFT: a caribou in the tundra.
RIGHT: Dall ewes on Mount McKinley.

THE FRAGILE WILDERNESS

To preserve Alaska's wilderness we have to tread carefully.
The tourist industry is bearing this in mind as it welcomes visitors

You don't really know what wild means until you've been to Alaska. With one-fifth of the land area of the contiguous United States and more shoreline than all the other states combined, Alaska includes 150 million acres (61 million hectares) of national parks and forests, wildlife refuges and other designated preserves – ample territory for wilderness adventure. Its 38 mountain ranges, 3,000 rivers and three million lakes fall within climate ranges from temperate rainforest to arid arctic. Much of this territory is barely charted, let alone touched by the human foot.

Of Alaska's 40 national parks and preserves, only 11 are accessible by road. Glacier Bay National Park (3.2 million acres/1,295,000 hectares), for example, can only by reached by boat or floatplane. North America's premier mountain wilderness and its largest national park, Wrangell-St Elias National Park and Preserve (13.2 million acres/5.3 million hectares), is home to nine peaks of more than 14,000 feet (4,270 meters), including the 18,010-ft (5,490-meter) Mount St Elias.

It also has the largest collection of glaciers in North America; the Bagley Icefield, which is the largest subpolar icefield on the continent; numerous wild rivers; and multitudes of wildlife. Yet only two unpaved roads, best negotiated by 4-wheel-drive vehicles, penetrate the park boundaries.

Gates of the Arctic National Park, the northernmost of the state's parks, is a remote and undeveloped 7.5 million acres (3,035,000 hectares) of crags and sweeping arctic valleys. Without roads or trails, backpacking, mountaineering and dog sled excursions are among the only ways of gaining access to these areas.

And in all Alaska's wide open spaces, you will encounter a profusion of wildlife. Grizzlies weighing as much as 1,500 lbs (680 kg) romp

PRECEDING PAGES: kayaking in Lake Clark National Park.
LEFT: walking into the Harding Icefield.
ABOVE RIGHT: stepping out with care.

about sand flats digging clams or snatching salmon from glacial-fed torrents. Caribou, numbering in the thousands, roam across sweeping tundra, seals sun themselves on ice floes, and whales ply turquoise fjords.

When federal geographer Henry Gannett, a founder of the National Geographic Society,

surveyed Alaska's expanse in 1904, he set the tone for today's ecotourism: "Its grandeur is more valuable than the gold or the fish or the timber, for it will never be exhausted." Alaska is a land where inhabitants and travelers sense that they can do no better.

Low-impact tourism

Unfortunately, the traditional tourist industry in the state often bypasses its great wilderness areas in favor of organized tours that take visitors by bus, train or airplane to cities, towns and developed parks. The majority of Alaska tourists see sights that are reached by road (such as Portage Glacier, Denali National Park and

Preserve, and cities such as Anchorage, Juneau and Fairbanks) – but rarely step into untouched wilderness. Only one road goes into 6 million-acre (2,430,000-hectare) Denali National Park – a 90-mile (145-km) strip that bars most private vehicles. While this road channels more and more visitors into the park each year via bus tours – which cause minimum disturbance – only 33,200 of the park's 500,000 visitors in one recent year registered for backcountry permits.

Guides such as Bob Jacobs, owner of St Elias Alpine Guides in McCarthy, feel that visitors to Alaska should see a lot more, but, at the same time, the land should be protected. "Alaska is a

ditions such as sea-kayaking, mountaineering and wildlife-watching.

In the late 1990s ecotourism – defined as low-impact vacations that allow people to learn about, enjoy, and help preserve the natural environment while disturbing local people as little as possible – is becoming a preferred manner of travel in Alaska. Traveling at nature's pace in a land that offers adventure and asks for respect, tourists gain an intimate awareness of life as it was 1,000 years ago. As privileged guests, they enter another civilization, where sea lions, loons, moose and whales are constant companions – and that is ecotourism's modern appeal.

wonderful classroom," Bob says. But, unlike school, "You don't need a schedule. In summer you can hike until 2 am and sleep until noon."

On Jacobs' trips into the heart of the Wrangell-St Elias National Park you climb unnamed peaks, raft down swift, milky rivers and backpack for weeks at a time, enjoying the rich wilderness traditions that typify the Alaskan way of life. Alaska's a whole new experience once you've touched the 1,000-year-old ice of a massive glacier, rafted a raging river and heard wild creatures calling across unpeopled lands.

Jacobs was one of the pioneers of a new industry labeled "ecotourism," which reveals to travelers the quintessential Alaska outdoor tra-

NATURAL WONDERS

When it comes to counting the most and the biggest, Alaska has some amazing statistics. It is one-fifth of the size of the contiguous United States, measuring 2,400 miles (3,860 km) from east to west, and geographers have named more than 1,800 islands. Its mountains include 19 that are over 14,000 ft (4,270 meters), and 17 of them are among the 20 highest peaks in the USA. The state also has over 5,000 glaciers, and more than three million lakes. The largest of these, Lake Iliamna, just south of the Lake Clark National Park in Southwest Alaska, encompasses 1,100 sq. miles (2,850 sq. km).

Since the early 1980s, the Alaska travel industry has reoriented itself toward this new brand of adventure where sea-kayakers, whitewater rafters, backpackers and nature photographers mingle with bald eagles, grizzly bears and caribou.

The Alaska Division of Tourism recently estimated that around 1.2 million non-resident visitors spend about $1.5 billion in the state annually. Fifty percent of these visitors indicated that they did some wildlife viewing – although only an estimated 10 percent strike out away from traditional tourist areas into the pristine wilderness.

parties of schoolchildren in spring and fall, the center works to foster responsible human interaction with our natural surroundings and to generate knowledge of the marine and coastal ecosystems of Kachemak Bay through its environmental education and research programs.

Ultimately, ecotourism relies on pristine country and wildlife as its chief commodity, so there is great motivation to maintain the health of the land and the well-being of its wildlife. It is a clean industry which could well take the place of some of its less-fastidious competitors.

Ecotourism initially was the province of a handful of small, independent operators and

Protecting the land

Essentially, ecotourism means using the tourist industry as a tool to protect and enhance Alaska's natural beauty so that visitors, and residents, may continue to enjoy the land for generations to come.

"It's important to understand that we're a part of nature and a part of the plan," says Penney Hodges, administrator of the Alaska Center for Coastal Studies in Homer. "We need to learn how to get back into balance with nature." By opening its doors to travelers in summer and to

outfitters that led groups into the outback, while the mainstream industry concentrated on marketing developed resort areas. Now many large-scale organizations have developed policies and principles that depart significantly from traditional commercial concerns and lean toward low-impact tourism.

The guidelines of the American Society of Travel Agents spell out the ecotourism ethos: visitors should support local cultures; avoid littering; walk only on designated trails; support conservation-oriented programs; learn about local customs; refrain from disturbing local habitat or buying products which utilise any part of endangered animals. ❑

LEFT: grizzly stop in Denali Park.
ABOVE: close encounter with a whale.

Eco-friendly options

Dozens of outfitters offer river rafting, tundra trekking, mountain climbing, bird-watching, whale cruising, wildlife photography safaris and sea-kayaking adventures, ranging from easy to strenuous. Some tour operators offer ecotours geared specifically toward senior citizens. Although some of these trips hark back to the days of the pioneers, they are usually made more comfortable by some of today's amenities. Visitors can take advantage of experienced guides without having to acquire all the necessary skills themselves; and many of the backcountry meals are of gourmet quality.

Wildlife viewing is a major draw, especially for those hoping to see the monarchs of the land: the grizzly and brown bears. One of the most notable areas is the McNeil River State Game Sanctuary, but visitors are strictly regulated by permit. This close supervision means that visitors have to apply in advance, and names are drawn out of a hat. You have a more realistic chance of good bear-watching at Brooks Camp in Katmai National Park.

Other renowned bear-viewing areas include Denali National Park and Preserve, home to 200–300 bears. Kodiak National Wildlife Refuge, designated a refuge by Franklin D. Roosevelt in 1941, is home to the largest bears

on earth. As much as 10 percent of Alaska's grizzlies live on Kodiak Island. "Big bears fill big hotels," says grizzly activist Timothy Treadwell. "People go to Alaska to see wilderness, to be part of what Earth used to be like. That's good for tourism. If you protect grizzly habitat, you protect your bread and butter."

Ethical guidelines

Although ecotourism industry operators generally follow environmental ethics, they don't all abide equally by the unwritten code of minimal impact. Some people are now advocating a "green rating" system so that it is possible to distinguish between good and poor operators on an ecological impact scale.

Currently, no such system exists, but Bob Jacobs has some suggestions to enable would-be visitors to pick the right company to travel with. "Do your homework. Look for organizations that go beyond making money. Talk to them. Get a feeling for their philosophy. Ask for references. That's the best policy."

Following some general guidelines will help make your trip ecologically friendly. Check to see if an operator limits the number of people it takes into fragile areas – because it should. Does the company practice low-impact camping and hiking and vary the location of campsites from trip to trip in order to avoid scarring the ground in certain areas? Does it supply a reading list about the area and the type of activities you will be pursuing?

Top ecotourism companies are staffed by experienced naturalists who always accompany their guests on journeys and offer extensive information along the way. Such specialists help minimize impact on wildlife by keeping groups at unobtrusive, safe distances. The companies should also be committed to energy conservation and recycling, as this helps preserve the environment that you have come here to enjoy.

Even if you're traveling on your own, you can do your part. Follow carefully the guidelines that come with backcountry permits from the park or forest service and write your own code for minimum-impact traveling, based on the points outlined above. It makes sense to preserve the grandeur of Alaska's wilderness and keep it wild for future generations.

ABOVE: autumn foliage along the Glenn Highway.
RIGHT: admirably low-impact camping.

WISE WORDS FOR SURVIVAL

The most successful explorers are those who take sensible precautions.

Don't skimp on them: remember that the elements are stronger than we are

This section is not intended to deter anyone from enjoying the wilderness. Great obstacles were overcome by early expeditions, which had no proper equipment, and there are so many things which make modern-day adventure a lot safer and easier. Yet even people with the best gear have disasters. These tips are intended to help you make the most of the wilderness and go home safely with some wonderful memories.

Traveling in Alaska need be no more hazardous than elsewhere if proper precautions are taken. Due to the latitude and varying weather conditions, travelers must have the appropriate equipment and be physically prepared for the activities they wish to pursue. Because there are so few roads and distances are so great, clear and precise communication is vital. This chapter isn't an exhaustive discourse on any one topic: its purpose is to cite several common problems and offer some simple solutions.

Weather

Coastal and Southcentral Alaska: The word to remember when selecting equipment for coastal Alaska is rain. Some of this area receives up to 200 inches (508 cm) annually, so reliable raingear is essential. If you plan to be outside for long periods, a rainsuit (jacket, pants, and hat) and a synthetic pile or fleece jacket, will be used frequently. Rain is also the prime consideration when selecting a tent and sleeping bag. Tents must be able to withstand long wet spells. Sleeping bags filled with synthetic materials are better than down because they retain more of their insulating qualities when wet.

The Interior: The Interior has dramatic seasonal contrasts. Summer temperatures are pleasantly warm while in winter the mercury can dip below -40°F (-40°C).

PRECEDING PAGES: on top of McConnell Ridge, Glacier Bay National Park.
LEFT: an ice climber negotiates a crevasse.
ABOVE RIGHT: taking a rest, Gates of the Arctic National Park.

Summer equipment can be lightweight, although mountain-goers will face much lower temperatures. A hat and at least one heavy long-sleeved shirt will be useful, as will a mosquito headnet, which takes up little luggage space.

The extreme cold of winter demands the best quality equipment. A good down jacket, a hat,

mittens and warm boots are essential. Camping in winter requires a sleeping bag that is comfortable at -40°F (-40°C) or colder.

Spring is the finest time, by far, to ski in the mountains. Temperatures are so comfortable that people ski without shirts – although the sensible ones cover themselves in sunblock. But snow-blindness is a very painful reality for unprotected eyes; mirrored sunglasses are best, but dark sunglasses will suffice.

The North Slope: If the key word for coastal Alaska is rain, the equivalent for the North Slope is wind. The area is technically an arctic desert with less than 5 inches (13 cm) of annual precipitation. But this meager amount should not be disregarded as it may fall as snow or freezing rain and be driven by gale force winds. Travelers to the North Slope need clothes that are windproof and warm and camping equipment that can withstand heavy winds.

Travel

Charter flights: Check first to see if there is a regular air service – there is to some small villages and communities, and this will save you a lot of money. But if you are bound for the wilderness, a charter flight is necessary.

Before departure, be sure someone knows where you are going. If you have no alternative,

tackle and a pistol or rifle with ammunition. A sleeping bag, snowshoes and a wool blanket are added to the list for winter travel.

Although most flights carry some survival gear, the requirements are sometimes ignored. Check the survival gear before taking off. If you decide to bring your own, keep as much of it on your person as possible. In winter fill your pockets; in summer, use a small waist pack. You may have to evacuate the downed craft quickly.

Every plane in Alaska is also required to carry a downed aircraft transmitting device (Emergency Location Transmitter or ELT). Learn how to operate this device before you set off. If the

inform the Alaska State Troopers of your destination and expected return date. Make firm arrangements to be picked up. Be certain that someone besides the pilot knows where you are going. In one case, a fisherman was dropped off in a remote location known only to the pilot. The latter had a fatal crash while returning to town, and it took several days' searching to locate the missing fisherman.

What happens if the plane crashes while you are in it? There is a legal requirement for all planes to carry emergency equipment. The required list includes food for each person for two weeks, an axe, first-aid kit, a knife, matches, mosquito headnets, gill net, fishing

LEARN THE RULES

Learning a few basics could save your life if you were stranded in the wilderness. There is a record of one man in a desperate situation who spotted an Alaska State Troopers airplane flying over his campsite. He frantically waved both his arms over his head. When the plane flew over a second time, he waved again. The plane flew off. It was only much later that the man realized his mistake; when he studied his hunting license, he saw that he had signaled, "Everything OK, don't wait." Sadly there was no happy ending: this information was recorded in a diary found when the man's body was discovered.

pilot becomes incapacitated, you can activate the ELT and be rescued more quickly. Don't be deterred by these dire warnings: almost everyone arrives at their destination safely. These precautions pertain to the 0.5 percent of flights during which an inflight problem does occur.

Automobile travel: There is no Alaska law which governs what survival equipment should be kept in a vehicle, yet the average car is maintained less frequently than a plane, which means that far more cars break down while traveling.

In sub-freezing weather, a breakdown can be life-threatening as well as inconvenient. The Alaska State Troopers recommend the follow-

When renting a car, inform the rental agency of your proposed route and confirm that maintenance is available along the way. Anticipating problems before traveling will avoid misunderstandings later. Most agencies have stringent rules about driving on gravel roads.

Avoidable dilemmas

Mosquitoes: Alaska may have been spared snakes, skunks and termites but this has been more than compensated for by the mosquito. Billed sarcastically as the "Alaskan State Bird," these insects are a wilderness force to be reckoned with. Use the most powerful repellents

ing survival kit: down coat, boots, mittens, hat, snow-pants, sleeping bag, flare, candles, extra spark plugs, extra belts, shovel, chain, flashlight and high-energy food.

Automobile maintenance is vitally important. Even if you come to no real harm, it is expensive and time-consuming to break down on the road – towing charges can be very costly. Check the car carefully before leaving the city, and remember winter essentials: snow tires or studded tires, an operating engine heater and ample electrical cord to reach a power source.

Left: landing at Lake Hood near Anchorage.
Above: well prepared for mosquitoes.

available, such as the musk types or those with a high concentration of DEET. Even in the face of these measures, the mosquito seems to thrive. Thick clothing will reduce the number of bites, but sometimes a headnet is the only means of relief. Carry a mosquito net – there are some neat, lightweight ones available – and make sure that it is impregnated with repellent as well.

Bears: When bears and people cross paths in the wild, only one side wins. Many Alaskans have stories about encountering bears at close quarters, but there are a few tragic accounts. Most bears turn tail and run upon encountering people, but in some instances the bear will stand its ground. At this point, advice differs widely.

One school of thought is to stay calm and speak softly to the beast, encouraging it to leave. The second line of thinking is that you should shout loudly to scare the animal away. Both schools agree that if the bear is a brown (coastal) or grizzly (interior), you should climb a tree if available. (Black bears may follow the climber.) Should a bear attack, the only course of action is to "play dead." Protect your head and neck and try to lie on your stomach, but do not struggle. Bears have been known to walk away if they think the prey is dead.

Three important strategies should be used to minimize chance meetings with bears. First,

Hypothermia: Beware of hypothermia, the sub-normal lowering of the body temperature. It is caused by exposure to cold, but aggravated by exhaustion, wind and wet clothing. Left untreated, a person suffering from hypothermia may become disoriented, incoherent, then unconscious, and may finally die. Never ignore shivering, it is the body's way of signaling for help. The time to prevent hypothermia is during the initial period of exposure. The following suggestions may help prevent an emergency:

Try to stay dry. Wet clothing loses most of its insulating value. Functional raingear is vitally important. Ponchos are almost useless.

TOOT HORN ONLY IF BEAR IN CAMP

make plenty of noise while walking in the wilderness. Some people tie bells to their shoes or pack: it may sound excessive, but it's worth a try. Bears will hear your approach and leave. Second, be careful with food. If possible, do not cook in the camp and always store food away from your sleeping area.

The third suggestion seems like common sense, but is easy to forget. If you see a well-worn path in the wilderness – it may even be grooved into the earth – remember the trail may belong to a bear. Be alert if you must walk along such a path, make lots of noise, and do not pitch your tent on the trail, or you may have an unexpected tent mate.

TREATING HYPOTHERMIA

If a member of your party develops hypothermia there are emergency measures you can take. Handle a victim gently, replace wet clothing with dry, and warm the core area of the body. The warming procedure consists of making a human sandwich: one person on each side of the victim, bare skin to bare skin, inside a warm sleeping bag. Do not give a victim any alcohol as this could prove fatal; forget stories about a sip of brandy being restorative. Avoid the mistake of rapidly warming the extremities, as it takes much-needed blood away from the core area and can result in unconsciousness.

Avoid the wind. Wind carries body heat away much faster than still air. Wind also refrigerates wet clothing by evaporation.

Understand the cold. Most people die of hypothermia when the temperature is between 30° and 50°F (-1 and 10°C). Most hikers underestimate the severity of being wet in Alaskan waters. It can be fatal and first aid measures must be taken immediately.

End the exposure. If a member of your party shows signs of hypothermia or if it becomes impossible to keep dry with existing clothing and conditions, make camp or end the trip.

Avoid over-tiredness. Don't be too ambitious.

below it. Spend as little time as possible near the zone. Choose the route carefully to avoid steep mountain faces, especially after a fresh snowfall. And remember, spring is an especially dangerous season for avalanches.

Tides: There are large tidal variations in Southeastern Alaska, Prince William Sound, Cook Inlet and Bristol Bay. The extreme diurnal variation occurs in spring in Cook Inlet near Anchorage where high tide can be 38 ft (11.5 meters) above low tide. Such tides present two dangers for sport fishing: swift incoming tides and strong currents, magnified in island areas.

Obtain a tide book from a fishing tackle shop,

Make camp before you get exhausted, and bring high energy food to replenish your reserves.

Avalanches: These pose a serious threat to winter mountain adventurers. Research has shown that most avalanches are triggered by people skiing through an avalanche zone.

An avalanche zone is a slope in which the gradient ranges between 27° and 45°. On shallower slopes, the snow usually won't accumulate. Avoid disaster by careful route selection and trip planning. Don't ski through a likely avalanche zone – make sure you pass above or

a hardware store, a bar or gas station if you plan to be on the water or along the shoreline. All too frequently, the fisherman standing on a rock working the incoming tide waits too long to retreat. This can develop into a life-threatening situation. People traveling along beaches in vehicles must also be aware of the tides or they risk losing their transportation – or worse. Large tides create swift currents in constricted areas, such as inlets. Avoid traveling in small crafts during these times – it's perilous.

Be aware of these warnings, take sensible precautions, listen to experts, and you will go home safely with unforgettable memories of the vacation of a lifetime. ❏

LEFT: repelling bears and insects.
ABOVE: an icy, unwelcoming glacier.

PLACES

*Alaska contains some of the last untamed wilderness areas
that are still within easy reach of an airport*

Alaska is, above all else, a land of remarkable diversity. It is the largest state in the union, and the most sparsely populated. With approximately 621,400 residents, there is an average of about 1 sq. mile (2.5 sq. km) of land for each of them.

There's urban Alaska, which usually means Anchorage, although the description is often enlarged to include Fairbanks and Juneau. The latter is the capital, but it's a much smaller city than Anchorage. There's rural Alaska, which comprises the villages scattered throughout the land, mostly along major rivers or near the coast. And there's wilderness Alaska, vast regions of relatively untouched ground – ground that knows only the whims of nature.

Communities have their attractions to be sure, and these are mostly friendly, easy-going communities, but it is the wilderness that beckons most travelers to Alaska. Where else in the world can you climb the highest of peaks, tread softly along an unexplored river bank, chill refreshments with ice broken from a glacier, or view hundreds of square miles of untrampled wildflowers, all with little more formality than a passport check when stepping from an airliner?

Almost all the cities and towns have companies which specialize in providing access to the wilderness. Charter air services, outdoor expedition ventures and a host of other related industries exist specifically to take travelers into remote regions – and to provide people with a way of earning a living in the wilderness, a factor which should not be overlooked, for it is a vital part of the state's economy.

Each Alaskan enjoys his or her own "special place," almost all of which are in the wilderness. Visitors to Alaska should make the effort to spirit themselves away from civilization and seek a special place of their own. Ask those who have been to Alaska whether it was the thought of glaciers and mountains, or of a city, that lured them north. Very few will say the latter. People may be pleasantly surprised by Alaska's cities, but almost without exception they come principally to explore the Great Land, the under-tamed wilderness that appeals so strongly to so many 20th-century urban dwellers. ❑

PRECEDING PAGES: traditional winter dog train; a more contemporary train near Denali; a cruise-ship at sunset. **LEFT:** which way to downtown?

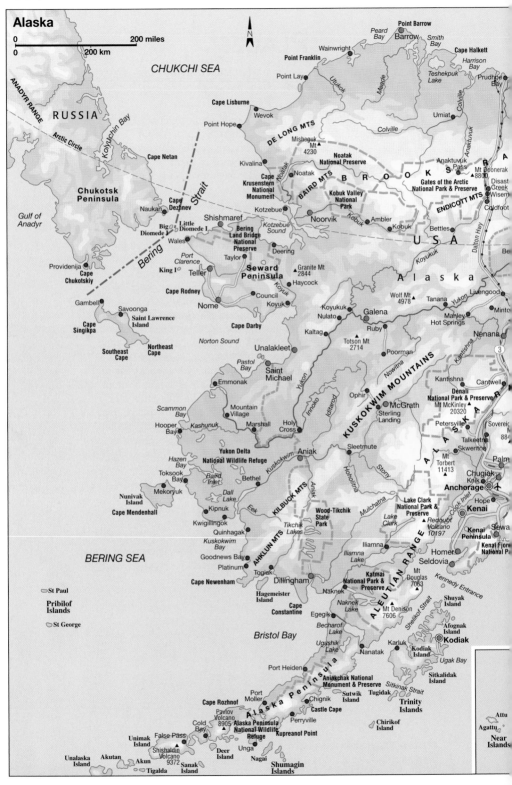

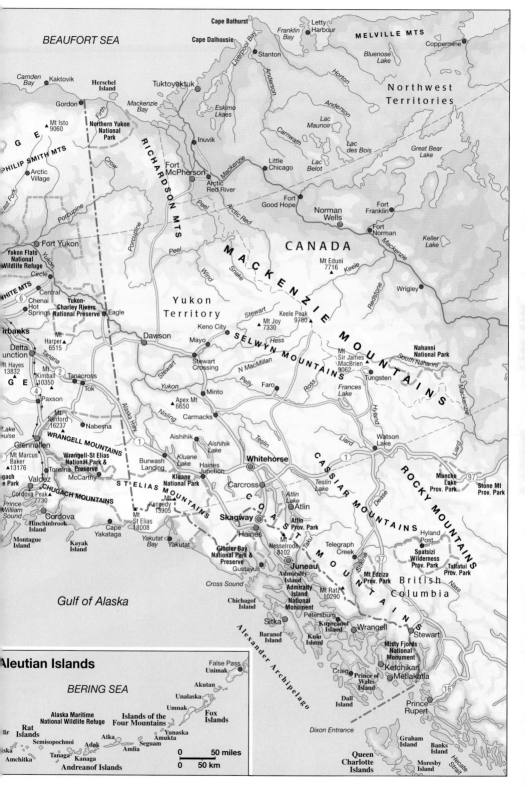

BEAUFORT SEA

Cape Bathurst
Cape Dalhousie
Franklin Bay
Letty Harbour
MELVILLE MTS
Coppermine
Stanton
Bluenose Lake

Camden Bay
Kaktovik
Herschel Island
Tuktoyaktuk
Mackenzie Bay
Eskimo Lkaes
Anderson
N o r t h w e s t
T e r r i t o r i e s

Gordon
Mt Isto 9060
Northern Yukon National Park
Firth
Lac Maunoir
Anderson
Great Bear Lake

PHILIP SMITH MTS
Arctic Village
Crow
Inuvik
Fort McPherson
Mackenzie
Little Chicago
Lac des Bois
Lac Belot

East Fork
Porcupine
Porcupine
RICHARDSON MTS
Arctic Red River
Peel
Fort Good Hope
Norman Wells
Fort Franklin

Fort Yukon
Porcupine
Peel
Arctic Red
Fort Norman
Keller Lake

Yukon Flats National Wildlife Refuge
Circle
Yukon
C A N A D A
Mackenzie

WHITE MTS
6
Central
Chenai Hot Springs
Yukon–Charley Rivers National Preserve
Eagle
Mt Eduni 7716
Keele
Wrigley

irbanks
Mt Harper 6515
Dawson
Keno City
Yukon Territory
Stewart
Keele Peak 9780
Redstone
Nahanni National Park
South Nahanni

Delta Junction
Tanana
Mayo
Mt Joy 7330
Hess
Mt Sir James MacBrien 9062
Tungsten

Mt Hayes 13832
2
Tanacross
Stewart Crossing
SELWYN MOUNTAINS
Mackenzie

GE
Mt Kimball 10350
Tok
Stewart
N MacMillan
Pelly
Faro
Frances Lake

4
Paxson
Yukon
Apex Mt 6650
Minto
Ross
Hyland
Watson Lake

Mt Sanford 16237
Nabesna
Nisling
Carmacks
Liard
1

Lake Louise
WRANGELL MOUNTAINS
Aishihik
Aishihik Lake
Teslin
ROCKY MOUNTAINS

Glennallen
Mt Marcus Baker 13176
Wrangell–St Elias National Park & Preserve
Burwash Landing
Kluane Lake
Haines Junction
Whitehorse
CASSIAR MOUNTAINS
Muncho Lake Prov. Park
97
Stone Mt Prov. Park

Tonsina
McCarthy
Kluane National Park
Carcross
Teslin Lake
Dease

gach e Park
Cordova Peak 7730
CHUGACH MOUNTAINS
ST ELIAS
Atlin Lake
Atlin

Valdez
Kennedy 13905
Skagway
Atlin Prov. Park
Stikina
37
Spatsizi Wilderness Prov. Park
Tatlatui Prov. Park

Prince William Sound
Cordova
Mt St Elias 18008
MOUNTAINS
Haines
Nesselrode 8102
Telegraph Creek
Hyland Post

Montague Island
Hinchinbrook Island
Cape Yakataga
Yakutat Bay
Yakutat
Glacier Bay National Park & Preserve
Gustavus
Juneau
Taku
Mt Edziza Prov. Park
B r i t i s h C o l u m b i a

Kayak Island
Cross Sound
Admiralty Island
Admiralty Island National Monument
Mt Ratz 10290
Nass

Gulf of Alaska
Chichagof Island
COAST
MOUNTAINS
Petersburg

Alexander Archipelago
Sitka
Baranof Island
Kuiu Island
Kupreanof Island
Wrangell
Stewart

Craig
Prince of Wales Island
Misty Fjords National Monument
Ketchikan
Metlakatla

Dall Island
Prince Rupert
16

Dixon Entrance

BERING SEA

False Pass
Unimak
Akutan
Unalaska
Umnak
Fox Islands

Alaska Maritime National Wildlife Refuge
Islands of the Four Mountains
Yunaska
Amukta
Seguam
Amlia

Rat Islands
Semisopochnoi
Adak
Atka
Andreanof Islands

ska
Amchitka
Tanaga
Kanaga

0   50 miles
0   50 km

Graham Island
Banks Island
Queen Charlotte Islands
Moresby Island
Hecate Strait

TOURING THE PANHANDLE

*A cruise or ferry tour of the Panhandle is a good
introduction to Alaska, giving the visitor
a taste of the scenery and the culture*

Map,
page 110

Ever since it emerged from the melting of the last great Ice Age – some 15,000 years ago – the great island-studded, 1,000-mile (1,600-km) passage of water that stretches from present lower British Columbia to the top of the Southeast Alaska Panhandle has been one of earth's treasures. The first Europeans to visit a portion of what is now called the Inside Passage did not get a friendly reception from the locals, however. In 1741 Alexei Chirikof, captain of the good ship *St Paul*, set sail from Russia. With his commander, Vitus Bering (who also was captain of the vessel *St Peter*), he left the Kamchatkan Peninsula in Siberia and headed east on a voyage of exploration and discovery.

What Chirikof and Bering were looking for was North America, which everyone knew was out there – Columbus had established that in 1492 – but Bering and his colleagues had only shortly before determined that it was not connected to Siberia and the European–Asian land mass. But the two captains were separated in a storm which struck soon after leaving port, and they never saw each other again. Bering, in fact, died after being ship-wrecked on his voyage home.

Chirikof and his crew sighted the high wooded mountains of what we now call Prince of Wales Island in Southeast Alaska on July 15, 1741. Two days later they dropped anchor near the present-day city of Sitka. It was there that tragedy struck, when two boat loads of sailors put ashore to reconnoiter disappeared without trace (*see* page 117).

These days, it is not often that visitors to the Panhandle fail to return to ship. When it does happen, it is probably because they lose track of time while hiking to the top of Deer Mountain in Ketchikan, get carried away in the pursuit of pleasure at the Red Dog Saloon in Juneau, or simply decide the fishing is too good to be hurried.

The sights along the Inside Passage are surprisingly varied and never boring. There are two capital cities along the length of the passage, one Canadian and one American, where life and lifestyle revolve largely around politics and bureaucracy. And there are tiny Native villages where the food on most residents' tables still depends on the harvest of sea, land and forest and the skills of the hunters and fishermen.

There are homes and condos and high-rise hotels as modern as can be found in any of the communities of the world, and there are tiny, hand-built cabins and camps which may be spotted – briefly, on a cruise or during a fly-by – in isolated wilderness settings far from roads, stores, television stations or daily newspapers.

The geography and the geology of the Inside Passage varies greatly as well. At its southernmost end, the passage is protected by Vancouver Island, a large, elongated landmass that begins near the northern border of the United States and stretches nearly 300 miles (480 km) northwest, nearly half the distance up the British

PRECEDING PAGES:
cruising the Inside
Passage.
LEFT: state ferry in
Lynn Canal.
BELOW: kayakers
on Pack Creek,
Admiralty Island.

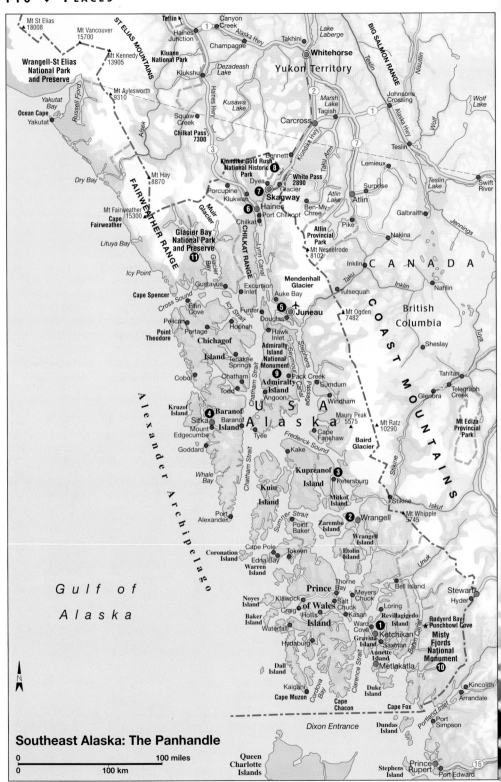

Southeast Alaska: The Panhandle

| 0 | 100 miles |
| 0 | 100 km |

Columbia coast to Southeast Alaska. Then comes the seaward protection of the Queen Charlotte Islands, not as large as Vancouver Island but a number of them – especially Graham and Moresby islands – quite sizeable nonetheless. And finally, about where US jurisdiction, and Southeast Alaska begins, there's the Alexander Archipelago, a 400-mile (645-km) long maze of 1,000 massive and minuscule isles which, along with a 30-mile (48-km) wide sliver of mainland, make up the Southeast Alaska Panhandle. In this book, only destinations within Alaska's state boundary are covered.

If the size and national colors of the islands of the Inside Passage vary, there is this commonality all along the way: lush green forests of hemlock, cedar, fir and other conifers cover whole islands and mountains except for snow-capped peaks and gravel beaches. Generous bays and exquisite little coves rival one another for attention, and major rivers course through great glacier-carved valleys, while waterfalls plunge from mountainside cliffs to the sea.

And everywhere along the way are watercraft: seine boats with crews of half a dozen or more; small trollers and gillnet fishing craft with a skipper and, maybe, a single helper; tugs pulling rafts of logs or barges or commercial goods; exotic yachts and simple open boats; cruise-ships; state ferries; freighters; even sailboats and kayaks.

The reason for this concentration of watercraft, of course, is protection. The same islands which provide near-continuous evergreen beauty to visitors along the way provide buffers from North Pacific winds and weather that could otherwise threaten all but the toughest vessels.

The islands also afford protection and nurture for a wide variety of wild creatures. Ashore, and beyond the gaze of spectators, thousands of animals make their homes within the forests and even atop the mountains of the Southeast Alaska Panhandle. Charter a light aircraft at Yakutat, near the very top of the Panhandle, and you are likely to see moose and perhaps brown bear as well. Near Juneau or Ketchikan or any of the other cities in the region, there is a good opportunity to spot herds of white mountain goats.

Take one of the kayak excursions in **Glacier Bay National Park** in the northern Panhandle (*see* page 126), and as you paddle alongside forest or beach you just might see the rare "Glacier Blue" – a subspecies of black bear. Cruise or fly to Pack Creek on **Admiralty Island** (*see* page 116) during the salmon spawning season and you can easily view and photograph dozens of huge, lumbering brown bears.

Spotting wildlife

Throughout the Panhandle, and down the coast of British Columbia as well, Sitka black-tail deer are numerous. This is one species of land animal you may be able to spot along the beaches from a cruise-ship.

Sea mammals are easier to see from a boat, of course. Humpback and killer whales, cavorting porpoises in twos and fours, and sea lions by the dozen are frequent sights, much appreciated by vessel-borne visitors along the Inside Passage.

Eagles are everywhere – the white-headed, white-tailed bald eagle which is the symbol of the United

Map, see opposite

BELOW: a guide to Dolly's House.

States. You see them diving and swooping from the heights to grab unwary fish swimming near the water's surface, you witness the strength of their powerful talons as they rip salmon carcasses to shreds alongside spawning streams, and you view them high in the spruce trees, standing guard over heavy nests which are lodged in the forks of great branches.

Besides the eagles, there are huge black ravens, tiny gray wrens and black-capped Arctic terns (who come to the northern climes from as far south as Antarctica), plus hundreds of different waterfowl, shorebirds and upland species.

The fishing here is world-class. Perhaps your goal is to haul in a lunker king salmon of 50 lbs (23 kg) or more. Or maybe you want to test your skill against diving, dancing and frothing steelhead trout. Whatever your heart's desire, the fishing in this region is simply unexcelled anywhere else. In addition to kings and steelheads, there are coho (silver) salmon – considered by many to be, pound for pound, the gamest fish in salt water – plus sockeye salmon, halibut, rainbow trout, Dolly Varden and eastern brook trout (these latter two are actually chars). With this concentration of fish, wildlife and scenic beauty, it's easy to see why increasing numbers of people choose to live in this region.

Ketchikan ❶, which Alaskans call "the First City" because it is the first major Alaskan community encountered on a journey north, is famous for at least three things: totem poles (more historic poles are located here than anywhere else in the world); salmon (caught in considerable numbers both by sport and commercial fishermen); and as the jumping-off place for **Misty Fjords National Monument** (*see* page 119) which in recent years has come to be appreciated as one of the mountain and maritime scenic wonders of Alaska. Ketchikan has one other small claim to fame: it is one of the few places where a brothel has been

A totemic hydrant.

BELOW: salmon fisherman in Ketchikan.

turned into a museum. **Dolly's House** on Creek Street, once the red-light district, is open most days during the summer months, and provides an interesting insight into one very important, if not much discussed, aspect of frontier life.

If you are more interested in totem poles, visit the **Totem Heritage Center** (601 Deermount Street; open daily in summer 8am–5pm; entrance charge) where you will be given a guided tour. As for Ketchikan's famous salmon: cross Ketchikan Creek to the Deer Mountain Tribal Hatchery (1158 Salmon Road, tel: 225-5158; open daily 8am–4:30pm; entrance charge) where each year thousands of coho and king salmon are raised and released. The new Southeast Alaska Visitor Center on Mill Street near the attractive Thomas Basin boat harbor is extremely helpful, particularly if you are planning walking trips on the various trails that start from the city, and contains a museum with extensive information about the area.

Wrangell ❷ is a town bypassed by most cruise-boats and most tourists. This is a pity, because it is a small untouristy patch of authentic Alaska. The fishing is excellent, and the people are genuinely anxious to help you enjoy their town. There is an interesting local museum and an easily accessible totem park and community house on **Chief Shakes Island** (opening hours vary; tel: 874-3770 or 874-2023 for details). Wrangell is also known for its petroglyphs, ancient rock carvings which can be seen at low tide on the beach at the north end of town, off Evergreen Avenue. A boat trip up the nearby Stikine River is a time-capsule voyage back into Alaska's unspoiled past. The forested scenery around the town is likewise spectacular – except for some big, ugly clear-cut logging scars on the side of some mountains, but that's part of what Alaska is all about these days.

Map, page 110

BELOW: totems at Ketchikan's Totem Heritage Center.

Banners in downtown Sitka.

Petersburg ❸, across the Stikine to the north and just a few minutes by plane from Wrangell, is likewise bypassed by most tour ships and visitors. Again, a pity, for this spick-and-span little community of Norwegian descendants (founded in 1897) offers yet another opportunity for visitors who enjoy poking around on their own.

As in Wrangell, there are ancient Native Alaskan petroglyphs to be seen on the beaches when the tide is low, and the small but tasteful **Clausen Memorial Museum** (2nd and Fram Streets, tel: 772-3598; open daily in summer 9am–4:30pm; entrance charge) offers insight into the history and art of fishing. Simply wandering the docks and wharves of the community will give the visitor a view of the large halibut fishing fleet.

Sitka ❹, the next port of call, dates back to 1799 when the Russian trader and colonizer Alexander Baranof established his headquarters there. Actually, Tlingit Natives had been there centuries before, and near the site of present day Sitka were fought two of the bloodiest battles between Alaska Natives and Russian colonists. The Natives won the first round, but the Russians, utilizing cannons as well as guns, won the second encounter. Today, the city is a pleasurable blend of Tlingit, Russian and American culture. The Russian Orthodox **Cathedral of St Michael**, on Lincoln Street, with its priceless icons and other religious treasures, is reason enough to visit this city. Another very good reason is the **Sitka National Historical Park** (106 Metlakatla Street, tel: 747-6281; open daily in summer 8am–5pm), which is located at the site of the second battle. Besides an excellent collection of totem poles, there is a museum on the battle and a workshop where you can see Tlingit artisans at work. Nearby, the **Alaska Raptor Rehabilitation Center** is the highlight for many people. Here you can

BELOW: the waterfront at Sitka.

see bald eagles and other birds of prey recuperating before being released into the wild. There are conducted tours (1101 Sawmill Creek Road, tel: 747-8662 for times and details; entrance charge).

Juneau ⑤, the state capital, is a port of call for virtually every cruise-ship, ferry and airline that comes to southeast Alaska. It will be covered in detail in the chapter on page 133.

Haines ⑥, 80 air miles (130 km) north of Juneau, is the northern co-terminus (along with Skagway) of the southeast segment of the Alaska state ferry system. From here you can drive the 150-mile (242-km) Haines Highway to Haines Junction (Canada) on the Alaska Highway which leads to the interior of the state. But do not leave for the Interior until you have seen what Haines has to offer. The town is rich in Tlingit Native culture and is best known for its majestic mountain scenery, king and sockeye salmon-fishing, bald-headed eagles, and Native art and dance.

Old Fort William Henry Seward to the south of town has massive turn-of-the-century officers' homes and command buildings still surrounding the old rectangular grounds. The biggest hotel in town is located in two of these buildings, as is the **Alaska Indian Arts Center**, a totem pole carving studio open for public viewing (open Mon–Fri 1–5pm; admission free). The **Chilkat Center for Performing Arts** nearby (open Mon–Sat 9am–12 noon, 1–5pm) stages dance productions throughout the summer months (tel: 766-2160 to find out times of performances).

In the late fall the world's greatest gathering of bald eagles – more than 3,000 of them, many of them coming from home territories hundreds of miles away – flies to a nearby river and woods to feast on a late run of salmon in ice-free

Map,
page 110

BELOW: distant packing house near Haines.

Map, page 110

waters. The **American Bald Eagle Foundation Natural History Museum**, at 115 Haines Highway (open daily 10am–5pm; admission free, donation requested) has a fascinating diorama.

Skagway ❼ is the northernmost of all the communities usually visited on a tour of the Inside Passage. For more details about this community, and the **Klondike Gold Rush National Historic Park ❽**, *see* page 142.

In addition to the major communities along the Inside Passage, there are throughout the region countless other settlements, Native villages and fishing camps equally worth a day's or a week's visit. Near Ketchikan, on Prince of Wales Island, colorful old **Waterfall Cannery** has been converted into what the owners call "the most civilized resort in Alaska." It's within easy reach of some of Southeast Alaska's hottest salmon angling. Similarly superlative fishing can be experienced near the Tlingit villages of Angoon, Kake and Hoonah, all of which offer modest but comfortable tourist accommodations.

Angoon is the only settlement in **Admiralty Island National Monument ❾**, a largely wilderness preserve which can be reached by air or sea from Sitka or Juneau, and which is famous for its salmon and, especially, its large numbers of brown bears – some reckon there are as many as 1,700 on the island. **Kake**, which has the tallest totem pole in the state, is the jumping-off point for trips to **Tebenkof Bay Wilderness**, where experienced kayakers can spend days paddling the waters around the bays and coves of many tiny islands. **Hoonah**, the largest Tlingit village in Southeast Alaska, has some good hiking trails and a Cultural Center and Museum, which exhibits Tlingit art. Small commercial fishing centers, like Elfin Cove, Tenakee Springs, with its hot thermal baths, and Pelican, though never touted as tourist towns, provide visitors with indelible memories of a very contented part of Alaska. Pelican can be visited on a day trip from Juneau through the Icy Straits, where you may well see humpback whales.

BELOW: catching Dolly Varden near Glacier Bay.

How to get around amongst all this wonderful wildlife, fabulous fishing, glacier grandeur and mountain-shrouded seaways? It's easy and the options are wide, but can be expensive. There are posh cruise-ships, for example. Some people choose to drive the family buggy aboard ferries of the Alaska Marine Highway System, which runs from the city of Bellingham, in Washington, with a stop at Canada's Prince Rupert, in British Columbia, before hitting all the major ports in Southeast Alaska, terminating in either Haines or Skagway. Passengers can get off and explore big towns and small villages along the way (*see* page 316 for more information). Still others jet in from Seattle to Ketchikan, Wrangell, Petersburg, Sitka and Juneau.

Once you've arrived, the options are even broader. Yacht excursions large and small are available at every turn. Alaska's bush pilots, some on wheels, some on floats, others in helicopters will take you wherever you want to go, and hiking trails fan out from almost every settlement. There are few visitors who are not satisfied with an Inside Passage sojourn. And Southeast Alaskans, never reticent about the attractions of their place on the planet, speculate that maybe, having sampled life ashore in this lush and bountiful land, even Chirikof's lost sailors didn't really want to leave. ❑

The lost sailors

To Alexei Chirikof, captain of the Russian ship *St Paul,* goes the prize for seeing Alaska first. His crew sighted the high wooded mountains of what we now call Prince of Wales Island in Southeast Alaska on July 15, 1741. Two days later he dropped anchor, probably in the vicinity of the present-day site of Sitka. It was there that tragedy struck – a tragedy recorded by Lt Sven Waxel, a Swede who served as first mate and pilot aboard the *St Paul.* The following account is his story:

The ship went to anchor a good distance from the shore and, being short of water, Chirikof decided to send a boat ashore. To command it he chose an officer called Avraam Demetiev, a very capable man, and gave him a crew of the best men he had. They were all equipped with guns and ammunition and also had a metal cannon. They were also given a signaling system and complete instructions about how to behave and act in the event of the unexpected happening. Besides all this, they were supplied with provisions to last several days.

The boat pulled away from the ship: they watched it disappear around a headland and some while later noticed various signal flashes corresponding with the orders given, so that they had every reason for thinking that the party landed safely. However, two days passed and then a third day, and still the boat did not come back.

Nevertheless, they could see the whole time that the signal fires continued to burn and so they began to think that perhaps the boat had been damaged on landing and that the party's return was delayed by having to repair it.

They then decided to send the little jolly-boat ashore with carpenters, calkers and all that they might need, so that the boat could be repaired if that should prove necessary. (A jolly-boat is an old term for a ship's boat. Its origins are obscure.)

This was no sooner said than done. Six men were ordered into the jolly-boat, equipped with guns and ammunition and well supplied with everything else they might need. They were to search out the boat and give all help that might be called for when they found it, after which both boats were to return to the ship immediately.

The next morning, two craft were seen coming out from land, the one slightly larger than the other. Naturally it was assumed that these were the long boat and the jolly-boat and very glad they were to see them. They began to get the ship ready to put to sea again. But as the two craft drew near the ship, they discovered the truth was the opposite.

These were American boats and they were filled with Natives. They approached to within three cable lengths of the ship. Then, seeing so many on deck, they turned back toward land. Those on board the ship had no boat left in which they could have put out after the Natives, and they had just to draw the melancholy conclusion that both the long boat and the jolly-boat were lost along with their entire crews. No one will ever know exactly what happened to the lost sailors, but we must assume they met a gruesome end. ❑

RIGHT: Vitus Bering died on his voyage home from Alaska.

MISTY FJORDS NATIONAL MONUMENT

Map, page 110

The southernmost of Alaska's national monuments is a magical place, carved out by the steady progress of huge glaciers

Misty Fjords was designated by the US Congress as a national wilderness as well as a national monument, and within the 3,570 sq. miles (9,240 sq. km) of its largely untouched coast and backcountry lie three major rivers, hundreds of small streams and creeks, icefields, glaciers, snowcapped mountains and mountain-top lakes.

Glacial scenery

Eons ago, great glaciers thousands of feet deep filled what are now Southeast Alaska bays and valleys. Slowly but relentlessly they ground their way seaward from mountain-top heights. In the process they carved and scoured great steep-walled cliffs that now plunge from mountain summits to considerable depths below sea level. The effect of this carving and scouring has never been more beautifully evident than it is in **Misty Fjords National Monument ⑩**.

It is the southernmost of Alaska's 18 national monuments and visitors to this 2.2 million-acre (890,000-hectare) wilderness experience every major ecosystem of Southeast Alaska, from the ocean swells on the outer coast to the alpine lakes. There are tiny coves, great bays, and forest groves so thick you can barely see daylight through them. Misty Fjords wildlife includes brown and black bears, Sitka black-tail deer, wolves, mountain goats, beavers, mink, marten, foxes and river otters. But it is not only a place of scenery and wildlife on a grand scale: it also has tremendous commercial value. Some of Alaska's most productive fish rearing streams are located here.

There are very few marks of human activity inside Misty Fjords. The area's first human inhabitants – the Native Tlingits and Haidas – are believed to have settled here many thousands of years ago, after crossing the land bridge from Siberia, but visitors to the monument may stay for some time without seeing any evidence of their passing.

LEFT: early light in Misty Fjords.
BELOW: a young brown bear in the wild.

Touring Misty Fjords

There are no roads leading to Misty Fjords, so there are only two ways to get there: by water or by air. Some travelers opt for a combination cruise/fly tour – going in by water and out by air, or vice versa. Some cruise-ships visit the monument as part of an Inside Passage experience (*see* page 109). You can fly there with one of several Ketchikan air charter companies; you can cruise there by charter boat; or (probably most convenient of all) you can sign on with an outfit called **Alaska Cruises** (tel: 225-6044 or 800-228-1905), and take one of the yacht tours which the company schedules daily in the summer time. These excursions, aboard one of the company's 32-passenger vessels, can either be a round-trip or one-way, with one part of the journey – either coming or going – done by air.

On a typical cruise/fly tour the boat will depart from near downtown Ketchikan at about 8:30am, but coffee is always ready on the galley stove and donuts are on the serving table for passengers who arrive on the ship early. These boats are wide, beamy, comfortable cruisers with plenty of walking-around room, big view windows, and table seating for 32. When the weather is nice about half that number can be seated on an open-air deck above the cabin.

Salmon route

*The insignia of
Alaska Star.*

The sightseeing begins as soon as the boat's lines are cast off and the vessel begins its southeasterly path toward the lower end of Revillagigedo Island (the locals abbreviate it to Revilla Island), on which Ketchikan is located. Passing dockside fish processors, supply houses and the town's main business district, the vessel soon cruises past the entrance to Ketchikan Creek. Late in the summer, thousands of salmon assemble here before ascending the creek – and formidable waterfalls – to spawn in the upstream shallows and then die.

Shortly after Creek Street (Ketchikan's former red light district), the boat goes past **Saxman**, a Native village containing one of the largest collections of totems in the state, before passing **Bold Island** where passengers line the port (left-hand) rails and windows of the vessel in the hope of seeing bald eagles perched in the island spruce trees. For Southeast Alaskans, such sightings are commonplace, though they never become dull. For visitors, the sight of America's national bird is a highlight of the trip. At one point or another during the morning's cruise, most passengers will crowd into the yacht's little wheelhouse and

BELOW: Misty Fjord
coastline.

talk to Dale Pihlman, sometimes the skipper and at one time the owner of the Alaska Cruises excursion firm. Dale generally welcomes the intrusion, as he is never reluctant to talk about the monument.

Dale is a former commercial fisherman and he was one of the committed people who traveled to Washington in the late 1970s to lobby for the bill that created Misty Fjords National Monument in the first place. The provisions of the bill do protect most of the monument today from destructive exploitation.

Porpoise companions

As the boat cruises toward the fjords, the on-board guide and naturalist may announce that there are porpoises both fore and aft of the vessel, and the passengers – half going in each direction in order to keep an even kilter – scramble for a view of the small marine mammals. The porpoises swimming behind the yacht are too far away for a close look – they are visible only as leaping, playing creatures 100 yards or more (just over 100 meters) astern. But the ones in front are only a few feet away, clearly visible, and just as clearly having a wonderful time pacing the boat. For brief moments their dorsal fins break the surface of the water; at other times they dive. It's obvious they could outdistance the 16-knot vessel easily, but they prefer to stay and play, and they will do so for a quarter hour or so.

By noon the vessel is in the monument and Dale guides it through a narrow channel into an exquisite little tree-shrouded cove on **Rudyerd Island**. The naturalist points out the steep granite rock formations on the shore and the occasional jet black vertical streaks, a few inches to a couple of feet or more wide, that appear among the brown granite walls.

Map, page 110

BELOW: touring the waterfalls by floatplane.

These were formed 60 million years ago when earthquakes in the region cracked the granite, and hot molten magma came up from below the earth's surface to fill the cracks. The black streaks that you see are magma.

Shapely rock

A little later, **New Eddystone Rock** comes into view. Depending upon the time of day when you see it and the angle from which you approach it, the rock can resemble several things: sometimes it looks like a man-made building, at others, a ship under sail, or it can look exactly what it is – a high-rising volcano "plug" from millennia past. It was called Eddystone Rock by the British navigator Captain George Vancouver (1758–98) (after whom the Canadian city is named), because he thought it looked very much like Eddystone Lighthouse off the shore of his native Plymouth, in England.

Overnight campers and kayakers who want to go into the fjords often travel along with the day visitors on Alaska Cruises vessels, and this is the time they leave the ship in their smaller craft to paddle the waters off Winstanley Island. There's a US Forest Service cabin there, one of relatively few located on saltwater sites in Southeast Alaska.

The comfortable, weather-tight shelter is popular with campers who paddle around **Rudyerd Bay** during the day. The cruiser enters the bay and often meets a welcoming committee of at least 20 seals which lie basking on the rocks of an island to port.

Minutes later, within the bay, the boat approaches the towering massive vertical walls of **Punchbowl Cove**. And it is here that you really feel the magical, mystical effect of the place.

A sharp-eyed owl.

BELOW: a misty waterfall in Rudyerd Bay.

Mists and mystique

It can be truly eerie hereabouts, especially when – as the monument's name suggests – there is mist or cloud or fog in the air. Steep, stark granite walls descend from heights hidden in clouds. Waterfalls which range from torrents to trickles plunge from unseen sources just as high. Trees both large and small cling tenaciously to many of the cliff-sides, on surfaces that don't seem to have enough soil to support a house plant.

The waters around and beneath the boat are a cold, slate gray, and they descend to depths of 750 ft (230 meters) or more. There have, as yet, been no sightings of sea monster reported in these waters – but it's exactly the right kind of place for them.

On board, thoughts turn to more practical matters: it is time for a luncheon of seafood chowder, rolls and tossed green salad. After lunch, the vessel leaves Punchbowl Cove and cruises toward the head of Rudyerd Bay. Along the shoreline that now replaces the steep cliffs, you may spot for bears, wolves or other wild creatures.

Creeks and waterfalls

The boat stops again an hour later, this time at **Nooya Creek** where, in season, 1,000 or more pink salmon descend to salt water each year from Nooya Lake in the high country. Here a trail leads to the uplands – although it is not as steep as the one which takes off, and up, from the Punchbowl Cove area visited earlier. The camping and trout-fishing opportunities at the ends of the trails are, according to our skipper, outstanding.

Then, if you are lucky, it might be time for yet another memorable experience. On some trips the skipper will edge his boat right up to a large plummeting waterfall, and passengers are given paper cups which they can fill with the icy water. Promptly at 2:30pm, it is time for those who fly back to Ketchikan to disembark and board the floatplane which taxis gently up to the boarding platform.

From the air

Fifteen minutes later, goodbyes are yelled to those remaining and the pilot drifts his plane away from the vessel. He then gives the aircraft full throttle, and within a minute it is airborne. Within three or four minutes more the airborne passengers may well be spotting white, furry mountain goats, usually nannies and their youngsters, negotiating seemingly impossible cliff faces to the right of the plane. It is a dramatic flight back through the fjords and the wildlife is only part of the excitement as the dark granite walls seem to be just inches away from the plane's wing tips – a bit too close for comfort, some may think, but passengers are in very safe hands.

By the time you arrive back at the floatplane dock in downtown Ketchikan, your mind's eye will be full of images and your camera bag full of film you are longing to get developed. Your stock of anecdotes will be piling up at the same rate, and you will be convinced that visiting Misty Fjords is, indeed, one of Alaska's premier experience. ❏

Map, page 110

BELOW: the verdant coastal rainforest.

GLACIER BAY NATIONAL PARK

The glaciers of the bay have retreated dramatically during the past two hundred years, a process which is continuing today

Alaska
Anchorage●

PRECEDING PAGES: setting up camp in Glacier Bay. **BELOW:** the willow ptarmigan, Alaska's state bird.

Glacier Bay National Park and Preserve ⑪ encompasses 3.3 million acres (1.3 million hectares). Located at the northern end of Alaska's southeastern Panhandle, the park's center lies approximately 90 miles (145 km) northwest of Juneau and 600 miles (965 km) southeast of Anchorage. Most visitors arrive at Glacier Bay on large cruise-ships or package tours, but you can reach Gustavus by air and boat charters from Juneau.

In a land comprising three climatic zones – marine to arctic – seven different ecosystems support a wide variety of plant and animal life. From the endangered humpback whale and Arctic peregrine falcon to the common harbor seal, black and brown bears, mountain goats, marmots, eagles and ptarmigans, Glacier Bay provides a rich overview of Alaska's wildlife.

Glacier Bay's physical environment is as diverse as any found in Alaska. Sixteen massive tidewater glaciers flowing from the snow-capped mountain peaks of the **Fairweather Range** plunge into the icy waters of the fjords. Besides the jagged icebergs, the ice-scoured walls of rock lining the waterways, the saltwater beaches and protected coves, numerous fresh-water lakes and thick forests of western hemlock and Sitka spruce are also found in the area.

History and exploration

Evidence of man's habitation in the Glacier Bay region dates back approximately 10,000 years. Researchers have outlined seasonal patterns of hunting, fishing and gathering from semi-permanent villages. Native Tlingit folklore includes tales of periodic village destruction from shock waves and other natural forces.

European exploration of Glacier Bay began in July 1741, when Russian ships (part of the Bering expedition) sailed the region's outer coast. French explorer Jean François de la Perouse arrived 45 years later, and in 1797 he published his detailed observations and map of Lituya Bay, with its five surrounding glaciers. These observations have provided scientists with valuable data, from which glacial changes over time are computed. Other explorers followed, such as Captain George Vancouver, who charted the waters of the Inside Passage in the 1790s. But it was the widespread publicity soon after naturalist John Muir's first reconnaissance of the area in 1879 that stimulated scientific investigations and early tourism. Where early explorers had found only a massive wall of ice, Muir paddled in waters newly released from glacial ice.

Visitors to Glacier Bay today see views very different from those which were observed in Muir's day, as glaciers have further changed the landscape in the past century. In Muir's time, the network of fjords had not

Map, page 110

yet been established; a huge glacier extended into the area which is now open water. Early steamship excursions during the 1880s carried up to 230 passengers, people who had come from around the world in order to sail close to the mighty ice walls. But the flock of curious scientists and tourists halted abruptly when, in 1899, a violent earthquake struck, causing huge amounts of ice from the Muir Glacier to calve, falling into the sea. An unbroken jam of floating ice choked the waterway and extended more than 10 miles (16 km) from the glacier's terminus.

When ships could no longer sail closer than about 6 miles (10 km) to the Muir Glacier, excursions to the area ceased. Touring slowly developed again after 1925, when the Glacier Bay National Monument was established.

Glaciers and icebergs

The glaciers of Glacier Bay National Park and Preserve have, over time, retreated and advanced due to severe climatic fluctuations. De la Perouse and Vancouver both observed glacier ice at the mouth of the bay in 1786 and 1794. During Muir's trip to Glacier Bay in 1879, however, the ice had retreated 32 miles (51 km) to a point near what is now the mouth of Muir Inlet. Ninety years later, the Muir Glacier had receded another 24 miles (39 km). Today the bay is 65 miles (105 km) long.

Glacier Bay visitors can often watch entire sections of glacier ice calve from 150-ft (46-meter) walls. The cracking ice produces a thundering roar, heard by those on the water. Huge bergs are set adrift, and waves sweep across sandbars outward from the glacier's tidewater base. Kayakers are warned to keep a safe distance from the glacier faces. Those on the water, close to ice chunks slowly

BELOW: cruise-ship in Glacier Bay.

Map, page 110

melting in the salty bay, may hear a crackling sound similar to breakfast cereal or champagne, which comes from the release of thousands of air bubbles which became trapped in the ice from high pressure during its formation. From the air, the sound cannot be heard above the drone of an aircraft engine, but the perspective of shimmering ice flowing from mountain top to sea is a dramatic one.

Plant and animal life

Two hundred years ago, when a glacier filled what is now a network of inlets in Glacier Bay, only a small number of plant and animal species inhabited the region. Since the retreat of the ice, life in the water and on the surrounding land has flourished. Today, the nutrient rich waters of the fjords are important feeding grounds for large marine mammals, and even the windswept, insect-free upper slopes of the glaciers provide welcome refuge for mountain goats and other animals.

A delicate tundra flower.

The four land and three marine ecosystems in Glacier Bay support life forms adapted to the environment. Near **Gustavus**, an ecosystem of sandy grassland, thick coniferous forests and damp marshes provides habitat for sandhill cranes, river otters, wolves, bears, coyotes and moose. **Bartlett Cove**, the park's only area of development, lies within a region dominated by coastal western hemlock and Sitka spruce. Watch for bald eagles flying overhead.

In the magnificent backcountry of Glacier Bay National Park and Preserve you may climb to elevations of 2,500 ft (762 meters). Here, in the alpine tundra ecosystem, the thick vegetation of lower elevations is replaced by shrubby plants – alpine grasses and dwarf blueberry. The terrain is rocky, and snow patches remain in early summer. Delicate flowering plants and lichens should be treated with respect, for regeneration in this environment is extremely slow. Glacial history can be computed by studying the steady rate of lichen growth.

Although few visitors venture onto the higher snowfields and glaciers, life in this seemingly barren, mountainous environment does exist. The ice worm, which is the only earthworm known to live on snow and ice, feeds on a red-pigmented green algae and organic debris swept onto the frozen surface. Slightly less than an inch (2.5 cm) long, these tiny black creatures hatch their eggs in sub-freezing temperatures and are extremely sensitive to heat. The glacier flea – a vegetarian insect – also lives above the treeline.

Possibly the most controversial species found within Glacier Bay National Park is the endangered humpback whale. A migratory marine mammal that winters near Hawaii or Mexico, humpbacks feed in the icy waters of southeastern Alaska and Glacier Bay in the summer. Killer and minke whales are sometimes spotted in the bay as well. Environmentalists fear that excessive numbers of cruise-ships may drive out the whales. Besides small intertidal creatures, Glacier Bay is also home to many fish and shorebirds. Sea lions and otters, harbor seals and porpoises are frequently sighted.

Park facilities and attractions

A small, free campground in Bartlett Cove fills to capacity only two or three times a season. **Sandy Cove**, approximately 20 miles (32 km) north, offers a good anchorage for those traveling by boat.

The National Park Service provides interpretive programs and activities to make visits even more exciting. Guided nature and walking tours on two well-maintained trails start from Bartlett Cove, and slide-lecture shows are given in the lodge and on concessionaire vessels. A floating ranger station in Blue Mouse Cove is open during the summer. The Park Service also staffs all cruise-ships entering the park with naturalists to inform people about the landscape. ❏

RIGHT: a sparkling ice cave.

JUNEAU, STATE CAPITAL

*Juneau is a small but busy capital, with museums,
galleries and bars downtown, and
trails and glaciers close by*

Map,
page 110

The going had been slow, sweaty, frustrating – plodding leadenly upstream beside the forest-rimmed waterway. Thick entangling underbrush, huge grasping devil's club plants (with thousands of tiny needles on every stalk and leaf), and great boulders in and alongside the stream. Then it got even worse, and the five men – two white prospectors who were guided by three Natives – had to abandon the stream entirely. They were forced to climb the mountain beside them in order to get to the gulch they sought. But as they descended from the mountain top into the watershed the labor was well worth the effort.

Before they even got to the mouth of the gulch, they took samples from the quartz lodes that cropped out of the mountain. And they were incredulous at what their pounding hammers yielded. One of the men recorded the experience in his journal thus: "We knew it was gold, but so much, and not in particles; streaks running through the rock and little lumps as large as peas or beans... I took the gold pan, pick, and shovel and panned $1.20 to $1.30 to the pan."

The two men were Joe Juneau and Richard Harris. The year was 1880. The place was Silver Bow Basin. And out of their discovery came a camp that became the capital city of Alaska.

PRECEDING PAGES: a
hiker above Juneau.
LEFT: banners on
the waterfront.
BELOW: cruising into
town.

City of gold and government

The delightful city of **Juneau ❺** today is a far cry from the wilderness site that Juneau and Harris encountered. About 30,000 Alaskans – whites, Native Tlingits, and other ethnic groups – call the community home. Most of them either work for the government (state, federal or local) or provide services for those who do.

The town is as modern as the state-of-the-art computer center in the State Office Building and as old-fashioned as the plantation-style Governor's Mansion a couple of blocks up the street. It's as sophisticated as its symphony orchestra and as earthy as the notorious Red Dog Saloon or the equally frontierish Alaskan Hotel bar nearby; as urban as its high-rise office buildings and high-comfort hotels, and as rugged as the northern wilderness of thick, lush forests, glacial ice and salt water which surrounds it. The wilderness begins literally where the houses stop.

Gold fever

The town was first named Harrisburg – some say because Harris, unlike his partner Juneau, was able to write and recorded it that way. But the name didn't stick: after news of the gold strike spread to Sitka and elsewhere, nearly 300 prospectors swarmed to the scene, and decided to rename the place Rockwell. Shortly thereafter it became Juneau. By whatever name, the camp was bustling with gold fever and, soon, gold

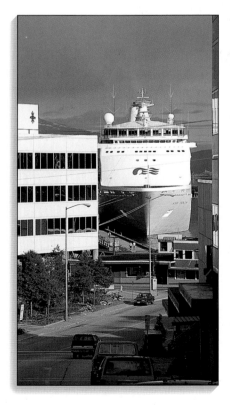

Stained-glass window in the library.

production. It didn't take long for simple gold pans, pickaxes and human labor to be replaced by miles-long flumes and ditches, carrying water to massive hydraulic earth-moving and sluicing operations. Within a decade of the Juneau/Harris discovery, wagon roads penetrated the valleys behind the camp-turned-town – roads you can hike on to this day.

Juneau is, of course, on the North American mainland. Across Gastineau Channel, on **Douglas Island**, even more furiously paced development took place. By 1882 the world famous Treadwell Mine was operational and expanding. Near it, the proud community of **Douglas** grew up, and indeed rivaled Juneau in population, industry and miners' baseball for a good number of years. Eventually, more than 50 years later, the two towns would merge, but the Douglas community remains distinct to this day, much in the way that Alaska is part of, but somehow set apart from, the rest of the United States.

Early on, politics assumed considerable importance in Juneau. The future state's first political convention was held here in the summer of 1881. The camp became a first-class municipality under the law in 1900, and in 1906 the district government of Alaska transferred there from Sitka.

In 1913, Alaska's first territorial legislature convened, in what is now the Elks Hall on Seward Street. Nearly life-size photo murals of that distinguished group can be seen today on the first floor of the State Capitol Building. The all-male representatives and senators in the pictures look exactly what they were, rugged frontier types, most of them probably uncomfortable in the stiff collars and ties they were forced to wear on the floors of their respective houses. As the city grew and prospered, enterprises such as fishing, saw-milling and trading became important in the economic scheme of things: important but not paramount.

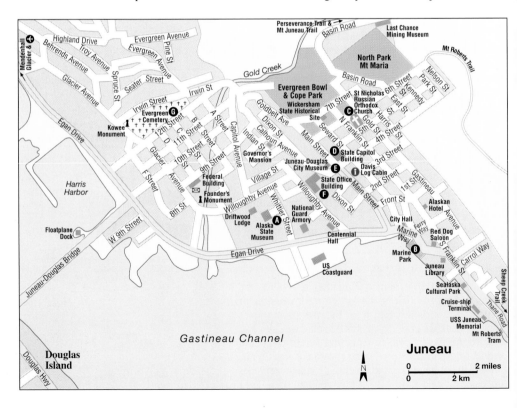

Gold was what Juneau was all about. Miners labored daily in miles and miles of tunnels that honeycombed the mountains both on the mainland and on Douglas Island. For recreation on days off they scoured the wild country beyond the urban centers, digging, panning, hoping against hope that they, too, might strike it rich like Juneau and Harris. Sadly, these two early prospectors, like many gold locators the world over, never realized much from their discoveries. Juneau died broke in the Canadian Yukon and a collection had to be taken up to send his body home for burial in the city he co-founded.

A frontier government

As the years passed there were ups and downs (definitely down when, in 1917, major portions of the Treadwell tunnels beneath the waters of Gastineau Channel caved in and flooded), but gold remained Juneau's, and Alaska's, mainstay, until relatively recent times. During World War II, however, the government ended an era when it closed down the massive Alaska-Juneau gold mine and milling operation for reasons of manpower and conservation.

But even with the mine closure, things didn't go too badly. By the time the 1944 shutdown came about, the city was experiencing something of a war boom, and with war's end there came a gradual but continuous rise in territorial government activity and employment.

By 1959, when Alaska became state number 49, government had all but filled the economic void left by mining's demise. And in the years since, Juneau has grown from a waterfront community hovering beneath the skeletal remains of the old Alaska-Juneau millsites, to a gregarious, upreaching, outreaching city spreading for miles to the north and south.

Map, see opposite

BELOW: a room in the Alaska State Museum.

The city's size was established in the mid-1960s when Juneau and Douglas and the Greater Juneau Borough were unified by a democratic vote into the City and Borough of Juneau. Since then, at least two additional communities in Alaska (Anchorage and Sitka) have consolidated their city and borough governments, but none have come close to ending up with as much territory.

Juneau is a small town in terms of population, but in square miles it is the biggest town in North America and second biggest in the world. In the international size sweep-stakes, Juneau's 3,108 sq. miles (8,050 sq. km) are exceeded only by the city of Kiruna, Sweden, which has 5,458 sq. miles (14,136 sq. km) within its borders. With that much land under its collective belt, it is little wonder that Juneau offers visitors so much to see and do.

Juneau is the only state capital in the USA that is not accessible by road.

Touring the capital

It's a good idea to start your tour of Juneau with a visit to one of its biggest attractions, the **Alaska State Museum** Ⓐ (open daily; entrance charge), within walking distance of downtown hotels and shopping. To visit the museum is to visit the whole of Alaska. Inuit culture is represented here in the form of small, intricate ivory carvings and a huge 40-ft (12-meter) *umiak*, or skin boat, of the type which were used for whale- and walrus-hunting along the ice floes of the Arctic Ocean.

Southeast Alaska's ancient Native way of life is reflected in the re-creation of an authentic community house, complete with priceless totemic carvings, and the Athabascan Natives, from the Interior, are represented with displays of a birch bark canoe, weapons and bead-decorated moosehide garments. There is also gold rush memorabilia, and natural history displays. Nor is the pre-gold rush Russian heritage ignored. Orthodox religious exhibits include precious

BELOW: Franklin Street in the heart of Juneau.

coins, priests' raiments, and the first American flag to be flown at Sitka when Russian America became American territory on October 18, 1867.

Map, page 134

Most notable of all the museum's exhibits is the "eagle tree," just inside the front entrance. There, in the middle of a spiraling staircase, a model of a towering spruce tree rises from ground level almost to the ceiling of the second floor. In a fork of the branches is a nest holding a very authentic-looking young bald eagle, with its magnificent 5-ft (1.5-meter) spread of wings outstretched.

Most of Juneau's other visitor attractions can be encountered in a walking tour along the community's docks and among its meandering, frequently narrow, streets and alleys. Go left along Egan Drive to **Marine Park ❸**, overlooking the city's dock and wharf area. It's a small, but pleasurable place of benches and shady trees situated near the ramp where cruise-ship passengers land after being lightered from ships at anchor offshore. This is where half of Juneau seems to eat its lunch, especially on sunny summer days. Street vendors in the vicinity offer entrées, literally *à la carte*, that range from halibut to hot dogs to tacos and Vietnamese spring rolls.

To the Capitol

Cross Ferry Way to South Franklin Street, where you will find art galleries and shops that feature Alaskan ivory, jade, totemic wood carvings and leatherwork. Also on South Franklin (turn right from Ferry Way) is the best-known bar in the city, the fun but touristy **Red Dog Saloon**. Further up the street is the **Alaskan Hotel Bar**, which retains its gold rush era decor and is well worth a visit. There are several seafood and other restaurants here, too, as well as the city's standard assortment of merchants and professional offices.

BELOW: the State Capitol Building.

Juneau's visitor information office – a re-creation of the town's first log school, which later became a brewery – is located on Seward Street, parallel with South Franklin, and on the way to the tiny **St Nicholas Russian Orthodox Church ❸**, one of the most picturesque houses of worship in Alaska.

The onion-domed, octagon-shaped church, located on Fifth Street, was constructed in 1894 at the specific request of Ishkhanalykh, the then principal chief of the Tlingits of Juneau. It is the oldest original Orthodox church in Southeast Alaska and one of the senior parishes of the entire state. The building is open to the public, but a donation is requested.

Downhill on Fourth Street is the **State Capitol Building ❶** where tours are conducted daily in the summer. The capitol was built in the 1930s and many of its halls and offices have recently been refurbished to reflect that era. You can see where the Alaska House and Senate meet during sessions; it's well worth a stop.

On the corner of Fourth and Main Streets is the **Juneau-Douglas City Museum ❸** (open daily in summer; entrance charge), which has interesting displays on the town's gold mining history. Across the road is the **State Office Building ❹** on Fourth Street, where you can stroll through the sky-lighted great hall. And on Friday, at noon, visitors to the SOB can enjoy a special treat. A giant old Kimball theater organ, a magnificent relic of Juneau's silent movie days, has been

Map,
page 134

A hopeful gold
seeker.

relocated in the atrium of the building; visiting organists and local musicians celebrate the coming weekend by playing its pipes from 12 noon to 1pm.

Two blocks beyond the SOB, on Calhoun Avenue, is the **Governor's Mansion**, which the state recently spent $2 million restoring to the glory of its 1913 opening. You can photograph the exterior, but you can't go in.

Beyond the Governor's Mansion and across **Gold Creek** – where Joe Juneau and Dick Harris panned their first gold in the area – you come to the **Evergreen Cemetery** ❻ where the two prospectors are buried. Cemeteries are not everybody's idea of sightseeing and the two founders' burial monuments are not overly impressive, but the partially wooded cemetery is a popular place for visitors to stroll and residents to walk their dogs. And after visiting the town, it's good to see where the two old prospectors ended up.

Glaciers – up close

Below: Mendenhall Glacier.

From Juneau, a number of impressive glaciers can be reached by auto or by trail, or viewed from the air. The best known is the **Mendenhall Glacier** which can be seen from a US Forest Service information center about 13 miles (21 km) north of town. The center sits on the edge of a frigid lake into which Mendenhall Glacier calves icebergs large and small. The face of the glacier is about one mile (2 km) from the visitor center, while its 1,500 sq. miles (3,885 sq. km) of ice and snow is called the **Juneau Icefield**. Perhaps the most exciting way to savor the glacier and its originating icefield is to take a trip organized by one of several air charter companies, or try one of the four helicopter carriers that offer 45 minutes or so flying over the great white deserts of snow, and a landing on the surface of the icefield. ❑

Juneau's trails

The most memorable thing about Juneau for many people is the rich variety of hiking trails which can be reached easily from the dockside and city center. All the starting points are clearly marked and you can get information about routes and the degree of skill and stamina needed, from the US Forest Service staff at the Centennial Hall on the corner of Egan Drive and Willoughby Avenue (open Mon–Fri; tel: 586-8751).

Among the best-known trails are Mt Roberts, Perseverance, and Mt Juneau. Mt Roberts takes off from a trailhead at the north end of Sixth Street. It's a steep climb, but a good one, with alpine ground cover above the treeline, and splendid views. If you want to cheat, you can hop on the Mt Roberts Tram, which takes you from South Franklin Street, near the dockside, up to the treeline, where you can commence your hike and browse through the visitor center or watch a documentary in the theater.

The starting point for the more gentle and most popular trail, the Perseverance Mine Trail, is only a few blocks further north, on Basin Road. Before setting off, pop into the Last Chance Mining Museum, near the trailhead (open daily; entrance charge; tel: 586-5338) to get an idea of what life used to be like when the mines were functioning. On the Perseverance Mine Trail you have the chance to see and explore the ruins of some of the early mining sites, including the Silver Bowl Basin Mine and the Glory Hole. Or you can continue along the Granite Creek Trail, and hike as far as the creek basin.

The experienced and thoroughly fit hiker can link up with the steep Mt Juneau Trail, which provides the best view that can be had with two feet on the ground. Mainland Juneau and Douglas Island are laid out 3,500 ft (1,066 meters) below the mountain summit, and the twisting, glistening Gastineau Channel seems to go on and on forever. This trail will bring you back full circle to join Perseverance near Ebner Falls. The less fit, or those with less time, can miss this loop, by retracing their steps from the Granite Creek Basin.

The Sheep Creek Trail, which starts in the southeast of the city, at Thane Road, takes you through the beautiful valley south of Mt Robert, then up to Sheep Mountain and back on the Mt Roberts Trail.

Several interesting trails start from Douglas, on the other side of the Gastineau Channel. The Treadwell Ditch Trail, which begins at D Street, is a 12-mile (20-km) hike to Eagle Crest, but it can become a much easier walk by going only as far as the Dan Moller Trail, then returning on the road. Only the really experienced should try the Mt Bradley Trail, which sets off from Fifth Street in Douglas. Mt Bradley is 3,400 ft (1,040 meters) high and the going can be tough, although the scenic rewards are great. An easier walk is 2-mile (3.5-km) Cropley Lake Trail, which starts at Fish Creek Road.

There are hikes to suit all abilities, ages and aspirations, but if you are a novice and feel nervous about setting out alone, contact the Juneau Parks and Recreation division, tel: 586-5226, which organizes hikes for groups and families two days a week. ❑

RIGHT: the glistening Gastineau Channel.

SKAGWAY, THE FUN CITY

*Skagway was founded on gold and dreams,
and its brief period of glory is re-created
for the enjoyment of visitors*

PRECEDING PAGES:
Skagway's 4th of
July parade.
BELOW: nostalgia
and youth in
Skagway.

The old familiar sounds are everywhere. You will hear them all the time in **Skagway ❼** where the rollicking past has been preserved. On a calm midsummer night when the sun has just skipped behind the last peak, you can't help but hear them coming from behind those false fronts as you walk up the boardwalk on Broadway. They are the sounds of a not-too-distant era: ragtime pianos, whooping cancan girls, ringing cash registers, songs and raucous laughter; the happy sounds of gold fever run rampant at the start of the trail. They are re-created for the tourist market, to give visitors a taste of the past, and to keep the local economy ticking over.

But if you tear yourself away from these diversions, stop at a corner and give your imagination free rein, you may think you hear other sounds too: horses panting as they slog through mud, whips cracking over their backs, hammers striking rail spikes, and the faint moans and cries of broken men. These sounds, which were every bit as much part of the Klondike Gold Rush, a century ago, are not evoked for the tourist trade, but are heard now only in one's imagination.

There's no town in Alaska quite like Skagway when it comes to blending history with natural beauty. Situated at the northern end of Southeast Alaska's Inside Passage, Skagway is the natural jumping-off point for anyone taking the shortcut over the coastal mountains into Canada's Yukon. A century ago, in 1897–98 stampeders took to the trail, and a town of 10,000–20,000 sprouted. Today, many of the old buildings still stand and the town's 800 residents cater to the needs of more than 400,000 tourists who hit the trail every summer in cars, campers, buses, bikes or, as in the old days, on foot, as well as those who arrive on cruise-ships.

Finding the pass

When you approach Skagway from the south – by Alaska Ferry, cruise-ship or air taxi – you see a tiny town at the base of a river valley surrounded by mountains which range in height from 5,000 to 7,000 ft (1,500 to 2,100 meters) above sea level, rising almost straight out of the salt-water fjord. You would not expect to find a pass to the closed-in valley, but there is one – the White Pass.

The first white man to discover it was Captain William Moore, a member of an 1887 Canadian survey party, a dreamer who had captained steamboats on rivers all over the Western Hemisphere At the age of 65, he came across the wooded tideflats of "Skagua" (a Native Tlingit word meaning "windy place") and envisioned a lively port with a railroad heading across the pass into the Yukon. The railroad

Map, page 110 & below

would haul miners in and bring gold out, and he would make the most of it. Moore and his son Bernard staked their claim, built a cabin (still standing) and a wharf, and waited for the rush to come. They had rather a long wait.

The big strike in the Yukon did not occur until August 1896, and word did not reach the rest of the world until *Portland*, the steamship with the famous "ton of gold," cruised into Seattle's harbor about a year later. Twelve days later, the first of many hundreds of steamers brought men and supplies to Skagway. The town boomed overnight in the fall of 1897. Miners pushed Moore aside, setting up their own system of streets (one going right through the captain's home), and allowed the old man to keep 5 acres (2 hectares) of the 160 he and his son had originally claimed.

When Skagway's first newspaper was published in October 1897, it reported 15 general stores, 19 restaurants, four meat markets, three wharves, 11 saloons, six lumber yards, eight pack trains, and nine hotels. Three other newspapers had been established by the summer of 1898. The stampeders arrived in Skagway with lots of money to tie up in supplies and various distractions made available to them by Skagway merchants.

As the town grew, so did its bad reputation. With no law to speak of, Skagway was ripe for con-artists. Jefferson Randolph "Soapy" Smith, who had earlier been chased out of Colorado, set up his gang in Skagway. For nine months, under the guise of a civic leader, he won the allegiance not only of prostitutes, gamblers and saloon keepers, but also of bankers, editors and church builders. But Soapy's downfall was quick once things got out of hand; one of his men had robbed a miner (a not unusual occurence), and Soapy refused to bow to vigilantes and return the gold. He died in a shootout while

BELOW: gold rush one-armed bandit.

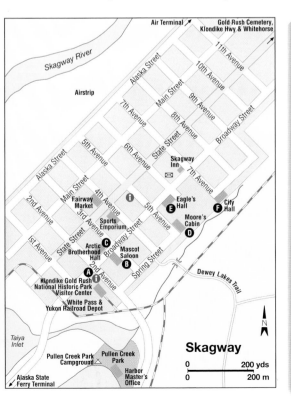

trying to break up the lynch mob. Frank Reid, the city engineer who killed him, also died in the fight.

Skagway was not alone in its quest to become the "Metropolis of the North." Dyea, a city on the bay 10 miles (16 km) to the west, sprang up as well. It sat at the foot of the Chilkoot Trail, an established Native route that was shorter but steeper than the White Pass Trail. Dyea and Skagway, each boasting they had the better trail, competed bitterly for the money of every stampeder heading into the interior.

The White Pass Trail, nicknamed "Dead Horse Trail" because of the 3,000 pack animals that perished in the canyon, was used by fewer prospectors, but Skagway won the battle for survival. The White Pass & Yukon Route Railroad laid its first tracks up the middle of Broadway in May 1898, and by 1900 the narrow gauge line was completed, 100 miles (160 km) to Whitehorse, future capital of the Yukon Territory. An easy route to the gold fields was established, and Dyea subsequently became a ghost town. Its sparse remains can be seen at the beginning of the Chilkoot Trail.

The Klondike Rush had subsided by 1900, but Skagway was set up for life as the port for Yukon. Its population has fluctuated between 400 and 3,000 in the years since, due to a continuous boom-and-bust cycle. Food, fuel, war supplies, minerals and tourists have all been hauled by the railroad in various volumes and numbers. In the early 1980s the railroad went through a bad patch and closed down, but was re-opened in 1988.

Riding the narrow gauge train over the White Pass is the best way to get a feel of what the gold rush was like. You travel in turn-of-the-century parlor cars, pulled by steam or diesel engines, which seem to cling to the small cut

Ride the railway.

BELOW: steaming into town.

in the mountain-side. Hundreds of feet below are the still visible remains of the old trails. Excursions are available to White Pass Summit (2,890 ft/880 meters) or passengers may book a one-way ticket from Skagway to Fraser, British Columbia, where they continue to Whitehorse by bus. Visitors can also drive the Klondike Highway, completed in 1978, which climbs the opposite side of the canyon from the railroad. It is paved from Skagway to the junction with the Alaska Highway near Whitehorse.

The 3-hour drive gives you much the same splendid scenery as is seen from the railroad: Skagway River Gorge, Pitchfork Falls, White Pass Summit, and the beautiful lake country of British Columbia and the Yukon.

Map, page 143

Nostalgia in Skagway

The center of activity in Skagway is along Broadway, which starts at the dock and ferry terminal, where more than 60 gold rush-era buildings still stand. The **Klondike Gold Rush National Historic Park** ❽, created in 1977, took over ownership of many of these buildings and has since spent millions of dollars on their restoration. Private restoration has also taken place, breathing life into old structures that surely would have fallen down without this assistance. Occupying the old buildings are curio shops, restaurants, saloons, hotels, art galleries, ice cream parlors, and other businesses, many of them staffed by people in period dress, all intent on creating a carnival-like atmosphere in a gold rush setting.

Start a tour of the town with a visit to the **Klondike Gold Rush National Historic Park Visitor Center** ❹ (open daily 8am–7pm; tel: 983-2921) on the corner of Second Avenue and Broadway. The center contains a small muse-

BELOW: the Mascot Saloon has a gold rush atmosphere.

A traditional 4th of July celebration in Skagway.

um, offers informative talks, shows an atmospheric movie about the gold rush days, and conducts free walking tours of the historic district three or four times a day.

Nearby, on the corner of Third Avenue and Broadway, and also under the aegis of the National Historic Park, is the **Mascot Saloon** Ⓑ. Built in 1898, when it was one of many bar-rooms designed to slake the miners' thirst, it has some well-displayed exhibits which conjure up the rough, tough atmosphere of the saloon's heyday.

The **Arctic Brotherhood Hall** Ⓒ is just across the street. The exterior of the building is covered with thousands of pieces of driftwood. Inside, it has become the home of the informative **Trail of '98 Historical Museum** (open daily in summer 9am–5pm; entrance charge) full of gold rush and Soapy Smith memorabilia.

Walk up Broadway and turn right on Fifth Avenue to **Moore's Cabin** Ⓓ, built by the city's neglected founder and his son in 1887 and transferred to this spot when stampeders trampled over their land. This, too, has been renovated by the National Historic Park Service.

On the corner of Broadway and Sixth is **Eagle's Hall** Ⓔ where "Skaguay in the Days of '98" re-creates the Soapy Smith story nightly. This one-hour historical melodrama follows an hour of live ragtime music and gambling. The dealers are cast members, the money is phoney, and some of the tables date back to the gold rush. The show's popularity has kept it going since 1925, and residents refer to it as "the longest running show on Broadway."

At the end of Seventh Avenue (turn right off Broadway just past the Post Office) is the **City Hall** Ⓕ, a century-old building which has been both a

BELOW: old-style buses in front of the Arctic Brotherhood Hall.

place of learning (the McCabe College, which is why it is often known locally as the McCabe Building) and a courthouse. Outside you'll find a display of historic rail cars.

Running parallel with Broadway is State Street; follow this northeast for just over a mile (2 km) and you will come to the **Gold Rush Cemetery**, where Soapy Smith and Frank Reid were laid to rest after reaching their violent mutual end.

In addition to the walking tours organized by the National Historic Park Center, there are tours arranged by several companies which will take you around the historic district and up to the Gold Rush Cemetery. Some use pony-carts, others old street cars or mini-buses.

Fun and festivities

Skagway has the reputation for being a party town, especially in summer. Ask any Yukoner who bolts for the coast on weekends. Skagway people are fun-loving and seem to enjoy the attention, as well as realizing that it is partly this that keeps their town's economy flourishing, but by the fall they are more than ready for the quiet months ahead. There are two saloons which are usually hopping, especially on days when the larger cruise-ships are in town. Jazz musicians working on the cruise boats sometimes jump ship in Skagway for a few hours to attend jam sessions, because, they say, it's the only day of the cruise that they don't have to play "old folks music." If business is especially good, the bars will stay open right through until 5am, which is the official closing time.

Visitors are welcome to join locals in the town-wide parties. Featured in late March, for instance, is the Windfest, a community celebration of the coming of spring and longer days, with its zany chainsaw toss, chili cooking contest and other events. The Summer Solstice Party, held on June 21, the longest day of the year, is an all-night event, with bands performing in city parks.

A traditional gold rush-style Independence Day is celebrated on July 4, complete with parades, races and contests of all kinds. Four days later, on July 8, is Soapy Smith's Wake, a party and a champagne toast to Skagway's notorious con-man, which is held at the Eagle's Hall.

The Klondike Trail of '98 Road Relay is held on the second weekend of September. About 100 10-person teams run a distance of 110 miles (176 km) from Skagway to Whitehorse, ending, naturally enough, with a party. In 1998, the centenary of the Klondike Gold Rush was celebrated in great style. The construction of the White Pass and Yukon railroad, known as "the railroad built of gold," began on May 28, 1898. It was Alaska's first railroad and still has an international reputation as a miracle of engineering. The railway is still something to marvel at.

The last two weeks of June every year see the Dyea to Dawson race, in which competitors re-create the 19th-century gold rush trek over the Chilkoot Trail to Lake Bennett, then by canoe on to Dawson City in the Yukon.

Map, page 143

BELOW: saloon girls were tough in Skagway.

Hiking around Skagway

Around Skagway, there is much to be seen. If you're reasonably fit, own a backpack, and have the time, hiking the **Chilkoot Trail** is the most adventurous option for tracing the route of the gold seekers. Managed by the park services of the United States and Canada, the trail extends nearly 35 miles (53 km) from old Dyea to Lake Bennett, British Columbia. Most hikers allow three to five days to fully capture the scenery and explore the thousands of gold rush relics left behind during the stampede. A limited number of permits (about 50) are available daily to cross the pass. Call Parks Canada, tel: 800-661-0486 for information.

As you approach the base of the Chilkoot Pass and look up at the steps carved in the snow by the day's hikers, you can't help but visualize the scenes of a century ago, when men went out, full of high hopes, to seek their fortunes, and so many returned empty handed. Fortunately for us, it was captured in photographs and in print.

Edwin Tappan Adney recorded the scene for *Harper's Weekly* in September 1897: "Look more closely. The eye catches movement. There is a continuous moving train; they are perceptible only by their movement, just as ants are. The moving train is zigzagging across the towering face of the precipice, up, up into the sky, even at the very top. See! they are going against the sky! They are human beings, but never did men look so small."

There are several other trails, most of them described in a booklet obtainable from the National Park Service Visitor Center on the corner of Broadway and 2nd Avenue (open daily; tel: 983-2921). The center will also advise you about camp sites and United States Forest Service (USFS) cabins.

BELOW: whole families tramped over the Chilkoot Pass.

Map, page 110

The **Dewey Lake Trail System**, comprises various trails, the shortest (about half an hour each way) being to Lower Dewey Lake, where pink and silver salmon run in August and September, and where there are picnic spots and space to camp.

From here you can continue up to the Upper Dewey Lake and the Devil's Punchbowl. For a tougher hike, try the **Skyline Trail**, officially called the AB Mountain Trail, which starts on Dyea Road, just over 1 mile (2 km) out of town, and takes a whole day from start to finish. The **Denver Glacier Trail** is another option. It takes you up the Skagway River to the Denver Glacier, but it's tough going and not for the faint-hearted.

The best weather for outdoor pursuits is in spring. Skies are clear, the sun is hot, and the snow is still deep on White Pass until mid-May. Cross-country skiers and snow-mobilers drive to the top of the highway, and go all day. Later in the summer, after the snow has melted, hundreds of small ponds form on the moon-like terrain.

Heading for the Interior

Since the opening of the **Klondike Highway** out of Skagway, more and more travelers have opted to drive the 360-mile (580-km) "Golden Circle" route to include both Skagway and Haines on their way to or from the Interior. Driving up the Alaska Highway from the south, you can cut off to Skagway on the Klondike, put your car on the ferry for the short ride to Haines, and then proceed north along the Chilkoot River on the Haines Cut-Off till you meet the Alaska Highway again at Haines Junction. This is the most direct road route to the interior of Alaska from the Panhandle. ❑

BELOW: a variety of options on the waterfront.

THE GREAT KLONDIKE GOLD RUSH

Gold was discovered in the Klondike in a period of economic depression, attracting the penniless, the adventurous and the unscrupulous

During 1897–98, 100,000 people poured into Dawson in the Klondike in search of gold. Although Dawson is in Canada, the best way to reach it was by ship from Seattle to Skagway, 600 miles (960 km) across one of two treacherous passes – the White Pass from Skagway or the Chilkoot from Dyea. The former was believed to be slightly easier, but it was controlled by "Soapy" Smith – a villain who virtually ran Skagway during the gold boom – and stories of men being robbed and murdered were rife. On the Chilkoot Pass it was the elements which were the killers. The journey was made more difficult by the fact that, after some of the early prospectors died of starvation, the Canadian government insisted that each man should take a year's supplies – which weighed roughly a ton.

HAZARDS OF SPRING

Once the winter and the hazards of the trail were over, prospectors had to face the rapids and whirlpools of lakes and rivers which they tackled in hand-made boats – denuding the forests to build them. Dreams of gold kept them going but by the time most of them reached Dawson, the productive claims were already allocated. While some people became rich, and others found just enough to give them security, many of the so-called stampeders, having sunk everything they owned in the enterprise, were ruined.

▽ **THE WEIGH-IN**
Prospectors eye the scales and weigh the gold that has been gleaned during a long winter's work.

▷ **HORSES' FATE**
Those who could afford it loaded their provisions and equipment on to pack horses, but many of the animals failed to survive the trip, hence the nickname given to the White Pass – Dead Horse Trail.

▽ **LAUNDRY SERVICE**
Services sprang up in the towns and along the route. This laundry set up in Dawson was a welcome sight to people who had spent months on the trail.

▽ **JUNEAU'S BEGINNINGS**
Gold was discovered in Silver Bow Basin almost two decades before the Klondike strike, and was a lot easier to reach. Gold pans and pick axes were soon replaced by hydraulic earth-moving and sluicing operations, and the camp eventually became the town of Juneau.

▷ **DISASTER IN THE SUN**
Prospectors crossing the Chilkoot and White passes to Dawson, during the coldest winter in living memory, set up makeshift encampments en route. On Palm Sunday, 1898 spring sunshine began to melt the snow and an avalanche engulfed a Chilkoot Trail camp, killing 70 people.

DISHING THE DIRT IN DAWSON

Mining was a laborious business and those who went to the gold fields thinking the precious metal was there for the taking were soon disillusioned. The early prospectors had struck lucky with the claims closer to the surface, but by the time the great influx of hopefuls reached Dawson they were digging for gold which could be some 50 ft (15 meters) beneath the surface. To reach it they had to force their way through permafrost, burning it to soften the land, then sinking shafts which might, or might not, hit the right spot.

Once the "paydirt" – the mixture of earth and gold – had been extracted it had to be separated and cleaned, and this was done in a primitive sluice. When the streams began to thaw in spring, water channeled through the sluice separated the precious dust from the dirt. The more sophisticated hydraulic sluicing methods introduced in Silver Bow could not be used in Dawson because of the difficulty of getting equipment across the passes. The sluice pictured above is "Long Tom" in Nome, where gold was discovered in late 1899. Many prospectors, still gripped by gold fever, made their way there, empty-handed but hopeful, after the Klondike gold was exhausted.

▽ **SOMEWHERE TO SPEND IT**
Mary's Hotel in Bonanza Creek was one of many roadhouses which sprang up along the Klondike creeks. These hostelries provided a few home comforts, and gave the lucky ones somewhere to spend their money, distributing the rewards of the gold fields.

MARY'S HOTEL

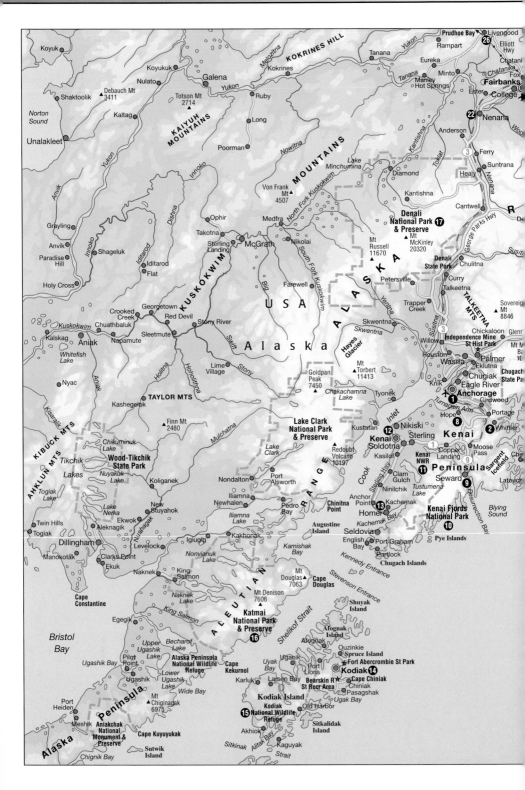

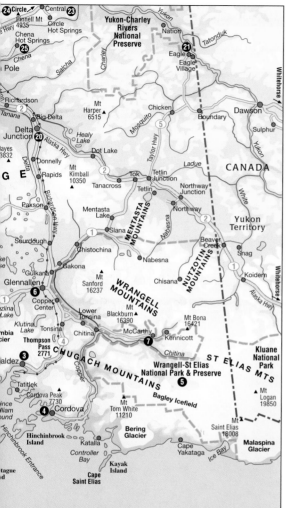

SOUTHCENTRAL AND INTERIOR ALASKA

S outhcentral and Interior Alaska is a vast expanse of land, which covers areas as diverse as Kodiak Island in the south and the borders of the Yukon River in the northeast.

Anchorage is the area's major city. Although it is not, in fact, Alaska's capital it has many of the attributes of a state capital city. For a start, it is where 42 percent of the population lives. There is also an interesting collection of museums, and some lively nightspots. And Anchorage is the hub round which most things radiate. From here you can drive south on the Seward Highway to the fjords and glaciers of the Kenai Fjords National Park. You can fly to Kodiak Island to see the brown bears; or to Katmai National Park where a volcanic eruption has left a strange, lunar landscape.

To tour Prince William Sound, go by road or rail from Anchorage to Whittier, and take a ferry or cruise-ship. And if you hope to explore two of the most popular national parks, you can drive the Glenn Highway to Wrangell-St Elias, or the George Parks Highway to Denali, home of the majestic Mount McKinley.

Anchorage is also a jumping off point for the Interior. Fairbanks, a university city which is lively in summer and has the northern lights to cheer the long winter days, is only a flight away. And from Fairbanks highways radiate out like the spokes of a wheel: to Eagle on the banks of the Yukon; to the hot springs of Chena, Circle, and to Manley. From Fairbanks you can also explore the gold dredges of the Steese Highway, or you can drive the Elliott Highway to Livengood, where the Dalton will take you as far north as it is possible to go. ❑

PRECEDING PAGES: the Anchorage skyline.

Southcentral and Interior

```
0                              100 miles
0                    100 km
```

ANCHORAGE

*Anchorage is a good jumping off point for many parts of the state,
but it has a lot else to offer, from interesting museums to lively
nightlife, and ski slopes right on the doorstep*

Map, pages 154–5

Imagine you're a passenger aboard one of the many domestic and international air carriers serving **Anchorage ❶** daily. About three hours out of Seattle, the pilot announces you'll be landing in Anchorage in a few minutes. You've been peering out of the window ever since your plane took off from the Seattle-Tacoma airport and, except for when you flew by the coast of British Columbia, you've seen darn few signs of civilization. Just as you're beginning to wonder if the pilot has lost his way, you see Anchorage.

Plopped down on a point of which sticks out into Cook Inlet, with Turnagain Arm bordering the southwest shore and Knik Arm the northwest one, the city of Anchorage sprawls out over a 10-mile (16-km) length, seeming to spread over most of the available land between the inlet and the Chugach Mountains to the east.

With over a quarter of a million residents, Anchorage is the largest metropolis and the commercial center of the state. This port city didn't get a good purchase on life until 1915, but in the decades since has developed from a railroad tent camp to a city of high-rise offices and ethnic restaurants.

Captain James Cook, the British explorer, sailed into Cook Inlet in 1778, while looking for a Northwest Passage to the Atlantic. Trading furs and fish with the Dena'ina Natives, he noticed that they carried iron and copper weapons, the first evidence of trade with the Russians who had set up trading posts in lower Cook Inlet and at Kodiak. Russian influences can still be seen today at Eklutna, a Dena'ina village inside the northern boundary of the municipality of Anchorage.

When Cook found no way out of the arm of Cook Inlet to the south of Anchorage, he ordered his ships, the *Resolution* and the *Discovery*, to turn around, hence the name "Turnagain." Knik Arm gets its name from the Eskimo word for fire, *knik*, which was used in reference to the Dena'ina people and their villages.

After Alaska was purchased from the Russians in 1867, gold seekers worked the land along Turnagain Arm and at Crow Creek and Girdwood, which is now the southern boundary of the municipality. The gold rush rapidly spread north and across Knik Arm. The old mining supply center of **Knik** is located across the inlet from downtown Anchorage.

During its short history, Anchorage, where 42 percent of the state's residents now live, has reverberated with the sounds of several major construction booms: laying track for the Alaska Railroad, building two adjacent military bases during World War II, the discovery and development of the Cook Inlet and Kenai Peninsula oil fields, and, most recently, the construction of the 800-mile (1,285-km) trans-Alaska oil pipeline from Prudhoe Bay to Valdez.

LEFT: air transport in Anchorage.
BELOW: the Oscar Anderson House.

Rugged individualism

The Good Friday earthquake of 1964, originally estimated at 8.7 on the Richter scale but now believed to have measured 9.2 was the most powerful earthquake ever recorded in North America, and it brought Alaskans together to work for a common cause. While the quake devastated many homes and businesses in Anchorage and in other communities, the reconstruction generated a mini boom and Anchorage emerged a new city. Quakes still shake Anchorage and South-central Alaska occasionally.

During the past decade Anchorage has striven to overcome the consequences of its boom-and-bust economy – unemployment, out-migration, poverty, to name a few. During the boom times, Alaska's population was a transient one. The majority of people were lured by the promise of high paying jobs. In the days when the trans-Alaska pipeline was being built (during the 1970s) the salaries for construction workers were in six-digit figures. Average salaries in Alaska are still slightly higher than those in the Lower 48, but services and goods tend to cost a little more here as well.

Some people move to Anchorage from other parts of the USA because they are attracted by the adventure of living at the "last frontier." This is a city where one needs only to walk out of the back door to find the wilderness. Although some residents take off weekends to pursue various outdoor activities, many others find no need to get away. Not surprising perhaps, when it is quite common to see a moose outside the living room window, or a bald eagle flying overhead. Wildlife is so abundant that no one who lives here blinks when they see a moose along the Glenn Highway. An estimated 2,000 moose, 200 black bears and 60 brown bears live in the metropolitan Anchorage area and nearby foothills.

Fireworks light up the Anchorage sky.

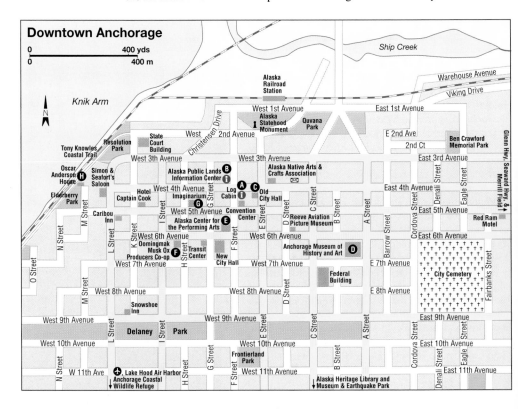

Discovering the city

Anchorage is the air crossroads of the world with several major airlines offering direct flights, primarily from Seattle, but also from other US cities, Tokyo and the Russian Far East. It is as close to London or Tokyo as it is to Houston. About 230 flights arrive daily at the Anchorage International Airport.

Local tour companies offer half-day and full-day tours of the city and surrounding area. The Anchorage Convention and Visitors' Bureau (tel: 276-4118), among others, will have details of reliable organizations. Another way to see Anchorage is to rent a car and explore it on your own. There are several car rental firms in town: Avis, Hertz, Budget and Rent-a-Wreck, with offices on the lower level of the airport's domestic terminal. There is a bus system, the People Mover, although its routes cater to the local residents rather than visitors. The transit center is located on Sixth Avenue between G and H streets.

But if you are staying downtown, you can easily explore this section of the city on foot. Laid out on a grid system, it is a very easy place to find your way around. Start at the **Visitor Information Center Log Cabin** Ⓐ (open daily) on the corner of 4th Avenue and F Street. Built in 1954, the log cabin is surrounded by flowering foliage in the summer. Note the 5,145-lb (2,333- kg) block of solid jade, the state's gem, outside the cabin. Here you can pick up maps and brochures, including a booklet outlining a suggested walking tour; or you could walk a block down the street and take one of the local trolley tours.

From here, cross the road diagonally to the **Alaska Public Lands Information Center** Ⓑ (open daily in summer; Mon–Fri in winter; tel: 271-2737). If you are planning on visiting national parks or taking part in any outdoor activities you will find it invaluable. You can see wildlife exhibits, watch videos on the various regions and activities available, and generally pick up all the information you'll need

Armed with this information, you can then continue your urban tour. First go back to the **Old City Hall** Ⓒ, a classic 1930s construction next door to the Log Cabin, where the lobby holds a display of photographs and other exhibits which will introduce you to the history of the city.

Continue your walking tour by heading east along 4th Avenue. You will pass the non-profit **Alaska Native Arts & Crafts Association** in the Post Office Mall on Fourth Avenue. Works include an array of carved walrus ivory, soapstone and horn, and intricately made baskets. Authentic Native-made handicrafts are identified by a tag, either showing a silver hand or stating "Authentic Native Handicraft."

Three blocks past the mall (and the main post office), turn right down A Street to the **Anchorage Museum of History and Art** Ⓓ (open daily in summer; Tues–Sat and Sun 1–5pm in winter; entrance charge; tel: 343-4326). Among the museum's permanent collections are the Alaska Gallery, with historical exhibits, and an excellent selection of Native art and works by travelers, explorers and early residents, displayed in skylit galleries. The museum shop sells books, prints and Alaska Native crafts.

Backtrack westwards along 6th Avenue. You will notice the **Reeve Aviation Picture Museum** (open

Map, see opposite

BELOW: the Visitor Information Center Log Cabin.

Mon–Fri), featuring photographs of Alaska's best-known bush pilots. Carry on two blocks more to the **Alaska Center for the Performing Arts E**. This building is viewed by some as a monstrosity and by others as architecturally innovative, richly adding to the beauty of the downtown area. Much of the interior, including carpets and upholstery, has been designed by Alaskan artists, and it is decorated with numerous Native masks. Try to join one of the tours which are organized on Monday, Wednesday and Friday in summer, at 1pm. There is no set charge, but a donation is appreciated.

The Alaska Center is a hub of activities for the arts. Performances by the Anchorage Symphony Orchestra and the Anchorage Concert Association begin in the fall. The Concert Association presents world-class performers in music and dance performances. Check local newspapers, especially the *Anchorage Daily News*, and visitors' guides for events.

One block further west, on the corner of 6th Avenue and H Street, you will find the **Oomingmak Musk Ox Producers' Co-op F** (tel: 279-9225) where you can buy, or just admire, garments of musk ox wool, called *qiviut* (kee-vee-ute) which are made in Eskimo villages.

From the Co-op, turn up H Street again to 5th Avenue, where you will find the **Imaginarium G** (open Mon–Sat 10am–6pm, Sun noon–5pm; entrance charge; tel: 276-3179). While primarily aimed at children, this award-winning science museum has a wealth of exhibits and hands-on experiences that are also popular with adults. If you want to know more about marine life, wetlands and the solar system, this is a good place to find out.

BELOW: the restored Old City Hall.

Continue west a few blocks along 5th Avenue to M Street, to the **Oscar Anderson House Museum H** (open Tues–Sat noon–4pm; entrance charge; tel:

274-2336) set in the attractive little Elderberry Park. Listed on the National Register of Historic Places, this is Anchorage's first wood frame house, built by Swedish immigrant Anderson in 1915.

Map,
page 158

Close by on L Street is **Simon & Seaforts**, an excellent place for seafood and a view of the inlet. Or you could try the neighboring **Elevation 92** (West 3rd Avenue) which also has a sea view and good food. Back down on 5th Avenue, **Sacks Café** offers an intimate atmosphere and very good seafood. While in Anchorage, don't miss trying the Alaskan specialties like baked halibut, salmon or steamed crab.

Leaving downtown behind

Outside the downtown area, but worth seeing, is the **Alaska Heritage Library and Museum** (open Mon–Fri noon–4pm, admission free; tel: 265-2834), in the lobby of the National Bank of Alaska on Northern Lights Boulevard and C Street. There is a large selection of Native art and artifacts and a number of works by Sydney Laurence (1865–1940), known as "the painter of the north."

Continue as far west as you can go along Northern Lights and you'll reach **Earthquake Park**, founded on the spot where, during the 1964 earthquake, some 130 acres (52 hectares) of land fell into the inlet, and 75 houses were destroyed. A walking trail and new, museum-quality interpretive signs make it well worth the stop.

Biking about

Anchorage is a great place for cyclists, with more than 120 miles (190 km) of paved paths, and plenty of bikes for rent (ask at the Visitor Information Center

BELOW: biking the Tony Knowles Coastal Trail.

A goose crosses the road.

Log Cabin, where maps of all trails are also available). The best known and most scenic route is the **Tony Knowles Coastal Trail** which starts near Elderberry Park on 2nd Avenue. The trail is 12 miles (20 km) long and parallels Knik Arm, continuing past Westchester Lagoon, and ending at Kincaid Park. In winter, the path becomes a cross-country ski trail. There are a number of other bike routes in town: trail maps are available from the Parks and Recreation department, as well as at the Log Cabin. Bicycling is an ideal way to get around, and offers great views of the city and the waters of the inlet, where migrating beluga whales are often seen on the surface.

Nightlife

If you are looking for something to do at night, when sightseeing is over, Anchorage has a variety of options. Try the **Crow's Nest** at the top of the Captain Cook Hotel (on the corner of 5th Avenue and K Street) if you want gourmet cuisine and a formal atmosphere, together with great views. But if you fancy a taste of nightlife in the last frontier, complete with sawdust on the floor, you won't do much better than **Chilkoot Charlie's** on Spenard Road. Don't bother with a coat and tie; this is where Alaskans go in their boots and jeans to dance, drink and be entertained.

Mr Whitekeys Fly By Night Club, also on Spenard Road, is best known for live blues and jazz and the ribald all-Alaskan floor show called the Whale Fat Follies. **Humpy's**, across from the Performing Arts Center, serves good beers, food and live music. Anchorage also has a number of cinemas and theaters, as well as the events which take place at the Alaska Center for the Performing Arts. Again, see the local press for listings.

BELOW: Merrill Field Airport.

Around Anchorage

If you want to experience the Alaska outdoor life, try a flightseeing trip. Excursions can easily be arranged by flight operators at **Lake Hood** or at **Merrill Field**. Not far from downtown near the international airport is **Lake Hood Air Harbor**, the busiest seaplane base in the world. On most summer days there are an average of 800 take-offs and landings. Channels on Lake Hood and Lake Spenard provide the runways for these seaplanes. Alaskans fly into the bush for fishing, hunting, hiking and a myriad other activities.

On the southern edge of town, visitors can view a variety of waterfowl at the **Anchorage Coastal Wildlife Refuge** (locally known as Potter Marsh). This 2,300-acre (920-hectare) wetland area is the nesting ground for migratory birds during the summer months. Bald eagles, Arctic terns, trumpeter swans and many species of ducks are commonly spotted. Canada geese and mallards raise their young here. From the boardwalk above the channel, huge red salmon are visible from mid-July to September as they return to spawn in nearby Rabbit Creek.

Not far from Potter Marsh, on the Seward Highway, visitors have a chance to view larger wildlife. During spring and summer it is common to see Dall sheep peering over the rocks of the adjacent cliffs at passing motorists. Several spots on this road allow visitors to watch the waters for belugas, the small white whales that chase salmon up the Turnagain Arm. Stop at **Beluga Point Interpretive Site** in spring and fall, where you will find spotting scopes, benches and information about the area.

Map, page 158

If you just want to contemplate the beauty and mammoth size of Alaska, you can grab a takeout lunch in town and picnic at nearby **McHugh Creek Picnic Area**, located just a few miles down the road from Potter Marsh. Here you can see miles down the inlet and view the majestic mountains on the other shore, and take a short hike along the trail.

At Anchorage's back door to the east is **Chugach State Park**; the park head-quarters are located across from Potter Marsh in the **Potter Section House Historic Site** (open daily 8am–4pm; tel: 345-5014). Here you will find a railroad museum and an old rotary snow plow on the track behind the house.

The park covers 495,000 acres (200,500 hectares) and offers visitors a wide variety of opportunities to experience the Alaska outdoors without being too far away from civilization. Between June and September, the park rangers and naturalists lead nature walks to various parts of the park. Each walk takes about two hours and focuses on a specific activity, such as wildflower observation or bird-watching. Call the Potter Section House for information.

The **Eagle River Nature Center** is north on the Glenn Highway from Anchorage. Only a 20-minute drive (14 miles/23 km) from downtown Anchorage, Eagle River is a pleasant area. The drive through the lake-dotted valley is worth the trip itself, and once at the center there are displays, nature videos, and a 3-mile (5-km) walking trail that takes you to the banks of the Eagle River. During August the berries are plentiful, and cross-country skiing is a popular winter activity. The center offers daily naturalist programs (tel: 694-2108).

BELOW: blanket toss at the Fur Rondy.

Winter activities

Winters are long in Alaska, but this is a special time of the year for visitors. On Thanksgiving weekend, the University of Alaska, located on several acres of wooded land in the city, hosts the **Great Alaska Shoot-Out**, an invitational college basketball tournament. Eight major college basketball teams from across the United States come to Anchorage to compete in a tournament which has gained national prominence and is televised via satellite.

After the Christmas holiday season, Anchorage residents prepare for their own 10-day carnival in February – **Fur Rendezvous** or, as the locals call it, "Fur Rondy." This annual festival celebrates Alaska's frontier past, when fur trappers met to sell and trade their goods.

Today the Fur Rondy features more than 150 events, ranging from the famous World Championship Sled Dog Race to the annual snowshoe softball tournament downtown between 9th and 10th Avenues on the Delaney Park Strip. Competition is held for the best snow sculpture (which draws competitors from as far away as Japan) and the fastest canoe in the Downhill Canoe Race. Other events include the traditional Eskimo blanket toss and the largest outdoor public fur auction in the United States. The highlight of the carnival is the **World Championship Sled Dog Race**. For three days competitors run heats totaling 75 miles (120 km). The racers start on 4th Avenue, and continue on the city streets to the out-skirts of town where they circle back. Dog mushing is the official state sport.

At the beginning of Fur Rondy, the **Miners' and Trappers' Ball** is held. This is not a black-tie affair and everyone in the city is invited. Tickets must be pur-chased in advance. It is held in a huge warehouse and people arrive in every conceivable attire, some hoping to win the contest for the most unusual cos-tume. Fur Rondy is a great time to experience what life is *really* like in Alaska. It is a time of camaraderie among the local people and they welcome visitors. As the event is becoming more popular, it is best to book well in advance. The Anchorage Convention and Visitors' Bureau can be contacted for the date of the festival, tel: 276-4118.

The last great race on earth – the **Iditarod Trail Sled Dog Race** – starts on the first Saturday in March. From downtown Anchorage competitors race to Nome, a distance of more than 1,100 miles (1,770 km). Generally the race takes about two weeks, but Doug Swingley, who won the race in 1995, set a record-breaking time of 9 days, 2 hours. Mushers compete with teams of 12 to 18 dogs against themselves, each other and the wilderness. The success of four-time win-ner Susan Butcher originated a T-shirt which reads, "Alaska, where men are men and women win the Iditarod!"

The race started in 1973 to commemorate the 1925 event, when 20 mushers relayed life-saving serum to Nome, which was fighting a diphtheria epidemic. Today, the race receives television coverage and residents line the streets to cheer on the competitors. The **Knik Museum and Sled Dog Mushers Hall of Fame** is 40 miles (64 km) from Anchorage in Knik. Open from June to Sep-tember, the museum tells the story of the Iditarod Trail and Alaskan mushers.

BELOW: the World Championship Reindeer Race.

In Girdwood visitors can join the **Glacier Valley Tour** and experience the excitement of riding in a dog sled. The run passes scores of ancient, hanging glaciers and stops in the wilderness for a homemade lunch. Visitors even have a chance to mush the dogs and snowshoe during the lunch break.

Downhill and cross-country skiing in Anchorage can be found in **Russian Jack Springs Park** with gentle slopes and rope tow for beginners. It also has 4 miles (7 km) of lighted trails. The **Hilltop Ski Area** has a chairlift and is an excellent facility for novice skiers. It also has night skiing and is accessible by public bus. For advanced skiers, **Alpenglow** at **Arctic Valley Ski Area** offers more challenging slopes. Two chair lifts, T-bar and three rope tows service the area which has over a 1,000-ft (305-meter) drop. Runs can be very steep and maintenance is sometimes questionable.

Alaska's largest and most popular ski area – **Alyeska Resort & Ski Area** – is 40 miles (64 km) southeast of Anchorage in Girdwood. With a vertical drop of 2,500 ft (760 meters), it caters to all levels of skiers and is a full-service resort with both day and night skiing. The area has six lifts, including a quad chair lift and four doubles, and a high-speed gondola which operates in the summer months, taking visitors to a restaurant on the mountain top. The new seven-story Alyeska Prince Hotel opened in early 1995, offering more than 300 rooms, formal and informal dining, an indoor pool, a health club and meeting facilities.

For the cross-country skier, Anchorage offers more than 140 miles (225 km) of trails. **Kincaid Park** on Raspberry Road has 34 miles (55 km) of Nordic ski trails, nine of them lighted. Near Service High School and Hilltop Ski Area, another trail is lit for skiers.

In Chugach National Forest more than 200 miles (320 km) of hiking trails, which extend from Anchorage to the Kenai Peninsula, are open to the cross-country skier. The trail at the top of Upper Huffman Road offers breathtaking views of the city and is manageable for skiers of any level. To get to it take the Seward Highway to the O'Malley turnoff going east, continue toward the mountains, turning on to Hillside Drive, and making a left on Upper Huffman to the trailhead.

An hour's drive north of Anchorage is an excellent cross-country ski area with a historical flavor. **Hatcher Pass** is at the heart of the majestic Talkeetna Mountains off the Glenn Highway on Fishhook Road. At the turn of the century **Independence Mine** was a hub of gold mining activity. Today it is a state historic park and its abandoned buildings and old mining machinery have become landmarks of the past. The area has miles of treeless groomed ski trails and on a clear day you can see all the way down the valley to the city of Palmer (20 miles/32 km). Accommodations are available at two small lodges, one of which also has individual cabins. For more information, call the Hatcher Pass Lodge, tel: 745-5897.

Heading south

With only two roads leading in and out of Anchorage, selecting a day trip is easy: you go north or south. Heading south on Seward Highway, visit Girdwood, Crow Creek Mine and Portage Glacier. The drive parallels the

Map,
page 158

BELOW: the start of the World Championship Sled Dog Race.

Turnagain Arm, an extension of Cook Inlet. Numerous spots along the 40-mile (65-km) drive to Girdwood offer spectacular views of scenery and wildlife: look out for Dall sheep, moose and beluga whales.

Girdwood is a quaint community which sees an influx of tourists in the summer and skiers in the winter. A ride on the Alyeska Ski Resort tram (*see* previous page) on a clear day provides an incredible view of the surrounding mountains and the inlet. The town has a variety of shops worth wandering around, which offer traditional Alaskan souvenirs.

A beady-eyed eagle.

Outside Girdwood, 3 miles (5 km) up Crow Creek Road, is **Crow Creek Mine**. The placer mine and its eight original buildings are listed on the National Register of Historic Sites. They represent the first non-Native settlement in the area. Visitors can pan for gold in this scenic setting. For the robust type, nearby Crow Pass Trail climbs through beautiful mountain valleys. Be sure to have some basic hiking gear before attempting any hike. Weather in Alaska can change dramatically and hikers should always be prepared.

Continuing down the Seward Highway, at **Twenty Mile River**, visitors may often see Arctic terns, bald eagles, mew gulls and moose from the observation platform. Plaques on the platform have information on the various species.

About 10 miles (16 km) past Girdwood is the turnoff for Portage Glacier. On the right side of the road is **Explorer Glacier** (there's an excellent photography vantage point). Stop at the bridge over Williwaw Creek to see salmon spawning from late July to mid-September. Portage Glacier is rapidly retreating, and with it the once dramatic view of Portage Lake with its huge blue icebergs.

BELOW: skiers at Turnagain Arm.

At the end of the road is the **Begich-Boggs Visitor Center** (open daily in summer; Sat–Sun only in winter; tel: 783-2326). The center has an interpretive dis-

Map, page 158

play on how glaciers are formed. It even has an iceberg on display so visitors can touch the ancient ice. Due to the great pressure during the formation of the glacial ice, it also melts slowly. Don't miss an award-winning documentary film called "Voices from the Ice," shown hourly during the summer months (entrance charge).

There are several glaciers in Portage Valley with a number of trails where visitors can view glacial features, including wildflowers and plant life. Take the short walk to **Byron Glacier**. Signs near Portage Glacier Lodge mark the road to the trailhead. Black bears are commonly seen in the area. Portage Glacier is the turnaround point for this trip to the south. From the visitor center there is a new road that will take you to the toll road and tunnel leading to the Prince William Sound community of Whittier.

Heading north

Traveling on the Glenn Highway north of Anchorage on a day trip, visitors have an opportunity to observe the cultural remnants of Alaska's past and to enjoy several scenic areas in Palmer and the fertile Matanuska Valley. In Eagle River, stop at the **Eagle River Nature Center** in Chugach State Park. Continuing on the Glenn Highway, you will see beautiful **Mirror Lake** wayside area on the right. Here, if you're brave, you can swim in the icy water on a warm day or ice fish in the winter. A mile further takes you to the entrance of **Thunderbird Falls Trailhead**. This is a pleasant 1-mile (2-km) walk to the rushing falls.

Eklutna Lake is Anchorage's largest. There is a campground and a wide, multi-use trail to **Eklutna Glacier**, whose waters feed the lake, and good wildlife-viewing and berry-picking in the area.

BELOW: bull moose in Chugach State Park.

Map, page 158

Fun at the fair.

BELOW: antiques for sale near Palmer.
RIGHT: flying high in Anchorage.

The Anchorage area's oldest building may well be the **St Nicholas Russian Orthodox Church**, which is part of **Eklutna Village Historic Park**, on the Eklutna turnoff, off the Glenn Highway. It was constructed with hand-hewn logs, and the surrounding spirit houses represent the interaction between the Natives and the Russians. This was the site of the first Dena'ina Indian settlement east of the Knik Arm, around 1650. The "spirit" houses show how the Native beliefs were mixed with Russian orthodoxy. Spirit houses were placed over traditional graves and contained personal items to help the spirit in the next world. A three-bar orthodox cross was placed at the foot of the grave. Small spirit houses indicate the resting place of a child and a large house with a smaller one inside means a mother and child were buried together. A picket fence around a spirit house means the deceased was not a Dena'ina.

Further down the Glenn are the **Palmer Hay Flats**. Moose are often spotted grazing in the area. This is the entrance to the Matanuska Valley, the breadbasket of South Central Alaska. Local markets sell Matanuska-Susitna Valley carrots, cabbage and potatoes. Here you will find the giant cabbages which are displayed at the annual Alaska State Fair in Palmer. Such large-sized produce is a result of the territory's long hours of daylight in the summer – the maximum being 19½ hours .

To really get a feel for the valley and have a specifically Alaskan experience, visitors can take a horseback ride and savor the beauty of the area while riding through the Bradley-Kepler Lakes system.

In **Palmer** stop at the **Visitor Information Center and Museum**. Many local artists have their works on assignment here. This small town of some 3,000 residents is set in a majestic rural setting, reminiscent of what many visitors expect Alaska to be. Palmer is the site each August of the **Alaska State Fair** (tel: 745-4827) which features the famous valley produce. The largest cabbage wins the blue ribbon – and it must weigh at least 75 lbs (34 kg) before it is even eligible to enter the competition.

Displays also include farm animals and hand made local items. A carnival operates and foodstalls line the runway so visitors can literally eat their way from one end to the other. The 11-day event, which ends on Labor Day, attracts more than 250,000 people a year and shouldn't be missed.

North of Palmer is the turnoff for Hatcher Pass and Independence Mine. A mile after the turnoff is the **Musk Ox Farm** (open daily in summer 10am–6pm; entrance charge; tel: 745-4151) with the world's only domesticated musk oxen. In the summer, visitors can watch the newborn creatures romping with their parents in the pasture. The coats of these shaggy animals produce *qiviut* – a rare musk oxen wool. The material is used by the Alaska Natives to hand-knit hats, mittens, gloves and scarves in traditional patterns. The *qiviut* is sent to villages around the state and then returned as finished articles to be sold. The Oomingmak Musk Ox Producers' Co-op in downtown Anchorage (*see* page 160), also sells a range of these products. It is believed that the light-weight wool is the warmest material in the world, and articles made from it are unusual presents, or mementos, to take home at the end of your trip. ❑

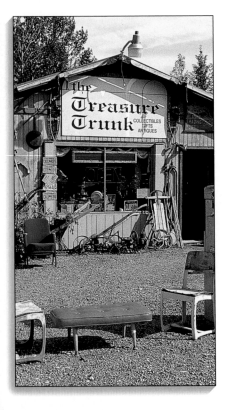

PRINCE WILLIAM SOUND

*The glaciers, the birds and the marine life
are the highlights of the Sound, yet its towns are
reminders that nature has its harsher side*

Map,
pages
154–5

Alaska
Anchorage

Few slide shows or promotional videos present pictures of rain in **Prince William Sound**. Usually, it's sunshine flickering in water cascading from the flukes of a breaching humpback whale. Kayakers wearing T-shirts are silhouetted in front of a brilliant blue-white glacier. Sea otters float atop glossy reflections and munch on Dungeness crab plucked from the ocean floor. But all those pictures are taken on clear days, when cameras are brought out during the times visitors call Prince William Sound a backcountry heaven.

Each year those pictures, along with stories told by the travelers who took them, draw more people to see the Sound's wonderful natural displays of animals, ice, forest and mountains. Few are disappointed, yet it is wise to remember that, as in much of Southeast Alaska, it rains a lot. Here in this wild country Southeast of Anchorage, where coastal peaks form a cloud-stopping arc from Whittier to Cordova, precipitation is measured in feet, not inches. Much of that moisture, driven into the Sound by the Gulf of Alaska's wicked winter storms, pours onto maritime rainforests. Even more precipitation falls as snow and adds substance to the Sound's numerous glaciers. Come summer, moisture, too thick to be called fog, hangs between gray-green glassy salt water and clouds the color of concrete.

Often enough, the clouds seems as durable as concrete, apparently anchored in place by gray, rocky peaks and black, green and gray forests of Sitka spruce and western hemlock. Horizons close in and the spirit of the Sound plays games with visitors. Newcomers camping in this cloud-shrouded funereal world may often feel tense or depressed, but more frequent visitors aren't particularly bothered by the weather. They recognize that rain accounts for much of the Sound's mystique, and they relish telling weather stories.

PRECEDING PAGES:
looking down at
Cordova.
LEFT: the flukes of a
humpback whale.
BELOW: secluded
inlet in the Sound.

Getting there

You can savor the atmosphere of Prince William Sound simply by crossing it on a ferry or tour boat (*see* page 314 for details of the Alaska Marine Highway ferry). **Whittier ❷**, is where many people begin a tour of the Sound. It is easily reached by road and rail from Anchorage (you can also put your car on the train) through tunnels in the Chugach Mountains. A new road connecting Whittier to the Seward Highway is scheduled to open in the spring of 2000. Historically, the site where Whittier now stands was a resting place for Native and Russian traders portaging their wares between the Sound and Cook Inlet. Later, gold miners and mail carriers crossed Portage Pass to reach the Iditarod Trail, which led to Alaska's far-west gold fields (and now better known for Alaska's big winter sled dog race). But Whittier didn't really develop until World

War II, when the army decided to use its ice-free harbor for a strategic fuel dump and the town became an important military port. Troops blasted two tunnels through the Chugach Mountains to connect Whittier with the Alaska Railroad depot at Portage.

In the 1964 earthquake (*see* page 39), Whittier was hit by three successive tidal waves, one of which crested at 104 ft (32 meters), and a huge amount of damage was done to the town and its harbor. There's not a lot to see in Whittier, a town of a few tall concrete apartment blocks built by the military, in which all the residents live, but if you have some time to spare between the train and the ferry the helpful Visitor Center staff near the Small Boat Harbor will give you information about the hiking trails around town. It's also a great place for sea kayaking, but it's best to organize this in Anchorage in advance. There are a number of kayaking guides and outfitters (*see* page 318 for details).

Passengers traveling by boat between Whittier and Valdez sometimes see bears and, occasionally, goats balanced on cliffs above them. Humpback and killer whales frequent the route, and Dall porpoises surf the bow wake. Sea lions haul out on rocks, and harbor seals rest on chunks of ice that drift with the wind and tide away from the glaciers. There are dozens of glaciers in the Sound, and some calve huge chunks of ice into the ocean in spectacular explosions of spray. **Columbia Glacier** is the largest among the many that drop down from the Chugach Mountains into the northerly fjords of Prince William Sound.

Fortunately, the enormous sheet of ice is situated almost due north of the site of the 1989 *Exxon Valdez* oil spill, upwind and upstream, so none of the black oil fouled the glacier's dazzling blue-white face. Fed each year by enough snow to bury a five-story building, Columbia Glacier covers an area the size of Los

There are more active glaciers and ice fields in the state of Alaska than in the rest of the inhabited world.

BELOW: harbor seals at the Columbia Glacier.

Angeles. It flows more than 40 miles (65 km) from the mountains to Columbia Bay, where its 4-mile (6.5-km) wide face daily drops hundreds of thousands of tons of ice into the sound.

The glacier's output of ice increased in 1983, when it began a rapid retreat. Now, glaciologists estimate that 50 cubic miles (210 cubic km) of icebergs could possibly be released during the next half century. So much ice has filled the bay in recent years that boats can't approach the glacier as closely as they could in the past, when passengers were provided with a close-up view of massive flakes peeling from the 300-ft (90-meter) wall. When the flakes come down, the harbor seals resting on bergs in the bay are rocked by the resulting swells. They don't even look up. Meanwhile, gulls and other birds swarm around the glacier face; the plunging ice stirs the seafood-rich water, bringing shrimp and other delicacies to the surface for their consumption. Thus, the glaciers are an intrinsic part of the life cycle of Prince William Sound.

Earthquakes and tidal waves

The land is also shaped by forces other than slow-moving glaciers. Earthquakes cause sudden, dramatic changes in the lay of the country. On March 27, 1964 – Good Friday – bedrock shifted just west of Columbia Glacier. The shock waves, believed to have registered 9.2 on the Richter scale, were the most intense ever recorded in North America. In just a few minutes, extensive new beach lines emerged as the land rose. The most dramatic geological adjustment occurred at the southern end of **Montague Island**, which tilted upward 38 ft (11.5 meters).

But most damage was done by undersea landslides that generated enormous tidal waves, called tsunamis. Whittier suffered badly, as already mentioned, but

Map, pages 154–5

among the worst human disasters was that at **Chenega**, a village of 80 on an island south of Whittier near the western edge of the sound. A wave enveloped all the buildings but the school and one house, and swept away 23 residents. The ruins were abandoned and the village rebuilt on another site 25 years later.

Many hard rock and placer claims are buried under rock slides and fast-growing alder and hemlock. In a few places, like the Beatson Mine on **La Touche Island**, piles of tailings stand out, along with a few unstable old buildings, rust-red lengths of steel pipe and pumps, and stripped trucks whose tires have been eaten by porcupines.

Valdez ❸, the next port of call for ferry and tour boats after Whittier, situated to the east of the earthquake epicenter, was completely destroyed, and had to be rebuilt on a different site. The tsunami that wiped out the waterfront also killed 32 people. Consequently there are no buildings of historic interest in Valdez, but it's a lively town, which grew to prosperity as the terminus of the trans-Alaska pipeline, and its setting, between the Sound and the Chugach Mountains, is splendid. Drop in at the Valdez Convention and Visitors Bureau on Fairbanks Drive (open daily in summer 8am–8pm; tel: 800-770-5954 or 835-4636) for information, and to see their film about the 1964 earthquake. The **Valdez Museum and Historical Archive** (open daily in summer 8am–7pm; entrance charge; tel: 835-2764) on Egan Drive is worth a visit to see a variety of exhibits, including one on the *Exxon Valdez* oil spill.

Valdez can also be reached by air from Anchorage (there are numerous daily flights) or by Alaskon Express bus (tel: 800-544-2206). You can also rent a car here and drive along the **Richardson Highway** toward Glennallen and the Wrangell-St Elias National Park (*see* page 183). It's a beautiful stretch of road.

The greatest recorded snowfall in one season – 81 ft (nearly 25 meters) – occurred at Thompson Pass, near Valdez, in the winter of 1952–53.

BELOW: Worthington Glacier near Valdez.

Map, pages 154–5

Leaving Valdez you pass the site of the original, pre-1964 town, although there's not much to see except a commemorative plaque. Some 12 miles (20 km) further on you come to the Keystone Canyon and the lovely Bridal Veil Falls. Drive on for another 7 miles (11 km) or so and the trans-Alaska pipeline comes into view. Nearby is an attractive camping spot with good trout fishing. Carry on up to **Thompson Pass**, perhaps Alaska's most spectacular mountain road. Passing the Edgerton Highway junction (82 miles/132 km from Valdez), you will reach Copper Center, a little village that was an early mining camp and is well worth a stop (there is accommodation available) before visiting the national park.

Railroad town

Cordova ❹ became a transportation center shortly after the turn of the century. The important mineral was copper, and the deposit, the richest in the world, was at **Kennicott**, 200 miles (320 km) up the Copper and Chitina rivers (*see page* 185). Cordova, still an attractive community of wood-framed houses, was born a railroad town with the arrival of a ship load of men and equipment on April 1, 1906. The railroad was the brainchild of Michael J. Heney, an engineer who had also pushed the White Pass & Yukon Route Railroad through the White Pass from Skagway to Whitehorse in Southeast Alaska in 1900.

For the next five years, Cordova was the operations center for the Copper River & Northwestern Railroad construction project. The CR & NW was an undertaking which, along with the oil pipeline, ranks among the greatest engineering achievements in history .

Heney had to contend with temperatures of -60°F (-50°C), a wind that knocked his boxcars off the tracks, drifting snow that buried his locomotives,

BELOW: Cordova harbor.

Foxes are no longer farmed for fur.

rampaging floods, and a fast Copper River current that sent massive icebergs crashing into the footings of a crucial railroad bridge.

On April 8, 1911, the first train returned to Cordova with ore from the Kennicottmines. The ore was almost pure copper, and it added to the fortunes of the railroad backers, a syndicate led by J.P. Morgan. The unfortunate Heney, though, had died of exhaustion a year before the railroad's actual completion. By the mid-1930s the price of copper had dropped drastically and all the high-grade ores had been mined. In 1938 the railroad was abandoned.

Cordova today is a pretty little fishing town where not much happens. You can't reach it by road. Whittier–Valdez ferries stop here, and a new dock has brought some of the cruise ship operators to town. Otherwise, it is reached by a short flight from Anchorage, and airport buses run you into town. The Chamber of Commerce on 1st Street will fill you in on things to do. The Small Boat Harbor is a lively spot and there's the **Cordova Historical Museum** (open Mon–Sat 10am–6pm in summer; Tues–Fri 1–5pm, Sat 1–4pm in winter; admission free) with historical and marine exhibits; and there's a marvelous view of the town and the Sound from the Mount Eyak Ski area. But the main attractions of the area are out on the 50-mile (80-km) Copper River Highway, which traces the railroad line across the biologically rich **Copper River Delta** to Child's Glacier. The delta is a birdwatcher's paradise, home to the world's entire nesting population of dusky Canada geese and swarms of migrating waterfowl.

BELOW: a railroad was necessary to transport copper to Cordova.

Industries in decline and ascent

The Sound is still rich in copper and gold, molybdenum, tungsten and silver. However, low mineral prices mean those resources will be left in the ground for

Map, pages 154–5

at least the next decade, according to executives with Chugach Alaska Corporation, a major private land owner in the Prince William Sound basin.

The mineral industry isn't the only one that has declined in the area. Fur harvesting also disappeared early in the century. Foxes, fed on salmon, were "farmed" for great profit on islands in the Sound until the fashion industry shifted away from the pelts, particularly as a result of anti-cruelty lobbying.

Sea otters, whose thick, warm fur originally attracted Russian and American colonists to Prince William Sound, were hunted to the brink of extinction. Now protected by law, these animals proliferated until thousands perished in the *Exxon Valdez* spill. Clean-up workers collected the bodies of 1,016 sea otters and figure at least that many bodies disappeared at sea. Nevertheless, otters remain common, even in town boat harbors.

The Sound continues to heal, but although wildlife officials have reported seeing returning animals, the long-term consequences for the ecosystem are unknown. Visitors won't see much sign of lingering oil, but scientists report that over a dozen wildlife species have yet to recover fully. But commercial fishing remains a major source of income for the 7,500 people who live along the Sound. In 1994, a record 14 million pink salmon returned to the port of Valdez.

Some of the Sound's most promising resources are its wilderness and its wildlife. After author Rex Beach documented the construction of the Copper River & Northwestern Railroad in his bestseller *The Iron Trail*, Cordova and its nearby glaciers became one of the greatest visitor attractions in Alaska. Some visitors moor their boats in Prince William Sound's coves and sleep on board. Kayakers and others often pitch tents on beaches. The increase in requests for cabin-use permits is one sign of a growing number of visitors to the Sound. ❑

BELOW: Forest Service outpost in the Sound.

WRANGELL-ST ELIAS NATIONAL PARK

America's largest national park has emerged from obscurity to become a mecca for those seeking backcountry adventure

Map, pages 154–5

U ntil the mid-1980s, **Wrangell-St Elias National Park and Preserve ❺** was an overlooked and undervalued mountain wilderness. Created in 1980, America's largest park – at 13.2 million acres (5.3 million hectares), the size of six Yellowstones – was also one of its least known, least visited. But some time in the late 1980s, Wrangell-St Elias was "discovered," and may well become "the next Denali," in terms of visitor use. Before visiting the park, stop off at the headquarters at **Glennallen ❻**, some 200 miles (320 km) east of Anchorage, for details and advice.

see also map on

A potted history

At the turn of the century, a couple of prospectors named Jack Smith and Clarence Warner spotted a large green spot on the ridge between the Kennicott Glacier and McCarthy Creek which proved to be mineral staining from a fantastically rich copper deposit. Mining engineer Stephen Birch bought the copper claims and won the backing of the Guggenheimer brothers and J.P. Morgan. Known collectively as the Alaska Syndicate, the investors formed the (misspelled) Kennecott Mines Co. – later the Kennecott Copper Corp.

The copper discovery sparked construction of the 200-mile (320-km) Copper River & Northwestern Railroad, connecting the mining camp to the coastal town of Cordova. When the mine closed in 1938 it had produced over 4.5 million tons of ore, worth a reported $200 million. At its peak, 600 people lived at Kennicott. The main settlement included all the operations needed to mill the ore, as well as houses, offices and stores, a school, hospital, post office, dairy and recreation hall. Just down the road, a second community, eventually named McCarthy, sprang up around 1908.

In a perfect complement to staid, regimented Kennicott, McCarthy played the role of sin city. Among its most successful businesses were several saloons, pool halls, gambling rooms and back-alley brothels. In its heyday, 100 to 150 people lived in McCarthy. But after the mine shut down, only a few people stayed on.

For decades after the mine's closure, McCarthy-Kennicott served as the quintessential haven for Alaska recluses. But more recently the region has become a major tourist draw, complete with two lodges, a hotel, several bed-and-breakfast inns, ice cream and pizza parlors, three air-taxi operators, three wilderness guide operations, and even an espresso bar – impressive for a community whose year-round "hard core" population numbers 20 to 30 people.

PRECEDING PAGES: Skolai Creek Valley. **LEFT:** glacial rock in the park. **BELOW:** a hiker approaches a glacier in the national park.

Access to the park

The northern entry to the park is the unpaved, 45-mile (72-km) Nabesna Road, which connects the state's highway system with the tiny mining community of **Nabesna** (population about 25). The entire road is now suitable for 2-wheel-drive vehicles, but motorists are advised to check for updated road conditions before making the drive, as sections of it are occasionally washed out during summer rainstorms. Planned improvements include more vehicle turnouts and wayside natural history exhibits.

Frost melts on spring flowers.

Although some gold, silver, copper, iron and molybdenum were discovered in the Nabesna area early in the 20th century, a much bigger attraction now is the wildlife. Caribou, moose and even grizzlies may be spotted in the open countryside bordering Nabesna Road, and large populations of Dall sheep are found in the hills surrounding the 9,358-ft (2,850-meter) Tanada Peak, about 15 miles (24 km) southwest of the road's end. (Trophy hunting for sheep and other species is allowed in the preserve, which encompasses about 37 percent of the unit's total area.)

The principal avenue into Wrangell-St Elias is **McCarthy Road**; 60 miles (95 km) long and unpaved, it stretches from Chitina, at the park's western boundary (where it connects with the Edgerton Highway) to the "gateway" community of **McCarthy ❼**, located deep within one of America's most spectacular wildlands. At its doorstep are rugged peaks that rise above raging rivers, fed by massive glaciers. The number of people funneled down McCarthy Road has grown dramatically over the past decade, from about 5,000 in 1988 to more than 20,000 in the late 1990s. Overall park visitation has increased at a slower pace, but has still jumped three-fold since the early 1980s.

BELOW: the interior of McCarthy Lodge.

Only a small percentage of those who drive the McCarthy Road actually visit the park's awesome backcountry. Most are content to hang out in McCarthy, take half- or full-day hikes to the nearby **Kennicott Glacier** and **Root Glacier**, or travel some 4 miles (7 km) to the historic and now abandoned **Kennicott** copper-mining camp. Until 1997 visitors could reach McCarthy-Kennicott only by crossing the glacially-fed Kennicott River on hand-pulled trams. These historic trams have been replaced by a foot bridge that makes the crossing considerably easier. Local residents remain adamantly opposed to any sort of vehicular bridge, however, fearing it might open up their community to large-scale "industrial" tourism, so visitors still have to leave their cars, trucks and RVs behind.

Treasures beyond the road

The park's real treasures lie in a wild and magnificent alpine world that wilderness guides call "North America's mountain kingdom." It's a kingdom that includes four major mountain ranges – the St Elias, Chugach, Alaska and Wrangells – and six of the continent's 10 highest peaks, including 18,010-ft (5,490-meter) **Mount St Elias**.

Here too is North America's largest subpolar icefield, the Bagley, which feeds a system of gigantic glaciers; one of those, the Malaspina Glacier, covers an area of more than 1,500 sq. miles (4,075 sq. km) – larger than Rhode Island. Hubbard Glacier, which flows out of the St Elias Mountains into Disenchantment Bay, is one of the continent's most active glaciers; in 1986, Hubbard was nicknamed the "Galloping Glacier" when it surged more than a mile and sealed off Russell Fjord. The ice dam later broke, but scientists speculate that Hubbard will eventually close off the fjord permanently.

Map, pages 154–5

TIP

In the backcountry, assistance may be miles or days away so travelers must be self-sufficient and schooled in wilderness survival skills.

BELOW: the abandoned Kennicott Mine.

The glaciers have carved dozens of canyons; some, like the Chitistone and Nizina, are bordered by rock walls thousands of feet high. Rugged, remote coastline is bounded by tidewater glaciers and jagged peaks. The park's alpine superlatives, along with those of neighboring Kluane National Park in Canada, have prompted their combined designation as a World Heritage Site.

Much of what's been "discovered" in Wrangell-St Elias by modern-day explorers was known to local residents centuries ago. This is especially true of the **Skolai Creek-Chitistone River** area, the most popular of the park's backcountry destinations. Those who hike the Chitistone "Goat Trail" – so named because it's a game trail that you need to be a goat to get across – are following in the footsteps of the Ahtnas, an Athabascan tribe that used the route for hunting and trading. They traded copper nuggets, used for jewelry, with the Eyak people on the coast, in return for which they would get shells or whalebone.

Later, both the Chitistone and Skolai Pass routes were used by stampeders traveling from McCarthy to **Chisana**, the site of Alaska's last major gold rush. Chisana's boom times lasted only a few years, from 1913 to 1915. But during that short period, as many as 10,000 people may have traveled through the mountains. Less than 20 people now live year-round in Chisana, located within the northeast corner of Wrangell-St Elias.

Modern explorers

Eighty-odd years later, the footsteps of the Chisana stampeders are being retraced by people attracted by wilderness values rather than gold. This newest rush into the Wrangell-St Elias backcountry is, so far, much smaller and more benign. Most modern explorers lured into this vast mountain landscape bring a minimum-impact ethic and leave little or no trace of their visit. Still, there's no question that they are having a cumulative effect.

In the first four years that he explored the Skolai-Chitistone area, wilderness guide Bob Jacobs saw only one set of footprints not made by his own parties. Now it's difficult to go more than a day or two without seeing signs of other backpackers, or at least hearing aircraft traffic. The increased use has taken a toll; there's been some trampling of vegetation, littering, crowding, and a growing potential problem with bears that have learned to associate humans with food. "It's a much more fragile environment than a lot of people realize and in places you can find evidence of degradation," says Jacobs.

It was only natural that the Skolai-Chitistone area became Wrangell-St Elias' heaviest-used backcountry area. It is one of the park's premier wilderness spots, ruggedly spectacular country in the heart of the mountains. Yet despite its vast, primeval richness, the area is easily accessible by plane, located less than 30 miles (48 km) from McCarthy – a short hop by Alaska backcountry standards.

This is "big country" in the truest sense of the word. The scale of things is immense. In every direction are stark, jagged, ice-carved peaks, most of them unnamed and unclimbed. Here, too, are massive, near-vertical rock faces thousands of feet high, hanging glaciers and waterfalls by the dozen; some are torrents, cascading

TIP

Even in summer the weather can change suddenly and storm systems may delay pick-ups by several days, so bring extra provisions, rain gear and warm clothing.

BELOW: lichen-covered rock, Wrangell-St Elias National Park

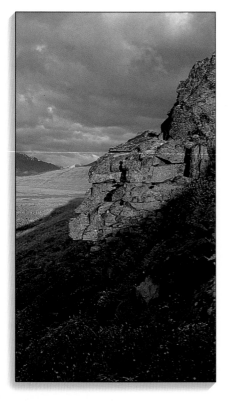

hundreds of feet to the valley floor, while others are more delicate mists. Among the glaciers' morainal deposits are "rock gardens" composed of huge boulders, covered with lichens, moss or grasses.

Yet for all the rock and snow and ice, this is not a barren or alien world. In the valley bottoms are alder groves and tundra meadows brightened with legions of rainbow-hued flowers: blue forget-me-nots, lupine and Jacob's ladder, purple monkshood, yellow paint brush, white mountain avens, tall pink fireweed and wintergreen. Ptarmigan hide in the alder, clucking in the early morning like roosters. Bands of Dall sheep inhabit high rocky places, while occasional moose, wolves and brown bears prowl valleys and hillsides. The valleys are also home to pikas, ground squirrels, shorebirds and robins. And overhead, eagles soar.

Preserving the wilderness

All these variables have dramatically boosted recreational visits to Skolai and Chitistone valleys, and park officials are understandably keen to protect them. Their biggest concern isn't the traditional wilderness traveler, but the novice explorer. Visitor education is one solution. Another is to spread the use to other beautiful but neglected areas. For instance Tebay Lakes, which are similar to the high sierras, with beautiful granite peaks, excellent fishing and hiking. Other areas that haven't been used as heavily include Goat Creek, which offers good hiking, and the wide-open, wildlife-rich upper Chitina Valley. There's also the remote and stark coastline of the park's southeastern edge, where sea-kayakers can paddle among seals, sea lions, sea otters and orca whales in Icy, Yakutat and Disenchantment Bays, or roam among icebergs loosed from tidewater glaciers.

Facilities

Many of Wrangell-St Elias' natural wonders are inaccessible to those who remain along the road system. Only in recent years have maintained trails been established, giving access to parts of the backcountry. The **Skookum Volcanic Trail** (Mile 38 of the Nabesna Road) leads to a tundra area with interesting volcanic dikes and basalt flows and is ideal for day hikers. There are also plans to improve trails along McCarthy Road. One trail will lead to the Crystalline Hills, which offer superb views of the surrounding mountains and the Chitina River valley. A longer, more challenging backcountry route, the Dixie Pass Trail, is planned, along with a path once used by prospectors and miners. Aside from those limited access points, air-taxi services provide transportation into the park and several guide outfits offer river-rafting, climbing and trekking opportunities. Increasingly popular are "flightseeing tours," out of McCarthy, Chitina, Gulkana and Nabesna. Overnight lodging is available at McCarthy and Kennicott and a "wilderness lodge" is located in the backcountry, but park facilities are intentionally minimal. There's a primitive campground along the McCarthy Road and several public-use cabins (built by miners, hunters or trappers) in the backcountry, available on a first-come first-served basis. A list of commercial facilities and services is available from park headquarters in Glennallen (*see* page 340 for the postal address). ❑

Map, pages 154–5

BELOW: view from the Goat Trail.

KENAI PENINSULA

Alaska in a nutshell: glaciers, salmon fishing, hiking trails, stunning scenery and friendly towns, all within easy reach of Anchorage

Map, pages 154–5

It's often said that Alaska is too big to see and do in a single lifetime, let alone a single vacation. But there is one place where one can sample most of the best of Alaska, and do it in a few weeks: the **Kenai Peninsula**. The entire peninsula is within easy driving distance of Anchorage, and people in the city like to refer to the Kenai as their backyard. But please, don't use that line on the peninsula.

On a map of the state, the Kenai Peninsula looks deceptively small. It's worth remembering that the peninsula covers 9,050 sq. miles (23,000 sq. km), making it larger than the combined areas of Rhode Island, Connecticut and Delaware. It is bordered by Prince William Sound and the Gulf of Alaska on the east and Cook Inlet on the west, and attached to the mainland of Southcentral Alaska by a narrow mountainous neck of land at the north.

The peninsula is home to one of Alaska's more artistically inclined cities, Homer. The population is also very socially aware, and for every development-minded resident, you'll find another who belongs to an environmental group. Some apparently belong to both camps, which is partly what makes it such a lively place.

The peninsula was originally home to Dena'ina Indians, a branch of the Athabascan family, and to Eskimos. Their descendants still live here, mostly in small, remote villages, but they now account for something less than 10 percent of the population. Modern ways have long since replaced those of the Natives; they speak and dress very much like their white neighbors, and have a lifestyle which melds traditional and mainstream American ways.

The Russians were the first whites to establish permanent communities on the peninsula. From their base on Kodiak Island, they sent out missionaries to found churches all along the eastern shore of Cook Inlet. The town of Kenai began as a Russian settlement in 1791. Other Russian-founded communities include Seldovia, which also dates to the 18th century, and Ninilchik, founded in the early 1800s. Seward didn't then exist as a town, but the area around Resurrection Bay was used as a shipbuilding site for the Russian-America Company. Early Russian influence is still to be seen in the onion-domed churches, and heard in the names of places and people in some peninsula communities.

Touring the peninsula

Driving from Anchorage, you will cross into the peninsula just south of **Portage**, a town which sat at the eastern end of Turnagain Arm, the thin finger of Cook Inlet that separates the peninsula from the Anchorage Bowl. Portage was completely destroyed by the 1964 earthquake, and only a few ruins remain. About 5 miles (8

PRECEDING PAGES: carved figures at Kachemak Bay. **LEFT:** king crab caught at Homer. **BELOW:** Russian Orthodox Church, Seldovia.

km) after passing the wreckage of Portage, you begin to climb through the Kenai Mountains, with a maximum elevation of about 3,500 ft (1,050 meters).

Mileage along the Seward and Sterling highways is measured from Seward. At about Mile 70 is the summit of **Turnagain Pass**, elevation 988 ft (296 meters). It's a popular spot for winter recreation, primarily cross-country skiing and snow-machining.

The town and highway of Seward were named after US Secretary of State William Seward, who negotiated the purchase of Alaska from Russia in 1867.

The pass and much of the area along the highway are part of the **Chugach National Forest**. Creeks, lakes and campgrounds are scattered through this area. The camps' opening dates can vary with the weather, but generally they are open from Memorial Day through Labor Day (for the information of non-American visitors, that is from the last Monday in May to the first Monday in September). Fees are charged for camp use. Facilities often include tables, fire grates, tent pads and some type of water and sanitary facilities. While fires are usually allowed in these sites, it's a good idea to carry a small camp stove with you. If you do decide to light a fire, you must take care to extinguish it properly, and try to restore the area before moving on.

The first town you encounter on the peninsula is **Hope ⑧**, a mining community of about 200, founded in the late 1890s. A trip to Hope requires a 16-mile (25-km) detour onto the Hope Cutoff, Mile 56 of the Seward Highway, but it's well worth the time. The town is the site of the oldest school house in Alaska – a red, one-room school still in use. Other facilities in Hope include the Hope and Sunrise Mining Museum (open Memorial Day–Labor Day Fri–Mon noon–4pm), a store, a couple of cafés, a bar and a lodge.

BELOW: Christmas lights on Seward Highway.

An ideal site for pink salmon fishing, moose, caribou and black bear hunting, Hope also is the head of the **Resurrection Trail**, one of the most popular hiking areas on the peninsula. The trailhead is located at Mile 3.5 of the Resurrection Creek Road. The entire trail is 38 miles (60 km) long, and hikers emerge at **Schooner Bend**, Mile 52 on the Sterling Highway. One option is to turn off the Resurrection Trail at Mile 20 and take the 10-mile (16-km) **Devil's Pass Trail**, which emerges at Mile 39 of the Seward Highway.

The Forest Service operates some cabins along the Resurrection Trail. Most have bunk space for six, and wood stoves. If a cabin is on a lake, it usually has a row boat and oars. Campers must bring their own food, utensils and sleeping bags. Because of the route's popularity, it is wise to make cabin reservations well ahead of time. Reservations can be made up to six months in advance (tel: 800-280-2267).

Depending on your stamina and interests, the Resurrection Trail can take between two and six days to cover. Trout fishing is possible in the several lakes along the trail. The trail also provides spectacular scenery for the photographer. If you don't want to hike the entire route you can take a wonderful day hike, starting at either end.

The Seward Highway

On leaving Hope and rejoining the Seward Highway, the first decision is whether to go west or south at the Seward Junction at Mile 40. To the south lie Moose Pass and Seward; to the west lie Cooper Landing,

Kenai, Soldotna, Anchor Point, Ninilchik, Homer and Seldovia, which can be reached only by ferry. There are several smaller towns as well, including Clam Gulch and Kasilof.

Heading south, the first community is **Moose Pass**. This is a quiet village of less than 200 people. Residents enjoy hiking, fishing and biking – the town has one of Alaska's relatively few bike trails. One of the highlights of the year is the annual Summer Festival, held to celebrate the solstice. The exact date of the festival changes from year to year, but is always held on the June weekend with the most total hours of sunlight. Activities include a barbecue, carnival, softball games and an auction.

Continuing south on the highway you come to **Seward ❾**, an attractive city of about 3,000 residents. Founded in 1903, it was for years the leading port city of Alaska. It was eventually eclipsed in that role by Anchorage, and the 1964 earthquake devastated the economy. Twenty years later, it began to regain its financial legs and now is once again a thriving port. A visitor center is located at the entrance to town, on the highway, and another one can be found at the Chamber of Commerce railroad car, located at 3rd Avenue and Jefferson Streets (open daily in summer). Almost diagonally opposite is the **Seward Historical Museum** (open daily in summer 10am–5pm; entrance charge). The town library, on 5th Avenue, features a summer book sale, photographs and a film on the effects of the 1964 earthquake on Seward.

One of the main attractions of the area is **Resurrection Bay**. Charter boats for sail or power excursions on the bay are available at the city harbor, as are kayak rentals. Boats can be hired for sightseeing or fishing. The state ferry system also has a dock in Seward, offering trips to Kodiak and the Prince William Sound areas.

Seward is the northern terminus for most cruise-ships crossing the Gulf of Alaska. These ships bring more than 180,000 visitors through Seward on their way to or from Alaska.

Another interesting stop is the Seward Marine Education Center, operated by the University of Alaska-Fairbanks. Tours are available weekday afternoons, except on public holidays. But Seward's newest and potentially biggest attraction is the **Alaska SeaLife Center** built on a 7-acre (3-hectare) site next to the Marine Education Center on the shores of Resurrection Bay. This marine science enterprise, which opened to the public in May 1998, combines research on saving marine species and aiding recovery from industrial damage, with the rehabilitation of maimed or stranded birds and mammals. It also aims to provide education and entertainment for the thousands of visitors who are expected to visit the center each year.

The highlight of the year in Seward is undoubtedly the annual 4th of July celebration, a festival which includes an all-town barbecue, a parade, acrobatic flyers, fireworks and the Mount Marathon foot race. Racers make a mad scramble up one side of a mountain located behind the town, and then take a wild slide down the mountain's back.

Another special event is the annual Silver Salmon Derby, a week-long fishing contest that offers more

Map, pages 154–5

BELOW: orca whales in Resurrection Bay.

Puffins inhabit the park.

BELOW: mountain goat at the Harding Icefield.

prize money than any other fishing derby in Alaska. It begins on the second Saturday of August.

Seward is also the gateway to **Kenai Fjords National Park** , which was declared a national monument in 1978 and designated a national park two years later. As well as the rugged coastal fjords for which it is named, and the glaciers which, for many, are its chief attraction, the park is home to porpoises, sea otters, sea lions, humpback and orca whales, puffins, bald eagles and other animals. Several local tour operators offer frequent wildlife cruises into the park, starting from Seward's Small Boat Harbor.

Most of the park is only accessible by boat: the only vehicle access is to the northwest of Seward, at Exit Glacier Road. Exit Glacier is the most easily accessible point of the **Harding Icefield**, a remnant of the Ice Age that caps a section of the Kenai Mountains 50 miles (80 km) long and 30 miles (48 km) wide. The glacier itself lies less than a mile (1 km) past the car parking area at the end of the road; you cross the bridge at the parking lot and head up the trail.

It's an easy walk to the face. There are ranger-led hikes but you can go it alone, taking care not to go beyond the warning signs. A challenging hike rises along the side of the glacier to the icefield above. For further information on this and all aspects of the park, contact the Visitor Center on 4th Avenue by the Small Boat Harbor in Seward (tel: 224-3874).

After leaving the park and initially driving north, it's time to head west on the Sterling Highway. Turn left at the junction; the road is marked as Alaska Route 1. Out toward **Cooper Landing**, you enter an area that's been closed to Dall sheep hunting. As a result, it's often a good area to spot them. But looking for sheep while driving can be dangerous, so pull off at one of many designated

Map, pages 154–5

stops before peering up to look for the white specks high up on the peaks. A spotting scope or powerful zoom lens is a big help.

Cooper Landing is a community of about 300 people, spread out along the headwaters of the Kenai River. Here the river is a beautiful turquoise color, and in the winter months the open stretches of water are a prime feeding ground for bald eagles.

Sport fishing – particularly for red salmon – hunting and tourism are the area's main industries, although the town began as a mining area.

At nearby **Kenai Lake**, you can fish for Dolly Varden, lake trout, rainbow trout and whitefish. The Kenai River has trout, king, silver and red salmon. Trophy rainbow trout, some weighing as much as 20 lbs (9 kg), are caught here by spin- and fly-fishing enthusiasts, and catch-and-release fishing is widely practiced. Rafting is another popular activity on the river, and several local businesses offer fishing and float trips. Hunting and fishing regulations vary: game regulation booklets are available free from the Department of Fish and Game. Many sporting goods shops also offer copies of the regulation manuals.

Continuing west, just outside of the Cooper Landing area at the confluence of the Kenai and Russian rivers, is the turnoff to the **Russian River Campground**. The site is easy to spot in the summer, as it's usually busy. The 20-mile (32-km) **Russian Lakes Trail** is a delightful and not over-demanding hike, with cabins en route. Reservations are essential (tel: 800-280-2267). The Russian River is the largest fresh-water fishery in Alaska, and draws more than 30,000 fishermen each year, all hoping to catch a red salmon.

Heading west on the Sterling Highway, you leave the Chugach National Forest and enter the **Kenai National Wildlife Refuge** ⓫, which is in a different

BELOW: marmot in an alpine meadow.

*Soldotna's Visitor
Center has many
colorful photographs
of the area, as well as
the prize exhibit, the
World Record King
Salmon, weighing
97 lbs (44 kg).*

federal game management area. Refuge regulations, as well as trail maps and information about things to do in the refuge, are available from the unit's Soldotna headquarters, tel: 262-7021, up Ski Hill Road from the Sterling Highway south of the Kenai River Bridge.

The refuge, which was established by President Roosevelt to preserve the moose population, is also the habitat of coyotes, grizzlies, caribou, and wolves. It comprises the western slopes of the Kenai Mountains, and spruce and birch forested lowlands bordering Cook Inlet. Among the major recreational areas in the refuge is the 20-mile (32-km) **Skilak Lake Loop**, which intersects the Sterling Highway near the Visitor Center. This road takes you to **Skilak Lake**, and also provides access to several other smaller lakes, streams and some 200 miles (320 km) of trails in the area. The most arduous trail is the Skilak Lookout Trail, which takes you up some 1,450 ft (440 meters) and provides stunning views. The Visitor Center provides details on the Swanson River Canoe Trail.

Skilak Lake itself has a surface area of 24,000 acres (57,600 hectares). It is prone to sudden and violent storms – warning signs should be taken very seriously. The lake offers fishing for salmon, trout and Dolly Varden.

Continuing west from Cooper Landing along the highway you come to **Sterling**, a community of about 5,000, based at the confluence of the Kenai and Moose rivers. It's a very popular salmon fishing area, and is the main access point to the Swanson River oil field and an endless string of lakes that are excellent for canoeing.

Another attraction of the area is the **Izaak Walton Recreation Site**. It is believed the area was an Eskimo village more than 2,000 years ago and several depressions mark the sites of ancient houses.

BELOW LEFT: ice-boating on Kenai Lake.
BELOW RIGHT: participants in Seward's 4th of July race.

Sterling is also the site of the Moose River Raft Race, an annual event that is held on the weekend after the 4th of July. Area businesses construct rafts in a variety of categories, then race down the Moose River to the Kenai River.

Heading on past Sterling, you come to **Soldotna**, seat of the borough government and home of about 4,000 people. With its central location at the intersection of the roads to Kenai and Homer, Soldotna has become the hub of the central peninsula. It is a popular spot to meet up with professional fishing guides, most of whom specialize in helping their clients find king salmon.

The amount of traffic on the Kenai River has become the subject of statewide controversy. Twenty-five years ago, only a handful of locals fished on the river for sport. Now the Kenai River system is the most popular fishing area in the state. Consult state park officials, or local officials from the department of fish and game for the most up-to-date information on river use. Information is also available from the Visitor Center, at the corner of the Sterling Highway and Kalifornsky Beach Road, which also houses the offices for the local Chamber of Commerce.

Soldotna's festivals include Progress Days, held the last weekend in July, a winter sports festival and sled dog racing championships in late February. Because of its location near the coast, Soldotna often doesn't receive enough snow to cover the sled dog course. For that reason, the city usually stockpiles snow scraped off the city streets, to spread over the course a few days before the races.

Located on the southwest edge of Soldotna is the **Kenai Peninsula College**. Among its major programs is petroleum technology, reflecting the area's tie to the oil industry.

Map, pages 154–5

BELOW: a good day's catch in Homer.

Contestant in the sled dog race.

BELOW: a kayaker in Kenai Fjords National Park.

Heading west from Soldotna on either the Kenai Spur Highway or Kalifornsky Beach Road, you come to **Kenai** ⑫, the largest city on the peninsula with a population of about 7,000, and also the oldest permanent settlement, founded by Russian fur traders and Orthodox priests in the late 18th century.

Kenai is home port to a good share of the peninsula's drift-net fishing fleet. In the summer a parade of boats can be seen coming in and out of the mouth of the river in their quest for red salmon.

During the spring, the flats along the mouth of the river are temporary nesting ground for thousands of snow geese. They stay in the area for about two weeks and are a popular subject for early-season photographers.

Kenai is also home to the peninsula's largest airport and has the most regularly scheduled flights. Airlines also fly in and out of Anchorage, Soldotna, Seward and Homer, and charter flights can take you almost anywhere else.

One of Kenai's main attractions is the **Kenai Visitors' and Cultural Center** on the corner of Main Street and Kenai Spur Highway (open daily in summer; admission free; tel: 283-1991). The center features exhibits and displays of Kenai's rich and diverse culture, from its Native and Russian history through the industries that currently fuel the area: oil and commercial fishing.

It's also interesting to head down Overland Avenue, where you will find Fort Kenay, although the present one is only a replica of the original 19th-century fortification. On the other side of Mission Street is the **Holy Assumption Russian Orthodox Church**, the oldest Orthodox place of worship in Alaska. If you follow Mission Street to Riverview Avenue you will come to the **Beluga Whale Lookout** where, in early summer, you can watch the white whales feeding on salmon in the river.

Special events include the 4th of July parade and the "Christmas Comes to Kenai" celebration on the weekend following Thanksgiving. That fête includes a fireworks display at about 4pm. Since the peninsula has very long days during the summer, the people of Kenai hold off on fireworks until November, when they can easily be seen against the black afternoon sky.

Continuing north of Kenai on the Spur Highway, you come to the **Nikiski** industrial area, with a large chemical plant, two oil refineries and a natural gas liquification plant. The plants aren't open to the public.

The area north of Kenai has several names. Some call it simply "North Kenai," while others say "Nikishka," "Nikiska," or "Nikiski." The latter name won a popularity vote in the area, but stick to what the locals say when talking to them.

North of the refineries is the **Captain Cook State Recreation Area**, a popular spot for hiking, camping, fishing, and snow-machining. There are a couple of good campsites and great views across the Cook Inlet. Much of what you see across the inlet is part of the **Lake Clark National Park**. Charter flights to the park can be arranged in Kenai – ask at the Visitor Center there for details.

From the recreation area, drive along the Bridge Access Road and connect with Kalifornsky Beach Road to return to the Sterling Highway. Farther south, the highway begins to parallel Cook Inlet and runs past some fine clamming areas in the appropriately named Clam Gulch. Clamming requires patience, practice, a shovel and pail, a fishing license and a current tide book. But for those who like to eat the mollusks – particularly the razor clams, said to be the best of all – a day in Clam Gulch could well be one of the highlights of their visit. You could stay at the local lodge, which serves very good clam chowder in its restaurant.

BELOW: turquoise lake, Lake Clark National Park.

At Mile 135 on the highway is **Ninilchik**, a fishing village founded by the Russians more than 100 years ago. Fishing is still popular here today, with many visitors coming in search of halibut or salmon. The town's 650 residents mostly live in recently constructed homes along the highway. The original village, which can be visited, is an attractive spot, sitting on the inlet at the mouth of the Ninilchik River. On a hill above the old village is the town's Russian Orthodox Church, not open for tours but still used by the parish. The modern community of Ninilchik hosts the Kenai Peninsula State Fair on the third weekend in August. Ninilchik is another good spot for clam digging.

Continuing south, you come to **Anchor Point**, the most westerly point in North America that is accessible by continuous road system. The 1,200-member community hosts a king salmon derby from Memorial Day weekend through the third weekend in June. In addition to kings, the area is a popular fishing spot for silvers, steelhead, halibut and trout.

Still farther south is **Homer** , the southern terminus of the Sterling Highway. Homer sits on the shore of **Kachemak Bay**, which is known for the variety of its marine life. Homer itself, a pleasant little town in a picturesque setting between mountains and sea, is best known for the Homer Spit, which extends 5 miles (8 km) out into the bay. Major attractions are boat tours and halibut-fishing trips, but call in at the Homer Visitor and Information Center on the corner of Sterling Highway and Pioneer Avenue (open daily in summer; tel: 235-7740) to find out what else is on offer. You will discover the **Pratt Museum** on Bartlett Street (open daily in summer; entrance charge; tel: 235-8635), a natural history museum which focuses on marine life in Kachemak Bay. It also has an excellent exhibit on the effects of the *Exxon Valdez* oil spill.

Blueberries for sale.

BELOW: the busy port at Homer.

Homer has quite a reputation as a local arts center. On Pioneer Avenue, which joins the highway, there are a number of art galleries, some displaying pottery and jewelry as well as paintings. In downtown Homer there are also several good restaurants and souvenir shops, and there are productions year-round by an amateur theater company .

The town is also the jumping off point for trips to the other side of the bay, including Kachemak Bay State Park, with the Grewingk Glacier, Halibut Cove – where there are more artists and galleries – and the pleasing little town of **Seldovia**. The state ferry service links Homer to Seldovia, Kodiak and Seward during the summer.

Seldovia is accessible only by air and water. You can bring a vehicle on the state ferry, but it isn't really necessary; all the town is within easy walking distance. It is home to yet another of the peninsula's historic and still active Russian Orthodox churches. Seldovia's Russian history predates the church, however. It was the site of one of the earliest coal mines, first worked in the late 18th century. By the 1890s, the mine had been exhausted and Seldovia had become a fishing and shipping center.

Unfortunately, much of the town's boardwalk area was destroyed during the 1964 earthquake. Town residents can show visitors where things were before the ground dropped. Seldovia also has a winter carnival, which brightens up the peaceful, quiet months. With the bulk of visitors gone and with plenty of nearby trails for hiking and cross-country skiing, winter is one of the nicest times to venture over to the southern shore of Kachemak Bay.

Whether you're searching for trophy-size halibut, Russian history or wildlife-viewing, the peninsula offers it all within an easy drive from Anchorage. ❑

Map, pages 154–5

BELOW: looking out toward Seldovia Bay.

KODIAK,
THE CITY AND THE ISLAND

Two-thirds of mountainous Kodiak Island is a wildlife reserve,
famous for its brown bears, while the city of Kodiak
has a strong and visible legacy from its Russian past

Alaska

Anchorage

A shift of the wind can change **Kodiak Island** from a desolate, windswept, rain-pounded rock isolated from the rest of the world by fog, to a shimmering emerald of grass, spruce trees and snow-capped mountains glowing pink in the sunrise. But while the winds may shift, they remain predominantly from the north. Both the island itself and the city of Kodiak are places whose characters change with the weather, the seasons and the observer.

At first glance the city of **Kodiak** seems to be somewhere near world's end, a town of 6,800 people perched precariously on a small ledge of land between ocean swells and mountains. A look into Kodiak's economy reveals a major fishing port – one of the top three in the United States. Kodiak is home to a multi-million-dollar fishing fleet which ranges from the Pacific Northwest to Norton Sound.

Over 200 years of recorded history have swept across Kodiak, each one leaving traces of its passing. Artifacts of the indigenous Koniag culture surface near remnants of the Russian period or World War II bunkers, derelict whaling stations, collapsing herring-rendering plants or fish-processing facilities. Just under the top soil is a layer of volcanic ash which covered the town in 1912 and still drifts about, leaving a coating of fine, white dust. White spruce tree skeletons guard the salt marshes, monuments to the land subsidence which occurred during the 1964 earthquake and tidal wave.

From the air Kodiak Island seems an empty wilderness, 3,588 sq. miles (9,293 sq. km) of rugged mountains deeply indented by bays. The north half of the island is covered with spruce trees, the south half with grass. Foresters say the spruce forest is advancing down the island at the rate of one mile a century.

Landing in Kodiak (there are frequent flights from Anchorage) can be an adventure. As the jet approaches the airport, it drops lower and lower over the water until its landing gear seems to skim the waves. Just beyond where the runway seems to emerge from the water, the plane sets down. At the other end of the runway sits **Barometer Mountain** (2,450 ft/745 meters), so called because the peak is only visible in good weather.

The airport is about 5 miles (8 km) from Kodiak City and there's a connecting bus. Spruce trees cast shadows across the highway, then the road twists in sharp turns around Pillar Mountain. In the winter bald eagles, sometimes 10 to a tree, perch in cottonwoods above the highway. The road then dips down into Kodiak.

The sea is Kodiak's front yard. Fifteen fish-processing plants line the city's waterfront. Flocks of sea birds bob on the swells and in the spring bald eagles wheel

overhead. The salt-tanged smell of fish announces that this is a port producing fish and shellfish for markets around the world. The blue onion domes of the Holy Resurrection Orthodox Church announces that this is the first Russian settlement in Alaska. Reminders of that heritage can be found everywhere.

The Russian legacy

Drawn by his search for sea otter pelts, Grigor Ivanovich Shelikof arrived in Three Saints Bay on the southeast corner of Kodiak Island in 1784 with two ships, the *Three Saints* and the *St Simon*. He was not welcomed by the indigenous Koniag people, who proceeded to harass the Russian party. Shelikof responded with appalling force.

The Russian monopoly of the Alaskan fur trade lasted until the 1830s when the British Hudson's Bay Company set up a post and began competing for trade.

"They said Shelikohov [*sic*] loaded two bidarkas [skin boats] with his people," wrote Ivan Peel, acting governor-general of Irkutsak and Kolyvan, to the Russian senate in 1789, "and with the armed band murdered about 500 of these speechless people; if we also count those who ran in fear to their bidarkas and trying to escape, stampeded and drowned each other, the number will exceed 500. Many men and women were taken as prisoners of war. By order of Mr Shelikohov, the men were led to the tundra and speared, the remaining women and children, about 600 altogether, he took with him to the harbor and kept them for three weeks."

Having established his authority, Shelikof founded the first Russian settlement in Alaska on **Three Saints Bay**, built a school to teach the Natives to read and write Russian, and introduced the Russian Orthodox religion.

BELOW: trading for oil.

In 1790 Alexander Adrevich Baranof arrived at Three Saints Bay to take over leadership of the Russian settlement. He moved the colony to the northeast end

TUSKI AND MAHLEMUTS TRADING FOR OIL.

of the island where timber was available, and which was closer to Cook Inlet and Prince William Sound. The site chosen by Baranof is now the city of Kodiak.

Russian members of the colony took Koniag wives and started family lines whose names still continue – Panamaroff, Pestrikoff, Kvasnikoff. Russian heritage in the city of Kodiak is also found on its street signs: Baranof, Rezanoff, Shelikof. The island's Native culture is also apparent, and can be observed at a performance by the Kodiak Alutiiq Dancers, a troupe formed by the Kodiak Tribal Council in 1988, which includes 50 dancers who wear traditional dress and perform ethnic songs and dances. The troupe performs throughout the state but schedules daily summer performances in Kodiak (tel: 486-4449).

Much of the rich culture of the Koniags was absorbed by the Russian culture and can only be guessed at through artifacts and the diaries of the early Russian settlers. The best window on Koniag culture is at the **Alutiiq Museum** (215 Mission Road, tel: 486-7004; open in summer Mon–Sat 10am–4pm; Sun noon–4pm; winter Tues–Sat only; entrance charge). This Native-owned research museum interprets artifacts from on-going Koniag-directed archeological digs. Visitors can also join digs on six-day sessions at remote sites in the Dig Afognak program (tel: 800-770-6014 or 486-6014).

The **Baranof Museum** (open Mon–Fri 10am–4pm, Sat–Sun noon–4pm; entrance charge; tel: 486-5920) is across from the Visitor Center which is on Marine Way, next to the ferry dock, and also contains displays of Koniag artifacts and clothing as well as items from the Russian and early American periods. The small museum is located in the **Erskine House**, once a store-house for furs, which has been designated a National Historic Landmark, and is the oldest Russian building in North America.

Map, pages 154–5

BELOW: the Baranof Museum.

Orthodox priests play a major role.

When the United States purchased Alaska from Imperial Russia, the Russian citizens left, but the Russian Orthodox church remained. The two blue onion domes of the **Holy Resurrection Church** on Mission Road are the town's most outstanding landmarks. Orthodoxy still plays a significant role in the Kodiak community, and is the predominant religion in the six villages in the island area.

In 1974 the **St Herman Orthodox Theological Seminary** was relocated to Kodiak: the white buildings stand near the church. Father Herman arrived in Kodiak in 1794 and settled on **Spruce Island**, where he established a school and became renowned as an ascetic and miracle worker. He was canonized in Kodiak in 1970, the first Orthodox canonization to take place on American soil. His remains are kept in the church and the Russian Orthodox faithful make pilgrimages every August to his shrine. Other treasures of the Holy Resurrection Orthodox Church include many brilliantly colored icons. Visitors are welcome to attend services.

The Russian Orthodox Church follows the Julian calendar, making Kodiak a town of two Christmases, December 25 and January 7, and two New Years, January 1 and January 14.

During World War II, Kodiak served as a major supply center for the Aleutian campaign. Military personnel and construction workers changed the city from a fishing village of 500 residents to a boom town of 4,000 people with another 20,000 in nearby areas. The US Navy built a major base on the site, which is now used as a US Coast Guard facility. Residents who lived in Kodiak during the war tell tales of sailors on liberty, submarine nets stretched across the Kodiak-Near Island channel and the difficulty of obtaining fishing supplies. Today all that remains of those years are silent, moss-covered bunkers.

BELOW LEFT: the Holy Resurrection Church.
BELOW RIGHT: Russian dancers.

Fort Abercrombie State Park, some 4 miles (6 km) from the city, is dedicated to the memory of those days. A large bunker and the remains of gun emplacements overlook the sea from a cliff. Other bunkers can be found by walking through an alpine meadow and along the cliff edge. There are guided tours several times a week, and some good facilities for camping within the park.

There are also bunkers on **Pillar Mountain** (1,270 feet/385 meters) behind the city. Hikers working their way through the alders and spruce forests along the tops of shale cliffs often find others. Crowned with radar towers, Pillar Mountain also provides panoramic views of the surrounding area.

Kodiak's US Coast Guard facility is the largest in the United States. Its cutters and C-130 airplanes keep track of the foreign fishing fleets working off the coast. For locals, the Coast Guard facility is the home of "angels" who arrive in helicopters to pluck men off their sinking vessels or search the coastline for survivors of marine tragedies.

Natural events have left indelible marks on Kodiak Island. Twice in the 20th century the landscape was altered, first by a volcanic ash fall in 1912 and again by the great earthquake and tsunami in 1964.

Humus has covered the ash that fell on June 6, 1912, when Mount Novarupta on the Alaska Peninsula exploded, but where roads have cut into the mountains the white layer of volcanic ash is visible under the soil's surface. In places the ash drifted several feet deep. Small lakes vanished. Wildlife died, and much natural vegetation was destroyed. Five hundred residents were evacuated on the revenue cutter *Manning*, and the town was choked by ash.

The Good Friday earthquake in 1964 which devastated much of South Central Alaska also set off a tidal wave which swept into the city of Kodiak and

Map, pages 154–5

BELOW: even the walls have bears.

destroyed the downtown buildings, canneries and the docks. Many residents fled up Pillar Mountain and watched helplessly while the sea ran out, leaving the harbor dry, and then rolled back in across the land. Those who didn't reach high ground were swept away.

Although a few fishermen managed to take their boats to sea – and safety – before the tidal wave hit, boats left in the harbor were pushed into town by the wave. The 100-ton power scow *Selief* ended up a half mile inland, still with 3,000 king crab in its hold. Along the shore the land and seabed subsided by as much as 5 ft (1.5 meters). Forested areas turned into salt water marshes, now identifiable by the still standing skeletal trees.

After the tidal wave, most of downtown Kodiak was redesigned and rebuilt. Fish-processing companies sent in floating processing plants to can king crab and salmon until new plants could be built. Residents who lived through the tidal wave and stayed to rebuild the town have formed a special bond. Though the tidal wave was a tragedy, it left behind a feeling of unity which still pervades the community.

A thriving fishing industry

Kodiak's economic dependence on the sea has been constant. The city of Kodiak provides temporary moorage and services for nearly 3,000 fishing boats a year. Fishermen deliver up to $93 million worth of fish and shellfish annually. Small skiffs, medium-sized salmon seiners, big shrimp trawlers and 100-ft (30-meter) midwater draggers steam in and out of the harbor bringing red, pink, chum and silver salmon, herring, halibut, black cod, Pacific cod, pollock and flounder.

BELOW: canneries at Kodiak's port.

Map, pages 154–5

Ask Kodiak residents what season it is and, if it is summer, they're likely to answer, "Salmon season." Fall is king crab season; winter's marked by the Tanner crab, marketed as snow crab; spring is herring season; halibut and black cod are harvested in spring and summer, and whitefish species most of the year.

Kodiak's fishermen work year round, switching from fishery to fishery as the seasons change. Between seasons the waterfront throbs with activity. Crane trucks and flatbeds move 500-lb (230-kg) steel crab pots from storage to the boat and back to storage. In spring, herring seines and gillnets are stretched out on the docks where crew men with shuttles can attach float and lead lines.

Visitors are welcome to wander down the ramp behind the Harbormaster Building and walk along the floats in **St Paul Harbor**. Across the channel, on **Near Island**, is **St Herman Harbor**. In St Paul Harbor there are two loading docks where skippers load gear on board their boats – crab pots may swing at the ends of booms or seines may be lifted to the deck. Just before a fishing season it seems there are more boats in a hurry to load than dock space for loading. Fishing boats line the loading docks – the ferry dock, the city dock and the sea-land dock where a huge crane lifts vans off barges.

Visitors expect to come to a major fishing port and eat seafood, but most of Kodiak's fresh seafood is in refrigerated vans waiting to be loaded onto barges for shipment. The fishing industry is geared to large volume production and sales, which has made it difficult for small, local buyers to establish a steady source of supply. The local supermarkets do offer fresh seafood in season and some restaurants include it on their menus.

Like its fishing industry, Kodiak's population is diversified, and you'll overhear a mixture of languages and accents as you wander around the harbor.

BELOW: Kodiak salmonberries.

Touring Kodiak Island

Except for several Native villages, the populated portion of Kodiak Island is confined to the road system, and there is less than 100 miles (160 km) of it. Some parts of the system are only fit for 4-wheel-drive vehicles, but other parts can be driven in an ordinary car. The six coastal villages on the island are accessible only by plane or boat; if you want to visit one of them, you need to make arrangements in advance.

There may be as many as 2,500 bears on Kodiak Island. A large male can weigh up to 1,500 lbs (680 kg).

It takes about an hour to drive to the end of the road at Fossil Beach. The road heads out of town past the **Buskin River State Recreation Area** where the headquarters and visitor center for the Kodiak National Wildlife Refuge is located. The Buskin River is a popular sport-fishing stream for salmon and steelhead. The road continues past the airport, the Coast Guard base, the fairgrounds, the neighborhood of **Bells Flats**, and then climbs headlands, curves around bays and crosses rivers.

In summer salmon can be seen jumping in the bays and swimming up the rivers. July and August are the best months for salmon-watching or fishing. Occasionally sea lions come into the bays to feed on the fish. It is very tempting to stop at every twist of the road, and there are no restrictions on exploring the beaches, walking in the forests, climbing the mountains, or simply smelling the wildflowers.

Eventually the road comes to a T-junction. To the left is the community of **Chiniak**. To the right the road travels through cattle country where Kodiak's ranchers run about 2,000 head of beef cattle.

BELOW: driftwood on Fossil Beach.

Ahead the ocean comes into view again by **Pasagshak**, a popular river for fishing silver salmon. There is a small campsite on its banks. The road continues

past a sand-duned, surf-beaten beach and ends at **Fossil Beach** where fossil shells lie loosely in the clay and rocks. During the fall, gray whales pass Pasagshak and Fossil Beach on their migration to California from the Bering Sea. In spring, the whales pass the island again as they migrate to their northern summer feeding grounds.

 Map, pages 154–5

Kodiak National Wildlife Refuge

By traveling along the roads you will see some of the loveliest scenery on the island. But if you want real wilderness, and bears, you must visit the **Kodiak National Wildlife Refuge ⑮**, which can only be reached by air or sea. This mountainous wilderness, covering two-thirds of the island, belongs to bears and foxes, rabbits and birds, muskrats and otters.

Most people come here to see the brown bears – the world's largest carnivores. The best and safest way to see them is to take one of the charter plane tours on offer in Kodiak, but be warned – they are not cheap. Alternatively, several wilderness lodges on the island have bear-viewing packages; and a wildlife refuge program offers four-day trips between July and September. Wilderness hikers should always remember to walk noisily through Kodiak's backcountry to reduce the chances of any confrontations with bears. During the salmon season, bears appear along the streams and beaches. As well as berries and salmon, the Kodiak bear enjoys a diet of calves and deer – much to the dismay of local ranchers and hunters.

Whether you are interested in Alaska's Native traditions, in the history of Russian settlers, or in wildlife and wilderness, a visit to Kodiak Island will be an enriching experience. ❏

BELOW: taking the family for a walk.

A SERENGETI OF THE NORTH

Wildlife-watching draws many visitors to the state, and they are rarely disappointed, for the seas, parks and wilderness areas are a treasure trove of wildlife

Alaska is sometimes called the "Serengeti of the North." That's a bit of an exaggeration, but not much, because the state is home to a huge diversity of birds and beasts. The seas are the habitat of humpback, beluga, minke and gray whales, porpoises and dolphins, walrus, sea lions, sea otters and polar bears; while the land is inhabited by 105 species of mammals, including hoary marmots, Dall sheep, little brown bats, flying squirrels and ferocious wolverines. The state also provides a seasonal home for more than 400 kinds of fish, nearly 300 bird species and seven amphibians. The Pribilof Islands in the Bering Sea are summer home to a million fur seals – the creatures whose skins lured Europeans to Alaska – and to millions of sea birds. The McNeil River, on the Alaska Peninsula, has the world's largest gathering of brown bears: more than 100 different individuals have been observed at McNeil Falls during a single summer, feeding on the salmon runs.

Farther north, some 400,000 caribou, members of just one herd, the Western Arctic Caribou Herd, roam the state's northwest region, perpetually on the move. And each fall between 1,000 and 4,000 bald eagles gather in Southeast Alaska's Chilkat Valley near Haines to feed on a late run of salmon.

△ **GRAY WOLF**
Gray wolves are symbols of the wild. They inhabit much of Alaska but are not always easy to spot, as they keep away from the company of humans as much as possible.

▷ **MUSK OX**
Musk oxen are a relic of the ice age. They live in open tundra. When predators threaten, they defend themselves by standing back-to-back, heads pointed out, in protective rings.

▽ **CARIBOU**
Alaska is home to some two dozen caribou herds totaling more than one million animals. They are called "the nomads of the north" because they travel so extensively, and seem to be in constant movement.

◁ **MOOSE**
The largest members of the deer family, moose are the most important game animals in the state. They are herbivores and feed on a variety of plants, including aquatic weeds which they nose out from the beds of lakes and ponds.

THE INHABITANTS OF BEAR COUNTRY

△ HOARY MARMOT

Members of the rodent family, marmots live among talus (scree) slopes or rock slides in the mountains. Their high-pitched alarm calls sound like whistles and carry for more than a mile.

▽ WALRUS

Two walrus bulls display their tusks as they engage in a territorial dispute along the rocky coast of Round Island, part of the Walrus Islands State Game Sanctuary in Bristol Bay. An adult male may weigh up to 4,000 lbs (1,800 kg).

There's a good reason why Alaska is called "bear country." It's the only one of the 50 states to be inhabited by all three of North America's bears: the black bear, the polar bear, and the brown bear – also called the grizzly. The populations of all these species are reported to be healthy, thanks in large part to the presence of vast wilderness areas. Polar bears roam the ice of the Beaufort, Chukchi and Bering seas. Both black and brown bears are found throughout most of the state, though the smaller black bears tend to be forest creatures, while browns and grizzlies prefer open areas like mountain meadows and Arctic tundra.

Brown bears and grizzlies are members of the same species: the former are coastal creatures while the latter live in the interior. Grizzlies have longer claws and a bigger hump and are generally smaller and lighter than their coastal cousins. Biologists believe brown bears grow larger mainly because they have access to energy-rich foods, especially salmon, like the one being devoured in the picture above. Though classified as carnivores, brown, grizzly and black bears eat both vegetation and meat; the polar bear is a true carnivore and its favorite prey is the ringed seal.

KATMAI NATIONAL PARK

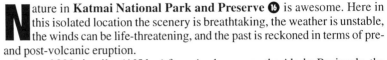

*Take a trip to Katmai on the Alaska Peninsula
to fish and paddle, and see the strange lunar landscape
created by a volcanic eruption*

*see also map inside
back cover*

PRECEDING PAGES:
mountain house on
the Ruth Glacier,
just south of Mount
McKinley.
BELOW: angler with
a king salmon.

Nature in **Katmai National Park and Preserve** ⓰ is awesome. Here in this isolated location the scenery is breathtaking, the weather is unstable, the winds can be life-threatening, and the past is reckoned in terms of pre- and post-volcanic eruption.

Located 290 air miles (465 km) from Anchorage on the Alaska Peninsula, the park is a haven for lovers of the unspoiled wilderness. No highway system touches this area; access is by small plane. Katmai can be reached by an hour's flight from Anchorage to **King Salmon**, and a 20-minute trip by floatplane or amphibian chartered from King Salmon to Brooks Camp, or you can hire an air taxi in King Salmon.

The park receives more than 50,000 visitors, sightseers and flightseers, fishermen, hikers, climbers and canoeists each year, most of them at **Brooks Camp** on **Naknek Lake**. You can pick up information at the nearby Visitor Center (open daily) which also runs evening slide shows. Book in advance if you hope to stay in Brooks Lodge (tel: 243-5448). Reservations open in January of the year before the date of the proposed visit, and all are booked up a full year in advance. There are several easy walks in the immediate vicinity, and bears can be viewed in summer from a safe viewing platform as they feed on spawning salmon. Bears congregate in July and September only, and may not be evident during other months. You can also book a place on a tour bus which provides transportation to the scene of volcanic devastation in the **Valley of Ten Thousand Smokes**. The bus takes visitors to Overlook Cabin, at the end of the road, from where you can see the valley and take a gentle, ranger-led hike, or set off on a more ambitious one on your own.

More than 85 years after the eruption, the valley remains awe-inspiring. Ash, pumice and rocks produced over 40 sq. miles (100 sq. km) of lunar landscape, sculpted by wind and water. The once-verdant valley floor, covered with shifting pumice, resists vegetation and quickly erases the imprint of hikers' boots.

Historic Katmai

Before the great eruption of 1912, a portion of the historic Katmai Trail would have passed through this valley. The trail was traveled by Russian fur traders and missionaries, then by a flood of gold seekers taking a shortcut to Nome. Prospectors and mail carriers used it to avoid a stormy sea passage around the Alaska Peninsula but by 1912 the gold rush had subsided and the trail was seldom traveled. Today it is no longer visible and its ancient route is a path of obstacles. Blowing ash, rugged terrain, dense undergrowth, quicksand and narrow canyons challenge the most seasoned hiker. During severe weather, travelers are warned against the old route at Katmai Pass at the head of the valley. The interchange of air between the Gulf of Alaska and the Bering Sea streams through this pass and can cause winds over 100 miles per hour (160 kph) – strong enough to blow hikers off their feet.

Map, pages 154–5

Earth tremors and eruptions

When the great eruption occurred in 1912, news was slow to reach the outside world because the area was so isolated. The closest account was furnished by a Native named American Pete, who was on the Katmai Trail only 18 miles (30 km) northeast of Mount Katmai when the violent explosions began. Earth tremors that preceded the eruption were so severe that the residents of Katmai and Savonoski, small Native villages on the Alaska Peninsula, gathered their possessions and fled to Naknek, on Bristol Bay.

Later research gave credit for the devastation not to Mount Katmai, but to **Novarupta Volcano**, a volcano formed by the eruption itself. The explosion was heard up to 750 miles (1,200 km) away in Juneau. Most heavily impacted were the Native villages of Katmai and Savonoski, later abandoned because of heavy ashfall, and the town of Kodiak on Kodiak Island, across Shelikof Strait.

Valley of Ten Thousand Smokes

In the following years several expeditions were sent to the eruption site by the National Geographic Society to satisfy worldwide interest and carry out scientific research. Scientists were initially prevented from reaching the source of the eruption by seas of mud, ash slides as deep as 1,500 ft (450 meters), and evidence of one of the most powerful water surges ever.

BELOW: a fisherman's idyll.

Map, pages 154–5

As ash began to fall, accompanied by nauseating gases, people believed they would suffer the fate of Pompeii and be buried alive.

BELOW: frosty flowers and feathers.
RIGHT: bears working up an appetite.

In 1916 the crater of Mount Katmai was reached and a smoking valley discovered at Katmai Pass. The valley, named the Valley of Ten Thousand Smokes by explorer Robert Griggs, covered up to 40 sq. miles (100 sq. km) and held thousands of steaming fumaroles. Some of these emitted periodic columns of steam that reached 1,000 ft (300 meters). Here, explorers found that by moving their tents in relation to a fumarole, they could regulate floor temperature. Steam from the fumaroles, they found, could not only fry bacon, but would hold the fry pan aloft.

In 1918 the Valley of Ten Thousand Smokes was made a national monument in order to preserve an area important to the study of volcanism. Later additions for a wildlife sanctuary brought the Katmai National Park and Preserve to its total of 4,268 acres (1,700 hectares). When the Katmai monument was first created it was believed that the Valley of Ten Thousand Smokes would become a geyser-filled attraction to rival Yellowstone National Park in Wyoming, because scientists thought that the geyser field at Yellowstone was dying. But the reverse has come about. The Yellowstone geysers are still active, but the fumaroles at the Valley of Ten Thousand Smokes have subsided.

A rugged wilderness

Katmai National Park and Preserve makes available to visitors not only an area of amazing volcanic involvement but a representative and undisturbed portion of the Alaska Peninsula. Great varieties of terrain in Katmai include the rugged coastal habitat of Shelikof Strait on one side of the Alaskan range and the rivers and lakes of the Naknek River watershed on the other. Mixed spruce and birch forests, dense willow and alder thickets and moist tundra are found at lower elevations, with alpine tundra on the higher slopes.

A series of small lakes and rivers provide opportunities for canoeing, kayaking and fishing. You can paddle to a group of tiny islands on Naknek Lake's north arm, but it's about a 60-mile (100-km) round trip. Rainbow trout, lake trout, char, pike and grayling are popular sport fish here, as well as sockeye, coho, king, pink and chum salmon. Nearly one million salmon return each year to the Naknek River. Park Service campgrounds and lodges at **Kulik** and **Grosvenor Camp** are available for serious fishing enthusiasts.

The brown bears are, of course, the main attraction, but there is a great deal of other wildlife that may be encountered – and you won't be quite so much part of the crowd as you would at the main bear-watching sites. Moose, caribou, land otter, wolverine, marten, weasel, mink, lynx, fox, wolf, muskrat, beaver and hare all inhabit the park. Off coastal waters, seals, sea lions, sea otters and beluga and gray whales can be seen. Birdwatching is also a popular pastime.

Weather in Katmai is variable, and heavy rain is characteristic of most areas in summer months. The northwestern slope of the Aleutian Range has the most comfortable weather: at Brooks Camp the average daytime temperature is 60°F (15°C). Here, skies are only expected to be clear or partially cloudy 20 percent of the time. Warm clothing, rain gear and boots are highly recommended at any time of the year. ❑

DENALI NATIONAL PARK

Map, pages 154–5

Dominated by the magnificent Mount McKinley, Denali, one of the world's greatest wildlife sanctuaries, is the most visited of all Alaska's national parks

Alaskan Indians called it Denali, "The Great One." In later years, the mountain was officially designated **Mount McKinley** by the US Government but Denali is the name still used by Natives and locals. It is the most spectacular mountain in North America. At 20,320 ft (6,195 meters), it is also the highest. It could be called the highest in the world: the north face of Denali rises almost 18,000 ft (5,500 meters) above its base, an elevation gain which surpasses even Mount Everest.

The mountain is surrounded by one of the world's greatest wildlife sanctuaries – **Denali National Park** ⓘ. A one-day trip through the park will almost certainly result in sightings of grizzly bears, caribou, Dall sheep, moose and perhaps a wolf. A visit to Denali Park is an adventure. It's like nothing you've ever seen. When you arrive, be prepared for the ultimate Alaskan experience.

Geology and history

Denali is part of the **Alaska Range**, a 600-mile (960-km) arc of mountains stretching across the southeast quarter of the state. The oldest parts of the range consist of slate, shale, marble and other sedimentary deposits formed under an ancient ocean. Approximately 60 million years ago, the collision and subsequent overlapping of two tectonic plates produced such intense heat that portions of the earth's crust began to melt. A gigantic mass of molten rock deposited beneath the current location of Denali eventually solidified into granite.

Overlapping of the plates caused the whole region to be uplifted. Granite and sedimentary rock were forced upward to form the Alaska Range. As the uplift tapered off, the process of erosion slowly wore down the range. As Denali is chiefly composed of erosion-resistant granite, it wore at a slower rate than surrounding sedimentary rock. A later period of tectonic plate collision and uplift began two million years ago and continues to this day. This ongoing uplift is responsible for the towering height of Denali.

The first humans came on seasonal hunting trips to what is now Denali Park about 12,000 years ago. Later, the Athabascans followed suit, but built their permanent villages in lower, warmer, sheltered locations, next to lakes or rivers which offered dependable fishing. Lack of significant numbers of fish in the Denali rivers limited Native use of the region.

The Athabascans of the Yukon and Tanana rivers gave Denali its name. They said the mountain was created during a battle between two magical warriors. The raven war chief, Totson, pursued his enemy Yako down a river. Totson threw a magic spear at his adversary but Yako turned a gigantic wave to stone and deflected the

PRECEDING PAGES: camping beneath Mount McKinley; fall colors in Denali. **LEFT:** skiing at Ruth Glacier. **BELOW:** going with the flow.

weapon. The solidified wave became the mountain they called Denali.

In another Athabascan story, Denali is called "the home of the sun." During the longest days of summer, the sun makes almost a complete circle in the local sky and drops below the horizon for only a few hours. From certain angles, it appears that the sun rises and sets from behind Denali. The first recorded sighting of Denali by a white man occurred in 1794. While sailing in Cook Inlet, the English Captain George Vancouver sighted "distant stupendous mountains covered with snow." Undoubtedly this was the Alaska Range. Other explorers, surveyors and adventurers in later decades commented on the mountain's great height.

"Surely we found the home of the sun, as we saw with our own eyes the sun go into the mountain, and saw it leave its home in the morning."
ATHABASCAN LEGEND

The naming process

Denali became known as Mount McKinley through a strange set of circumstances in 1896 when William Dickey went on a gold-prospecting expedition in the area just south of Denali. While camped within sight of the mountain, he met other miners and they argued at length whether gold or silver should back US currency. (They were against the gold standard while Dickey was for it.) When Dickey later returned to the Lower 48 states (less than 48 at the time), he wrote an article about his Alaskan adventures, and proposed that the highest mountain in the Alaskan Range be named after presidential candidate William McKinley, the champion of the gold standard. McKinley won the 1896 election and the name stuck.

The first white man to explore the Denali region, Charles Sheldon, was also the first to suggest that it be set aside as a national park. Sheldon made two extensive trips through the area in 1906 and 1907–8, and thought that the opportunity to see and study wildlife was the most impressive feature of the region. After leaving Denali, he used his influence as a member of the powerful Boone

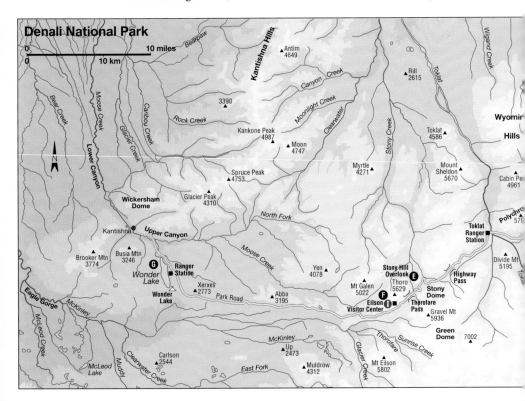

Denali National Park

and Crockett Club to gather support for his proposed Denali National Park. Largely due to Sheldon's efforts, the park became a reality in 1917. To his disappointment, Congress chose to call it Mount McKinley National Park.

While Sheldon was campaigning for the park, others were endeavoring to make the first ascent of Denali. In late 1909, four miners (Billy Taylor, Pete Anderson, Charley McGonagall and Tom Lloyd), not intimidated by the fact that they had never climbed a mountain before, decided to scale Denali. They figured if they had survived the Alaskan winters they could do anything.

The so-called Sourdough Expedition set off from Fairbanks. ("Sourdough" was the nickname given to prospectors because of the yeasty mixture they brought with them to make bread.) On the morning of April 6, 1910, Taylor and Anderson set out for the summit from their camp at 12,000 ft (3,700 meters). By mid-afternoon they were standing on Denali's North Peak: they had achieved their goal despite their total lack of experience. Unfortunately for them, the North Peak is 850 ft (260 meters) lower than the South Peak, Denali's true summit. Taylor and Anderson were never credited with being first on the top.

In 1913 Hudson Stuck and a party of three climbers mounted the first successful Denali expedition. Using maps and route descriptions made by earlier parties, they ascended the Muldrow Glacier which flows down the east side of Denali. After a long and difficult climb, they reached Denali Pass, the saddle between the North and South Peaks, only 2,100 ft (640 meters) below the summit. The high elevation, low oxygen and extreme cold made those last few hundred feet the hardest part of their climb. Walter Harper, a young Athabascan Native employed by Stuck and the strongest member of the team, was the first to stand on the summit of Mount Denali.

Map, see below

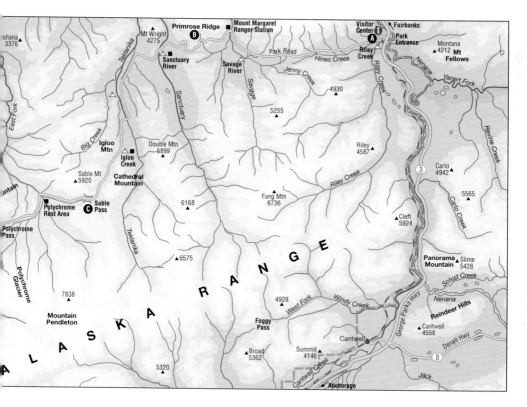

Recent changes

From 1917 to the early 1970s, few people visited Mount McKinley National Park. The park's remoteness and lack of direct access by vehicle combined to limit tourism. In the five years prior to 1972, the average annual number of visitors was about 15,000. In 1972, the Anchorage–Fairbanks Highway was completed and it suddenly became much easier for tourists and Alaskan residents to get here. In a short time, the numbers jumped to more than 140,000 a year, almost a ten-fold increase over the previous figures.

National Park Service Rangers were concerned about the effect this dramatic rise would have on the park and the quality of visitors' experiences. One major problem was that the single dirt road which bisects the park was too narrow to handle the increased traffic. Another concern was the park's wildlife, which in the past had always been readily visible from the road. The extra traffic and noise created by a ten-fold increase in numbers was likely to drive the animals out of sight; and huge influxes of people could result in more encounters with the park's dangerous animals, grizzly bears and moose.

The creative solution to these problems was the initiation of a shuttle bus system. Private vehicles must be parked at the park entrance and visitors board buses which run throughout the day, causing little disturbance to wildlife.

In the late 1970s, Congress considered a number of proposals to establish new national parks in Alaska. Most of the proposals also called for an expansion of Mount McKinley National Park to include scenic areas and critical wildlife habitat which had been left out of the original boundaries. The Alaska National Interest Lands Conservation Act was finally passed in 1980. One section of the act partially resolved an old controversy. Recognizing the longstanding Alaskan

The highway to Denali is known locally as "the Parks," but its full name is the George Parks Highway, and it's named for a state governor, not for its destination.

BELOW LEFT: a wolf in Denali.
BELOW RIGHT: a ranger gives advice.

use of the name Denali, Congress renamed the area Denali National Park, although the mountain is still officially McKinley.

Arriving in the park

The entrance to Denali Park is on George Parks Highway, 240 miles (385 km) north of Anchorage and 120 miles (193 km) south of Fairbanks. Access to the park is also provided by the Alaska Railroad which has a daily service from both Anchorage and Fairbanks. The train depot, the **Visitor Center Ⓐ** (tel: 907-683-1266), Denali National Park Hotel, the Riley Creek Campground, the general store and the youth hostel are all within walking distance of each other. The Front Country Shuttle also provides a free service between them every half hour.

Denali National Park Hotel, which has the only room accommodations inside the park, offers an array of services. Visitors can book private wildlife bus tours, river rafting and flightseeing excursions. Complete packages are available including transportation to the park. Accommodations are available from late May to mid- or late September, but should be booked in advance (tel: 800-276-7234 or 272-7234). The park road is closed beyond Mile 3 in winter, but a campground loop is plowed for campers.

Campground and backcountry camping registration also takes place at the Visitor Center. Denali Park has seven public campgrounds containing a total of 215 sites. A couple of them: Igloo Creek and Sanctuary River, are very small and have no water laid on. Some advance reservations are accepted for these campgrounds (tel: 800-622-7275 or 272-7234) and the rest are available on a first-come, first-served policy. During the peak summer season (late June to mid-August), all sites are often occupied by mid-morning. Private campgrounds

BELOW: shuttle bus dwarfed by Mount McKinley.

located just outside the boundary normally have space, even when the park campgrounds are filled, so you can take a site in one of these and book a couple of days ahead for one inside the park.

While in the park entrance area visit the sled dog kennel, located behind the park headquarters building at Mile 3 of the Park Road. Since the 1920s, park rangers have used sled dogs as a means of patroling the park, as they are the most practical means of getting around Denali in the winter months. The dogs have become so popular with visitors that rangers put on four dog sledding demonstrations every day during the summer season.

The adventure begins

The adventure of experiencing Denali National Park really begins when you step on a shuttle bus for an all-day trip into the park. There are several different bus trips, which all start at the Visitor Center. The rangers can give you a bus schedule, explain how the system works. The green shuttle bus trips, which go the whole 80 miles (128 km) to Wonder Lake, do not provide a formal program, although drivers will answer questions and help spot wildlife. Passengers can get on and off anywhere along the road, space permitting. The buses get very full in summer and should be booked well ahead (tel: 800-622-7275; *see also* page 337), or at the Visitor Center two days in advance. The Denali History Tour bus goes to Primrose Ridge and the Tundra Wildlife Tour to Stony Overlook. Snacks are included in the ticket price and there are periodic rest stops, but passengers may not get off the bus (tel: 800-276-7234 for reservations).

Your chances of seeing wildlife, as well as Denali itself, are increased by taking as early a bus as possible. The first few depart at 6am. During the rest of the

TIP

There are special rates on shuttle buses for 3- and 6-day passes, plus discounts for young people under16, and children under 12 travel free.

BELOW: bus load of photographers.

morning they leave every half hour. The early buses are often in high demand. No food or drinks are available along the bus route so be sure to take with you what you'll need for the day. Always be prepared for cool temperatures and rain regardless of what the early morning weather might be like.

The first leg of the bus route is the 14-mile (22-km) stretch between the entrance and the **Savage River**. The first views of Denali occur in this area. This section of the Park Road goes through prime moose habitat. Any time a moose or other animal is spotted the bus will stop to allow the passengers to watch and photograph it.

Moose are the biggest animals in the park – mature bulls can weigh as much as 1,500 lbs (680 kg). During the spring, watch for calves in this area. Cow moose usually have one or two calves each year. At birth, a calf weighs about 30 lbs (14 kg). Moose calves are one of the fastest growing animals in the world. By their first birthday, they often weigh over 600 lbs (270 kg).

Each September and October this portion of Denali Park becomes the rutting grounds for moose. The huge bulls challenge each other over harems of cows, and they are deadly serious. A bull can kill his opponent with his sharp antler points. Rutting bulls and cow moose with calves should always be considered extremely dangerous and avoided. If they are approached too closely, both cows and bulls will charge a human.

As your bus continues beyond the Savage River, you will pass a mountain to the north known as **Primrose Ridge ❽**. Dall sheep are often seen on the higher slopes of Primrose. They have pure white wool, perfect winter camouflage, but in summer, they readily stand out against the green tundra or dark rock formations. Like all wild sheep, Dall are generally found on or near steep cliffs, which

Guard on the McKinley Explorer.

BELOW: moose are often seen along the park road.

Tundra flowers.

BELOW: bear at the crossroads.

are their security, as no predator can match their climbing speed or agility. Enemies such as wolves or grizzlies can only catch weak or injured sheep, or those that have wandered too far from the crags.

The Dall ewes utilize the steepest cliffs in this area as lambing grounds. With luck, you may be able to spot young lambs on the higher slopes. Within a few days of birth, the lambs can match their mother's climbing ability. The lambs spend hours each day playing games of tag, king of the mountain and head-butting, which helps them develop their strength, agility and coordination.

Bands of rams may also be seen in the Primrose Ridge region. Rams are very concerned with the issue of dominance. A band will establish a pecking order based on the size of their horns, which are their most important status symbol. The older rams have horns of such size that they can easily intimidate the younger ones. Head-butting contests determine which animal will be dominant. The reward comes during the fall rutting season when the top rams are the ones who get to do most of the breeding.

By the time **Sable Pass** ● is reached at Mile 39 you are surrounded by tundra, which is any area of plant growth above the treeline. Sable Pass has an elevation of 3,900 ft (1,188 meters), well above the average local treeline of 2,400 ft (730 meters). The cool temperatures and strong winds at these altitudes are too severe for trees. The low growing tundra vegetation survives by taking advantage of the slightly warmer and less windy micro-environment at ground level.

Sable Pass is grizzly country. So many bears use this area that the Park Service has prohibited all off-road hiking here. Denali's grizzly population is estimated at 200–300 bears. Grizzlies are omnivores: like humans, they eat both meat and vegetation. They would prefer to eat large animals such as moose, caribou and Dall sheep but they are not often successful as hunters. Tundra plants make up at least 90 percent of their diet. The tundra vegetation in places like Sable Pass offers a dependable, easily obtainable source of nutrition.

Grizzly cubs are born in January or February in the mother's hibernation den. The sow gives birth to between one and four cubs weighing about 1 lb (½kg) each. Sable Pass is one of the best places in the world for viewing grizzly families. You may see the cubs being nursed, or racing across the tundra, play-fighting with each other. The sow usually drives off her young when they are 2½ years old, when they may weigh 100–150 lbs (45–67 kg). She then breeds again and gives birth to another litter the following winter.

Without a doubt, the grizzly is the most dangerous animal in North America. Its behavior and reactions toward humans are very difficult to predict. In grizzly country, you are responsible for doing everything you can to avoid provoking a bear. Most of them seem willing to avoid humans if given the opportunity. The few attacks by bears on people in Denali have almost always been provoked attacks – many made by mother bears on people who had deliberately approached their cubs. Park rangers can give you information on avoiding problems with grizzlies.

Your bus will stop for a rest break at **Polychrome Pass** ● at Mile 45. The brightly colored Polychrome cliffs are volcanic rocks formed 50 million years ago.

Map, pages 228–9

The spectacular view to the south includes part of the Alaska Range as well as a vast area of tundra.

Wolf observation

Polychrome Pass is a good place to watch for wolves. A local pack uses these flats as its hunting grounds, especially in spring when caribou are in migration. The Denali wolves range from white to black but most are gray. They may be traveling singly or in small groups. If a pack is sighted, look for a wolf with its tail in the air. This will be the alpha wolf, the leader of the pack, although he may well be bringing up the rear. The alpha male often delegates the lead position to the beta wolf, his second in command.

In a wolf pack, the only members who breed are the alpha male and the alpha female. Their litter is born in the spring and all other members of the pack help to feed the young pups. Feeding a litter of five to 10 pups is a difficult job, even for the entire pack. If all its members tried to breed, the territory could not support the offspring. The pack is better served by limiting breeding to the dominant pair, who have proved themselves to be the fittest animals.

Much of what is now known about wolves was discovered by Adolph Murie, a biologist who was assigned to the park in the 1930s: he was the first scientist to do extensive study on wolf behavior in the field. Much of his observation took place in the Polychrome area. In 1944, Murie published *The Wolves of Mt McKinley*, one of the great classics of animal behavior. He concluded that wolves, who were primarily preying on the sick and weak Dall sheep, caribou and moose, were a necessary part of the Denali ecosystem because they ultimately helped to keep their prey species in a strong and healthy state.

BELOW: caribou are sociable animals.

Caribou country

Caribou, the most social of the large Denali animals, are commonly seen in the Highway Pass area at Mile 58. In the spring, herds of several hundred pass through this area, heading toward their calving grounds to the east. Later in the season, they migrate back, moving toward their wintering grounds in the western and northern portions of the park. The herds are constantly on the move. Even as they feed, they rarely browse for more than a few moments. If they spent too long in one area, they would kill off the fragile tundra vegetation.

Caribou, like moose, have antlers rather than horns. Antlers are formed of bone and are shed every year, while sheep horns consist of keratin, the same material as our fingernails, and are never shed. The caribou bulls' antlers are fully developed by September and are used to fight for harems. These matches usually occur between Highway Pass and Wonder Lake. After their rutting season is over, the antlers drop off. Without their massive weight the caribou have a better chance of surviving the winter, the most stressful time of the year.

Denali Park is a paradise for watching and photographing wildlife. Binoculars and a telephoto lens will allow you to observe and photograph the animals from a safe distance and in a way that won't disturb them. As already mentioned, grizzlies, bull moose and cows with calves should never be approached. Dall sheep and caribou bulls are fairly tolerant of people if you allow them to spot you when you are still a long way off, so they know you are not a predator.

As your bus approaches **Stony Hill Overlook E**, Mile 61, be prepared for a spectacular view of Denali. From the overlook, it is 37 miles (60 km) to the summit. On a cloudless day, the crystal clear Alaskan air makes the mountain appear far closer. After a stop at Stony Hill, the bus will continue 4 miles (6 km) to **Eiel-**

TIP

A walk around the tundra ponds between Eielson and Wonder Lake will turn up many great photo compositions. Lighting on Mount McKinley is best in the early morning or late evening, when it is most likely to be cloud-free.

BELOW: wonderful Wonder Lake.

Map, pages 228–9

son Visitor Center , where the view of Denali is equally awesome. Park rangers here can answer your questions and suggest good hiking routes in the local area. Restrooms, drinking water, maps and books are available here.

If you are on a shuttle bus which continues on to **Wonder Lake G**, an additional 20 miles (32 km) beyond Eielson, this will add about two hours to your day. If the weather is clear, it's well worth the time. Denali remains in full view along the entire route. On the way, many species of waterfowl are seen in tundra ponds. In the evening, beavers can be seen swimming across these small ponds.

Walks and hikes

Denali National Park is a true wilderness. There are few official trails and these are mainly in the entrance area. Elsewhere, you are on your own. Despite the vast size of the Denali wilderness, route-making is not difficult. Since most of the park is open tundra, it is easy to choose a destination visually and hike straight to it. You may leave the shuttle bus wherever you choose, hike for a few hours and then catch a later bus anywhere along the road. Good areas for day hikes include the Savage River, Primrose Ridge, Polychrome Pass, the Eielson area and Wonder Lake. Before you begin a day-hike, talk to a ranger at one of the visitor centers about safety tips. Maps of the area are available at both centers. Permits are required for overnight hikes.

National park rangers offer a wide variety of interpretive programs to help you appreciate the area. Schedules of activities are posted throughout the park. Slide shows and movies are presented in the auditorium behind the Park Hotel. Most campgrounds have nightly campfire talks. Nature walks and half-day hikes are given each day in different sections of the park. ❏

BELOW: naturalist leads a nature walk.

THE ALCAN

*Built as a military route in World War II,
the Alaska Highway now takes tourists all the way
from Seattle to Delta Junction*

In 1942, while the world was at war, thousands of American soldiers wielded bulldozers instead of tanks, as they spent eight months building a 1,500-mile (2,400-km) highway from Dawson Creek, British Columbia, to Delta Junction, Alaska, just south of Fairbanks.

Construction of the Alaska–Canada Military Highway (the Alcan) was approved by President Franklin D. Roosevelt after the bombing of Pearl Harbor in 1941. The road linked the contiguous United States to Alaska, the nation's most recent addition and the one many feared would be the next military target. (In a propaganda broadcast, the Japanese forces thanked workers for opening a way for their own troops.)

Some said it couldn't be done, but construction, which began in March 1942, was completed in October. Soldiers battled the untracked wilderness of western Canada and Alaska, along with spring mud and mosquitoes. Rather than following the most direct route, the road linked existing airfields at Canada's Fort St John, Fort Nelson, Watson Lake and Whitehorse. At the project's peak, more than 11,000 military troops and 7,000 civilians were at work on the highway.

Today, the former military road provides a leisurely and scenic way for visitors to reach Alaska year-round. The Alaska Highway still more or less follows

BELOW: fall colors in the Mentasta Mountains.

its original path, wiggling its way northwest through British Columbia and the Yukon into Alaska's Interior. But what was once a wilderness adventure road is now a mostly paved highway. The scenery is still breathtaking and the chances of seeing wildlife are good, but continual road improvements have eased many of the dangers that once made driving north to Alaska an ordeal.

Which is not to say the road is a Sunday drive. It's only two lanes wide, often without a center line, and although the entire length is asphalt surfaced, sections have to be repaved continually. Drivers should watch for wildlife and construction workers on the road as well as chuckholes, gravel breaks and deteriorating shoulders. On the northern portion of the highway, frost heaves – the result of the freezing and thawing of the ground – cause the pavement to ripple.

It's a long drive. Numerous towns dot the map along the highway, but stretches of wilderness threaten drivers with tiredness or boredom. And the "towns" are often no more than a collection of houses clustered around a store/gas station/hotel. When accidents happen, particularly in winter, it can be a long time before someone happens along to rescue a stranded or injured driver.

Despite the rigors of the road, the trip is made by more than 100,000 people every year. In Alaska, you'll often see cars sporting bumper stickers that proclaim "I survived the Alcan Highway." Most travelers make the journey during the summer months – June, July and August, when the days are long and the weather poses fewer hazards. From Seattle it's about 2,300 miles (3,700 km) (including the route along Interstate 5 to Trans-Canada Highway 1 and BC Highway 97 to Dawson Creek) and it takes most people about a week. An excellent guide is the Alaska *Milepost*, a 700-page map book that documents the Alcan, plus almost every mile of every major highway in the state.   ❑

Map, pages 154–5

BELOW: watch out for bison.

FAIRBANKS

*Fairbanks offers the clearest view of the northern lights,
and the museum at the University of Alaska-Fairbanks
is one of the best in the state*

On August 26 1901, E.T. Barnette had just been deposited, along with 130 tons of equipment, in the wilderness, on a high wooded bank along the Chena River. How did this river boat captain, dog musher and aspiring entrepreneur become marooned on this desolate piece of real estate? The answer has all the ingredients of a true Alaskan story.

The birth of Fairbanks

Barnette journeyed to the Klondike in 1897, taking what was considered the rich man's route. He sailed from Seattle to St Michael, then was to travel by sternwheeler to Dawson. But when he arrived in St Michael, the sternwheeler had already departed. Undaunted, Barnette and several others bought a dilapidated sternwheeler, and set off for Dawson. Barnette piloted the craft to Circle and finally arrived in Dawson via dog sled, after freeze-up. He prospered that winter selling much-needed supplies to men in the gold fields, but the Klondike was too tame for the likes of this man.

During the winter of 1901, Barnette traveled south to Seattle, arranging the deal which, he speculated, would make him a rich man. He and a partner purchased $20,000 worth of equipment to outfit a trading post, not in the Klondike but at the half-way point on the Eagle-to-Valdez trail. Barnette considered this to be a strategically sound location upon which to create what he hoped would be the "Chicago of the North," the industrial hub of the territory. It was at this point that the trail crossed the Tanana River, and he planned to accommodate the overland traffic, as well as that on the river.

Barnette shipped the equipment to St Michael and departed for Circle to purchase a sternwheeler. He arrived in St Michael without incident, but there the sternwheeler struck a submerged rock, and the bottom was torn from the boat. At this point, Barnette was more than 1,000 miles (1,600 km) from his destination with 260,000lbs (120,000 kg) of equipment, including a horse, a quantity of food, no ready cash and a worthless sternwheeler. It was time for another partner. He convinced the customs agent in St Michael to co-sign notes and made him a full partner.

Barnette struck a deal with the captain of the sternwheeler *Lavelle Young* to take him to Tanacross (Tanana Crossing). The fine print on the contract stated that if the *Lavelle Young* went beyond the point where the Chena joined the Tanana River and could go no farther, Captain E.T. Barnette would disembark with his entire load of supplies, no matter where they were.

PRECEDING PAGES:
winter scene in
Fairbanks. **BELOW:**
duet at the Male-
mute Saloon.

As destiny would have it, the *Lavelle Young* could not float through the Tanana shallows called Bates Rapids, so the captain steamed up the Chena River, convinced by the increasingly desperate Barnette that it would join up again with the Tanana River. It did not.

The scene was set on August 26, 1901. Captain Barnette off-loaded his full kit on a high bank with a good stand of trees. It seemed that his string of ill-luck could get no worse.

The new gold rush

Two down-and-out prospectors watched the progress of the sternwheeler in the Chena from a hillside, now called Pedro Dome, about 20 miles (32 km) north of Fairbanks. The miners had found some "color" but no major strike, and were faced with the frustration of a 330-mile (530-km) round-trip hike back to Circle City to replenish much-needed supplies. The prospectors, Felix Pedro, an Italian immigrant, and Tom Gilmore, eagerly set off for the stranded boat, hoping to purchase necessities.

Barnette was surprised to see the prospectors but pleased to sell them anything they needed. Still possessed by his wild scheme to establish a trading post at Tanacross, Barnette sent to Montana for his brother-in-law Frank Cleary. Frank was to guard the cache of supplies while Barnette and his wife returned to Seattle to obtain a boat capable of traveling the remaining 200 miles (320 km) up the Tanana to Tanacross. Braving the -40°F (-40°C) temperature, the Barnettes departed for Valdez and points south in March 1903.

In their absence Cleary decided to outfit Felix Pedro again, on credit this time because Pedro had no collateral. Although this broke Barnette's rule, Cleary's

Map, see below

BELOW: chainsaw carving.

Downtown Fairbanks

- Creamers' Field & University of Alaska-Fairbanks
- Alaska Railroad Station
- Driveway Street
- Illinois Street
- Church Street
- Immaculate Conception Church **B**
- Griffin Park
- Clay St
- Front Street
- Old Steese Hwy
- Chena River
- Graehl Landing
- Clay Street
- Golden Heart Plaza
- St Matthew's Episcopal Church **C**
- Chena River
- Fairbanks Convention and Visitors' Bureau **A**
- Wendell Street
- 1st Avenue
- Dunkel Street
- Hall Street
- Fox
- 1st Avenue
- Key Bank
- Barnette Street
- Cushman Street
- 2nd Avenue
- Lacey Street
- Noble Street
- Dunkel Street
- 2nd Avenue
- Steese Expressway
- 3rd Avenue
- 4th Avenue **D**
- Northward Building
- Street
- City Hall
- 5th Avenue
- Transit Park
- 6th Avenue
- 7th Avenue
- 7th Avenue
- 8th Avenue
- 8th Avenue
- 9th Avenue
- Lacey Street
- 10th Avenue
- Steese Expressway
- 10th Avenue
- Alaskaland &
- North Turner St
- Cushman Street
- 11th Avenue
- 12th Avenue
- Log Cabin Ct
- Federal Building
- Vista Travel
- Gafney Road
- Noble Street
- N
- 0   250 yds
- 0   250 m
- Gray Line Office
- 14th Avenue
- 14th Avenue
- Airport Way
- Delta Junction

decision proved wise and changed the history of the Interior. Just three months later, Pedro quietly announced to Cleary that he had struck paydirt.

The Barnettes returned to the Chena camp six weeks later and immediately abandoned all thoughts of moving to Tanacross. They had two ship loads of supplies and they were on the brink of the next gold rush. Clearly, there was money to be made.

Before descending the airport escalator, study the series of paintings entitled "Our Heritage" by Rusty Heurlin, the history of the Eskimos which he sketched in 1946.

Hundreds of gold-hungry prospectors swarmed out of Circle City, Dawson and Nome, scurrying to the new and, they were told, the richest gold fields in the north. By the time they arrived, much of the promising land was already staked, most of it by "pencil miners" like Barnette who secured the claims only for the purpose of selling them later. These clever businessmen staked as many as 100 claims of 20 acres (8 hectares) each, thus controlling vast amounts of potentially rich ground. And still the stampede continued.

On the return trip from Seattle, Barnette had spoken with Judge Wickersham about naming his little settlement. The judge offered his support to Barnette if he would use the name "Fairbanks," after Senator Charles Fairbanks from Indiana, who later became Vice President under Teddy Roosevelt. So Fairbanks it was.

The community of Fairbanks in 1903 consisted of Barnette's trading post, numerous tents, a few log houses, and wooden sidewalks where the mud was particularly deep. What a fine tribute to the senator from Indiana.

Fairbanks today

BELOW: arriving at Fairbanks International.

Unless you have driven up the Alaska and Richardson Highways you will arrive in **Fairbanks** at the Fairbanks International Airport. Be prepared to handle your own luggage as there are no porter services. Many hotels offer guests free trans-

Map, page 243

port and will send a vehicle if called. Taxis are usually plentiful, and there is also a so-called limousine service (although it is more likely to be a van).

While 31,600 people call Fairbanks home, nobody ever visits the town in winter, unless they absolutely have to. Three hours and 42 minutes of sunlight is simply not enough. Temperatures plummet to -30 and -40°F (-40°C), with the average December temperature registering -14°F (-26°C) in the city. A rather unpleasant side effect of temperatures below -20°F (-29°C) is ice fog, which hangs in the still air. The fog results from a temperature inversion trapping ice crystals, smoke and exhaust fumes in a blanket of cold air which stays close to the ground.

But then there's summer, with daylight lingering for up to 22 hours. In July, when the average temperature in Fairbanks can be more than 61°F (16°C), it is hard to recall the cold winter nights when the aurora borealis screamed across the clear, crisp sky and everyone huddled by the wood stove for warmth and reassurance that they were not alone in the dark.

So, welcome to Fairbanks in summer. Once you are settled in your hotel, head for the **Fairbanks Visitor Bureau and Information Center Ⓐ** at 550 First Avenue (open daily in summer 8am–8pm; Mon–Fri 8am–5pm in winter; tel: 456-5774 or 800-327-5774). This well-constructed log building offers hundreds of brochures on Alaskan attractions, and there is a visitor information telephone number, 456-INFO. The recorded message is available at any hour, is updated daily, and may include information on events as diverse as an evening opera performance or the starting time of a dog race. The bureau also provides a free, comprehensive visitor's guide to the Interior and a brochure for a self-guided tour of the town.

BELOW: bridge over the Chena River.

Here you will notice the monument to E.T. Barnette, marking the place where the town was born, which also makes it a good starting place for modern-day explorers. Here, too, is the obelisk that marks Milepost 1,523 (2,450 km) of the Alaska Highway. The milepost is hidden behind posing tourists most of the summer. Even with the completion of the Dalton Highway to Prudhoe Bay, Fairbanks has, since World War II, been touted as the end of the highway. Residents like to say that this is where the road ends and the wilderness begins.

The borough of Fairbanks now has a population of 77,000 people and includes the towns of North Pole, Fox, Ester and Salcha.

A stroll through town

Several commercial sightseeing tours of Fairbanks' downtown area are available, but one good way to see the town is to turn right across the Cushman Street Bridge pausing for a look at the Chena River. The **Immaculate Conception Church** ⓑ stands directly across the river from the Information Center. The church originally stood on the opposite side of the river at the corner of First and Dunkle. In 1911, Father Francis Monroe decided it should be closer to the hospital on the north side of the Chena. Many good Catholics pitched in to move the building across the frozen river. Visitors are welcome to come inside and enjoy the stained-glass windows and the pressed tin ceiling paneling.

Half a block north on the opposite side of the street is the *Fairbanks Daily News Miner* building at 200 N. Cushman Street. The *News Miner* publishes seven days a week, carrying on a long tradition. Judge Wickersham published the first paper, the *Fairbanks Miner*, on May 9, 1903. All seven copies sold for $5 each, making the first edition one of the most expensive in the world.

Recross the Chena River to **St Matthew's Episcopal Church** ⓒ at 1029 First Avenue. The altar of St Matthew's was carved from a single piece of wood, but

BELOW AND RIGHT: milepost in Golden Heart Plaza, and, nearby, *The Unknown First Family.*

no one is quite sure of the origin of the huge chunk. The stained-glass windows are of special interest; they portray images of Jesus, Mary and Joseph with dark hair and Alaskan Native features.

Almost opposite the church at the corner of First and Cushman, is the **Key Bank**, which was started as a First National Bank on that very site in June 1905. "Square Sam" Bonnifield and his brother John founded the bank, now the oldest national bank in Alaska. "Square Sam" was given his nickname because he had been an honest gambler in Circle City, and miners could turn their backs while he was weighing a poke of gold.

Head south down Cushman Street, the heart of downtown Fairbanks – although not exactly a fast-throbbing one. The **Old Federal Courthouse** stands near the intersection of Second Avenue and Cushman. When Judge Wickersham (the man who originally suggested to Barnette that the town should be called Fairbanks) officially moved the Federal Court here in 1904, he built the courthouse on this piece of real estate, donated by Barnette, securing the future of the young settlement. The original wooden structure burned down, and the present building was completed in 1934. It included the first elevator in the Interior. Federal offices soon required more space and were relocated, leaving the building open for tasteful remodeling into office space and shops.

The next stop is **Co-op Plaza** at 535 Second Avenue. Of 1927 vintage, this building was Captain Lathrop's gift to the people of Fairbanks. Before then, the structures in Fairbanks were constructed of wood because, it was believed, no other material could withstand the test of a -60°F (-51°C) winter. This concrete affair was originally the Empress Theater, outfitted by Captain Lathrop with 670 seats and the first pipe organ in the Interior. Fairbanks' locals tend to use

Map, page 243

BELOW: sub-zero temperatures in the city.

The golden heart of Fairbanks.

"the Co-op" as a meeting place, so be sure to take a look. People visiting Fairbanks from the villages often eat at the diner and visit the specialty shops.

During the mid-1970s, while the trans-Alaska oil pipeline was under construction, Second Avenue was the scene of incessant activity. Bars were packed at all hours, and the avenue's reputation rivaled that of **The Line** during gold rush days. Workers flew to town during rest periods from remote construction camps, only to spend most of their time (and money) along Second Avenue.

If you carry on down Cushman you will come to the area which was known as The Line, the block of Fourth Avenue to your right, as far as Barnette Street. To ensure that no one unwittingly wandered into this sinful area, the booming city of Fairbanks erected tall, Victorian wooden gates at both ends of the avenue. Both sides of the scandalous boulevard were lined with small log cabins housing prostitutes. The Line is gone now, replaced by the less-colorful downtown post office, Woolworths, the Elks Club and a parking lot.

Cross Cushman Street again and continue on Fourth Avenue past Lacey Street. These names also originated from Judge Wickersham, always alert for an opportunity to win political friends, who requested that the streets be named for Congressmen Francis Cushman of Tacoma and John F. Lacey of Iowa.

On the next block, bounded by Lacey and Noble streets and Third and Fourth avenues, towers the "Ice Palace." Officially the **Northward Building** , it was the first steel-girded skyscraper built in the Interior, and became the inspiration for Edna Ferber's novel *The Ice Palace*. The "palace" in the novel is a modern skyscraper built by a ruthless millionaire named Czar Kennedy. Fairbanks' locals recognized in Czar Kennedy the reflection of prominent businessman, developer and politician, Captain Austin E. Lathrop.

BELOW: barbecue at Alaskaland.

That's about all there is to downtown Fairbanks, except for the attractive park known as Golden Heart Plaza, next to the Visitor Center, between Wendell Street and the Chena River (go south up Lacey Avenue from the Ice Palace), where you'll find the bronze statue entitled *The Unknown First Family*.

Map, page 243

City shopping

Fairbanks offers a cornucopia of gifts for the traveler. Gold-nugget jewelry, always a favorite, is priced by the pennyweight (dwt) with 20 dwt equal to one troy ounce (1 dwt = 1.555 grams). Remember that nuggets used in jewelry command a premium price which is higher than that for raw gold.

Native handicrafts from the Interior are also treasured souvenirs. The Authentic Native Handicraft Symbol assures visitors that they are buying the genuine article. Be careful, as counterfeits abound. Favorite items include beaded slippers, beaded mittens and gloves, birch bark baskets, porcupine quill jewelry and fur dolls.

The Alaskan Interior produces some of the finest lynx, marten, wolverine, fox and wolf fur in the world. Many people disapprove of buying furs; if you are happy about it, Fairbanks is the place to purchase raw or tanned furs and fur coats, jackets and hats – although you should be aware of customs regulations if you are taking such items out of the United States.

Alaskaland

Alaskaland, a 44-acre (18-hectare) city park at the corner of Airport Way and Peger Road, to the south of the city, is a snapshot of life in the Golden Heart of Alaska (open year-round daily 11am–9 pm; admission free; tel: 459-1087 or write to PO Box 71267, Fairbanks, AK 99707). You can get a shuttle bus to the park from the Visitors' Bureau and from many of the main hotels in town.

BELOW: grizzly on display at University of Alaska Museum.

The **Mining Valley** on the west end of the park contains many machines used in the hills around the area to extract gold. Sluice boxes, dredge buckets, a stamp mill and other equipment lend an air of authenticity to the display.

Stroll through the **Mining Town**, which includes an assortment of original structures rescued from the boom-town period. Every building is a piece of history, including Judge Wickersham's home, the first frame house in Fairbanks, which was built by the judge in 1904 as a surprise for his wife. It is a rather melancholy reminder of life in early Fairbanks: the bedridden Mrs Wickersham spent most of that summer sleeping in a tent as fresh air was thought to help cure tuberculosis.

Even the building now housing the **Park Office** had a spicy past as a brothel in Nenana. The **Gold Rush Town** is packed with small shops containing an interesting array of crafts.

The **Sternwheeler Nenana** is listed in the National Register of Historic Places because so few of these vessels remain. It was a classic paddlewheeler with a colorful history on the waterways of the Interior. Imagine leaning back in the captain's chair, the stack belching sparks, and the crew scurrying about the deck as you maneuver the craft through the Yukon River. Within the park you'll also find the **Alaska Native Village**, with artifacts and demonstrations of crafts still carried out in remote parts of the Interior.

If you get hungry, follow your nose to the **Alaska Salmon Bake** (open daily in summer 5–9pm), great value for a tasty Alaskan meal. King salmon, halibut and ribs are grilled over an open alder fire to give them a very special flavor. After dinner, you could saunter over to the **Palace Saloon** and enjoy a drink while cancan girls entertain you.

The temperature keeps dropping.

University pursuits

The **University of Alaska-Fairbanks** (UAF) is located on a bluff overlooking Fairbanks and the Tanana Valley (take a Red or Blue Line bus from the town center). Established in 1917 as the Alaska Agricultural College and School of Mines, UAF is the main campus for a system that operates 4-year satellites in Anchorage and Juneau. Emphasis on high latitude and Alaskan problems have earned UAF an excellent reputation.

The 2,500-acre (1,000-hectare) campus is a town unto itself, complete with its own post office, radio station, TV station, fire department and the traditional college facilities. A trip to the UAF campus is well worthwhile, and it's also a good opportunity to relax en route at the turnout on Yukon Drive and absorb the view of the Alaska Range. The large marker, complete with mountain silhouettes and elevations, helps you identify the splendid peaks fringing the southern horizon. It's the best Fairbanks view you'll get of Mount McKinley. Free guided walking tours are offered most days during the summer (tel: 474-7581).

BELOW: University of Alaska-Fairbanks.

The **University of Alaska Museum** on the UAF campus is a must for visitors to the Interior (409 Yukon Drive, tel: 474-7505; open daily 9am–7pm; entrance

charge). The museum is one of the best in the state, dividing Alaska's regions with an interdisciplinary approach to each which includes cultural artifacts and scientific equipment. Displays include prehistoric objects extricated during mining operations from the permanently frozen ground. A huge, 36,000-year-old bison carcass found near Fairbanks, preserved in the permafrost, is displayed, complete with skin and flesh. The Native Cultures displays are an educational introduction to the Athabascan, Eskimo, Aleut and Tlingit cultures. The collections date back to 1926, when the president of the school assigned Otto William Geist the task of amassing Eskimo artifacts. In the summer, there are daily shows on the aurora and Native culture.

Map, page 243

Tours are also provided at the **Geophysical Institute**, a world center for arctic and aurora research, during which a spectacular film of the aurora borealis is shown. A free UAF off-campus tour is offered on Yankovich Road about 1 mile (2 km) from Ballaine Road at the **Large Animal Research Facility**, formerly known as the Musk Ox Farm. These woolly prehistoric creatures graze in research pastures together with moose, reindeer and caribou.

A wildlife trail

Save a little shoe leather for a very special wildlife trail situated within the city limits of Fairbanks. **Creamers Field** at 1300 College Road was originally Charles Creamers' dairy farm, started in 1920. The 250 acres (100 hectares) remained in active production until the land was purchased by the state and was set aside as a waterfowl refuge in 1967. While hiking the nature trails you can see many species of animals, including diving ducks, shorebirds, cranes, foxes or even a moose. The real show, however, takes place in late April to early May

BELOW: musk oxen at the Large Animal Research Facility.

Reindeer meat for sale.

and again in August and September when the sandhill cranes, Canadian honkers and ducks congregate in the field. It really is something to see. Take a Red Line bus to the trailhead, where the Department of Fish and Game office will provide you with a trail guide.

Wheel into the past

Riverboats have never been far removed from the history of Fairbanks, since E.T. Barnette's load of supplies was put ashore. Jim and Mary Binkley continue the tradition with river tours aboard the 700-passenger *Discovery III*. The 4-hour, twice-daily excursions cover 20 miles (32 km) on the Chena and Tanana rivers. The Binkleys' narration brings history to life along the river banks. To reach the sternwheeler's port of departure at the landing off Dale Road, take Airport Way toward the airport, turn onto Dale Road, and watch for the signs. Reservations are recommended (tel: 479-6673).

As you float along, take note of the **Pump House Restaurant**, where you might like to eat later. Excellent family-style meals, mining relics and turn-of-the century decor combine to create a pleasant and unusual atmosphere. This historical site was built by the F.E. Company to supply water to diggings in Ester.

Special events in Fairbanks

The winter festival spirit has been revived in Fairbanks and is now called the **Winter Carnival**, celebrated during the second and third weeks of March. Fairbanks has traditionally hosted the **North American Open Sled Dog Championship** at this time. The North American, as locals refer to it, is not to be missed. The sprint race is run on three consecutive days, with the start and finish line in

BELOW: *Discovery III* on the Chena.

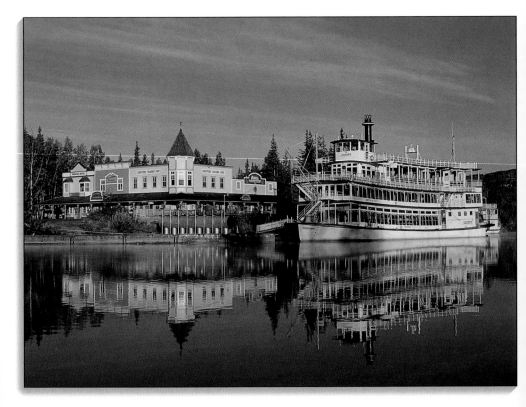

downtown Fairbanks on Second Avenue. It attracts the finest sprint dog mushers, racing teams of up to 20 dogs.

Another sled dog race, not a sprint, is the **Yukon-Quest**, a grueling 1,000-mile (1,600-km) race between Whitehorse, Yukon Territory, Canada, and Fairbanks, which ends in Fairbanks in odd-numbered years and runs in the opposite direction in even-numbered years. The Quest challenges the sturdiest of long-distance mushers.

A full slate of events continues throughout the festival including, of course, ice carving. The Festival of Native Arts takes place in February, along with Native-style potlatches.

Fairbanks residents do not allow the summer solstice to slip by uncelebrated. The Fairbanks Gold Panners baseball team plays the Midnight Sun game at Growden Field with the first pitch crossing the plate at 10.45pm – under natural light. There is also an arts and crafts fair, and speedboat racing, when sleek racing boats propelled by twin 50-horsepower outboard motors zoom down the Chena, Tanana and Yukon rivers to Galena, returning at breakneck speed to Fairbanks and the finish line at Pike's Landing.

Felix Pedro, the prospector who hit gold back in 1903, sported a beard, and so does most of the male population during the third week of July when Fairbanks celebrates Golden Days. One event is a Felix Pedro look-alike contest. The largest attraction is a parade through downtown Fairbanks complete with antique cars, clowns, marching bands and Felix Pedro himself dragging his reluctant mule through the streets. Beware of the roving jail, for those not wearing a fundraising button could be incarcerated for the time it takes to bribe the jailkeeper.

For those in Fairbanks during July, the **World Eskimo-Indian Olympics** is a

Map, page 243

BELOW: contestants in the Pedro look-alike contest.

must. Among Alaskan Natives, great value and respect have always been awarded to physical fitness. The wide variety of games and contests have become traditional Native pastimes. Many of the games require excellent coordination, quickness of hand and eye, as well as great personal strength.

The list of games includes some surprises as well as the expected. The blanket toss competition is fun to watch, as is the Native Baby Contest. The Knuckle Hop, Ear Pulling and Ear Weight competitions are exactly what they say, and seem excruciatingly painful. The *muktuk*-eating contest (muktuk is whale blubber), fish-cutting and seal-skinning competitions are opportunities to learn more about the Native cultures. It is also a rare opportunity for travelers to buy arts and crafts directly from Native artisans – beadwork, baskets, skin garments, masks and carvings.

Hard hats for sale on Steese.

Although officially called the **Alaska State Fair** on even years and the **Tanana Valley Fair** on odd years, almost everyone uses the latter name every year. The fair, held at the College Road fairgrounds during the second or third week of August, has grown to be the most popular event in the Interior, with attendances of more than 100,000 people. The prime attraction for travelers is the Harvest Hall filled with colossal vegetables. Here you will see what the long hours of summer daylight can produce in the Interior, including huge radishes and 70-lb (32-kg) cabbages.

BELOW: leaping for victory in the World Eskimo-Indian Olympics.

Then there is nature's own special event, the northern lights, or aurora borealis, which are seen more often and more vividly in and around Fairbanks than anywhere else. In winter this extraordinary show can last for hours; in mid-summer the sky is too light for it to be visible; but if you are in Fairbanks in late August or September, and don't mind staying up late, you may be able to watch the wonderful dancing lights night after night.

The fringe

To enjoy a trip back in time, head for the settlement of **Ester**, 7 miles (11 km) from Fairbanks off the Parks Highway. To the outsider, Ester is just another faded mining community, but during the summer, the **Malemute Saloon** swings open its doors to vaudeville shows and evening readings of Robert Service. The latter usually silences even those lively *cheechakos* (newcomers to the north) who hang around near the door. The sawdust floor and sourdough bartenders pushing beer across the bar mingle in a frozen moment and past and present become one, as the deep-voiced rendition of Service's *The Shooting of Dan McGrew* rings out.

So the stranger stumbles across the room, and flops down there like a fool.

In a buckskin shirt that was glazed with dirt he sat, and I saw him sway;

Then he clutched the keys with his talon hands –

My God! but that man could play.

Locals hang around the **Red Garter**, and everyone enjoys the **Ester Gold Camp Restaurant**. The rest of the year, the 200 residents of Ester sink into the solitude of small-town Alaska.

The gold dredges in the Fairbanks area have been mute since 1966 and now stand like aging, silent dinosaurs, with necks outstretched, waiting. The dredges, like so many pieces of Fairbanks history, are strewn about the hills waiting for some new purpose.

The easiest of the dredges to visit from town is **Gold Dredge No. 8**, rusting at Mile 9 (15 km) Old Steese Highway. The five-deck ship is over 250 ft (76 meters) long and displaced 1,065 tons as it plied the gold pay dirt of Goldstream and Engineer creeks. Tours of the dredge are available daily during the summer (tel: 457-6058). The 1999 admission fee was $13–$20 which includes gold panning; you keep what you pan.

The dredge is only 200 yards (184 meters) from the best view of the **trans-Alaska oil pipeline** (at Mile 8.4/13.5km), which parallels the highway above the permafrost-rich ground.

The big ditch

Large-scale mining demands lots of water. J.M. Davidson proposed building an 80-mile (130-km) water system to bring water from the Chatanika River to the diggings on Fox, Cleary and Goldstream creeks. A 5,000-kilowatt power plant was erected, as well as six or seven dredges, and shops and camps to maintain the equipment and house the crews.

During construction of the **Davidson Ditch**, portions of the Steese Highway were built to facilitate access. The Ditch was completed in 1930 and was capable of carrying 56,000 gallons (254,500 liters) of water per minute. After the dredges were put to rest, this system continued to generate electricity until the flood of 1967 destroyed it. Remnants of the Ditch are visible in several places along the Steese Highway, along which we will travel in the next chapter on the way to the towns of Central and Circle.   ❏

Map, page 243

BELOW: gold dredge on Steese Highway.

THE WORLD ESKIMO-INDIAN OLYMPICS

The annual games in Fairbanks may seem pretty whacky, but there's a good reason why the participants are proud of their skills

To those unfamiliar with Alaska Native tradition and lifestyle, the athletic feats performed during the annual World Eskimo-Indian Olympics in Fairbanks may seem bizarre. What are those people doing hopping around on their toes and knuckles? And why are they playing tug-o-war with their ears? You won't see conventional events here, such as the pole vault or the 100-meter dash. Instead, be prepared for games of raw strength, endurance, agility and concentration.

GAMES OF SURVIVAL

Survival has been the name of the game for Alaska's Native people for thousands of years. It was essential to be disciplined both mentally and physically, to be ready for the unexpected. It was also important to work together for the common good.

The four-man carry, for example, represents the strength needed to haul firewood or moose or caribou carcasses back home. During this game four men hang from a fifth, who walks as far as he can before collapsing. The one- and two-foot high kicks require contestants to jump off the floor and kick a suspended object before landing on the kicking foot. The kicks are said to have originated as a means of signaling to a village, while the messenger was still some way off, that a whale had been taken and the villagers should help haul the massive animal to shore. Other events include the blanket toss, fish-cutting competition, and seal-skinning contest.

The games bring to life a time when Native people would gather in villages for friendly competitions, storytelling, dancing and games of pure entertainment. The host village provided food and lodging and visitors brought news from the surrounding areas. The six interwoven rings of the WEIO represent Alaska's six major tribes: Aleut, Athabascan, Inupiat, Yup'ik, Haida and the Tlinglit and Tsimshian.

▷ **A NOT SO PLAYFUL TUG**
The ear pull, among the most painful of the games' events, is strictly a game of endurance. Elders say the ability to withstand great pain was necessary for survival. Contestants sit on the floor facing each other with a piece of twine looped over one of their ears. A tug of war begins. If the twine slips from a participant's ear, the other contestant wins the round. The winner is the one who wins two out of three rounds.

▷ **BREAK DANCE**
A Native woman dances to the infectious beat of the drums during a pause between competitive events.

◁ **HIGH JUMP**
A woman competes in the one foot high-kick. Native women began participating in the annual games in the 1970s and now make up a significant proportion of the competitors.

△ OLD-FASHIONED BEAT

A village elder drums and sings during the games. The drums are made in the traditional style, using animal skin stretched tightly across a wooden frame.

◁ TEAM SPIRIT

Traditional dancing has always been an important aspect of the Eskimo-Indian Olympics, and contestants are lured onto the floor to join spectators during any breaks in the competition. There are also performances by various dance groups.

◁ BALANCING ACT

A young competitor concentrates hard as he tries to maintain his balance on the greasy pole, one of the events most popular with the games' onlookers.

△ DANCE COSTUMES

Spectators often wear elaborate dance costumes, whose material depends on which part of the state the wearer comes from. Many feature intricate bead work.

SNOW SCULPTING: AN EPHEMERAL ART

What do dancing salmon, skating penguins and a bearded back-woods trapper have in common? Each of them has been sculpted out of snow during Anchorage's annual Fur Rendezvous. Snow sculpting is among the event's most popular attractions and holds its own against zany games of snowshoe softball and sled dog races. The finished creations draw hundreds of spectators to the display site north of downtown.

Sculptors, working alone, in pairs, or as a team, create their whimsical masterpieces from giant blocks of soft, clean, hard-packed snow. Each block stands 10 ft (3 meters) tall and stretches 8 ft (2.5 meters) across. Towering lights allow participants to work round the clock during the week preceding the festival. The rules are pretty straightforward: no power tools, props or extra snow; other than that, almost anything goes.

Unlike ice sculpting, which is more precise and requires greater skill, snow sculpting attracts a wide variety of participants, from scout troops and high school students to corporate executives – anyone crazy enough to spend hours in the cold turning a block of show into a gold rush-era saloon, a trapper's cabin or a replica of The Three Bears.

THE INTERIOR

*Follow in the footsteps of the gold prospectors
and discover the beauties and the hardships
of Alaska's Interior*

The cry of "Gold!" has lured men and women to the Interior for nearly a century. At first, the passionate hunger was surfeited by a stampede and a handful of valuable nuggets. The golden dreams are history now, but the spirit of the Interior still summons the adventurer.

There *is* gold in the Interior, gilding every aspen leaf in the autumn explosion of color, glancing off the wingtips of geese, shimmering in the river current as it flows into a blazing sunset. It splashes across the midnight sky as the aurora and dances as moonlight over the hulking white shoulders of mountain peaks. And for a few days each spring, this gold lies strewn like nuggets, captured for a moment in a carpet of wildflowers. Many who visit the Interior also find that the people have what can only be called hearts of gold. There is a longstanding tradition of caring, generosity and warm-heartedness which welcomes the traveler back again and again to the edge of the frontier.

Land of great contrasts

The Interior of Alaska, that one-third of the state north of the Alaska Range and south of the Brooks Range, is an area of stark contrasts. Mount McKinley, 20,320 ft (6,195 meters) and snowcapped year-round, towers above the temperate Tanana and Yukon valleys. The Alaska Range is girdled with miles and miles of glaciers, while in the valleys rolling hills of white spruce, birch and aspen fold into straggly stands of black spruce, willow tangles and muskeg.

PRECEDING PAGES: traveling into difficult territory. **BELOW:** floatplane on the Chena River.

If you are visiting the Interior in summer, as most people do, try conjuring up an image of what it would be like in winter, with low light reflecting blue off the snow-covered riverbed, and temperatures plumeting to -40°F (-40°C). Summer weather is glorious, with temperatures sometimes as high as 96°F (36°C). Travelers often experience difficulty sleeping because of all the light. The most practical advice is: don't even try to sleep until you're really tired, but enjoy the late evening light – this is the season that makes the cold dark winter worth enduring.

You will also discover that the later evening is a wonderful time for photography. Light of this quality is experienced at lower latitudes for only a few moments around sunrise and sunset. In Alaska's Interior, the special glow hovers for hours, casting gigantic shadows and ethereal reflections.

Over the river and through the woods

Outdoor adventure is the glue that binds people to the land in the Interior. The mountains, rivers and valleys offer unparalleled opportunities for hiking, canoeing, hunting and fishing. The best source of outdoors information is the Alaska Public Lands Information Center at 250 Cushman Street, Fairbanks, tel: 456-0527. This multi-agency information center and museum sells maps and answers visitors' questions about all categories of land.

One stimulating trek, the **Pinnell Mountain National Recreation Trail**, a 24-mile (40-km) spine connecting 12 Mile Summit and Eagle Summit on the Steese Highway, is a challenging example. The trail is defined with rock cairns along mountain ridges and high passes. Be prepared for sudden, severe weather conditions even in mid-summer. Caribou migrate through here in summer, and an occasional moose or bear may claim the path. The trail promises stunning vistas of the Alaska Range, the White Mountains and the Tanana Hills. Due to the elevation, 3,600 ft (1,100 meters) at Eagle Summit, hikers are treated to nearly 24 hours of daylight during the summer solstice.

The usually blue skies of summer coupled with hundreds of miles of wild and scenic rivers make water travel a natural pastime. Canoeing offers an idyllic opportunity to observe game animals undisturbed as the boat slips silently past. In Fairbanks, Canoe Alaska, Beaver Sports, Independent Rental or 7 Bridges, Boats and Bikes, have canoes for rent.

With the entire Interior river system at your paddle tip, deciding where to explore depends on ability and time. The Chena and Chatanika rivers offer a multitude of easily accessible possibilities for day trips or longer expeditions. For experienced wilderness canoeists, the more challenging clear waters of the Birch Creek can be accessed at Mile 94 (150 km) Steese Highway, or experienced on a 5-day sojourn on the broad sweep of the **Tanana River** from Delta to Fairbanks. These rivers are all conveniently accessible by road. If you own a collapsible kayak, numerous remote rivers can be reached by plane.

Map, pages 154–5

TIP

Portions of the easily accessible Nenana River contain Class IV and V rapids and should be attempted only by seasoned rafters, or experienced kayakers able to perform the Eskimo roll

BELOW: Interior landscape.

The Interior is a fisherman's promised land, and the Arctic grayling is its manna. The flash of the strike and the fight of the silver streak on light tackle is a treasured memory for many. The Clearwater, Salcha, Chantanika and Chena rivers are superior grayling producers and are accessible by road. In fact, all clear-flowing creeks and rivers in the Interior are well-stocked with grayling. Northern pike, rainbow trout, burbot and lake trout abound in the clear, cold waters throughout the Interior.

TIP

Chartered airplane operators can be contacted in Fairbanks, North Pole, Delta and Tok. Fly-in fishing is an expensive proposition, but the spectacular scenery and bountiful catches make it good value.

BELOW LEFT: welcome to Santaland.
BELOW RIGHT: North Pole refinery.

Exploring the Interior

Trails, like the threads of a spider's web, spun into Fairbanks from every direction in the early 1900s. The more popular routes were eventually transformed from dog sled tracks to the paved and gravel roadways that now link the rest of Alaska to Fairbanks, the commercial hub of the Interior. The first trail-cum-highway in all of Alaska, the **Richardson**, was originally a pack trail between the then-bustling mining settlements of Eagle and Valdez. Following the gold rush, the trail was extended to Fairbanks, linking the Interior to an ice-free port. Today, the Richardson joins with the Alaska Highway for the 98 miles (157 km) between Fairbanks and Delta Junction.

If you take the Richardson Highway, your first stop may well be 14 miles (22 km) southeast of Fairbanks at **North Pole** ⑲, the home, children are delighted to learn, of Santa Claus. Urban renewal forced Santa to move closer to the highway, where he's situated today. He poses year-round for pictures at **Santaland**, a thriving commercial enterprise on the Richardson Highway, and one that gives visitors an idea of the enterprising types who homesteaded this area during the 1930s and 1940s.

Map, pages 154–5

They were a new wave of pioneers who found Fairbanks too crowded and who didn't mind living in this low-lying basin where winter temperatures are severe enough for the nickname "North Pole" to stick and become official.

Today, North Pole is home to some 1,500 people and a surrounding population of 13,000. It has its own utilities, brand-new shopping malls and a large MAPCO petroleum refinery taking crude from the nearby trans-Alaska pipeline. It is best known as the town where it's Christmas all year round, where the **Santa Claus House** sells every kind of festive item you could dream of, and the post office is swamped with children's letters in December.

As surely as there is gold in the hills, there are buffalo and barley in **Delta Junction ⓴**. The **Tanana Valley** is one of the largest agricultural areas in the state, with most of the farming centered in the Delta area. Despite the typical Interior winter climate, the valley supports the Delta Barley Project, a state-sponsored attempt to introduce large-scale grain production to the Interior. Although beset by troubles, at 90,000 acres (36,450 hectares), this farming venture, begun in 1978, is yet another example of the exuberant pioneering spirit in the Interior.

But what about the buffalo? Although they could be the spirit watchers of the shaggy bison who ranged the Interior millennia ago, this herd was actually imported from Montana and introduced to the area specifically as a game animal. The original 23-member herd now numbers about 400. They have even been granted their own farm of 90,000 acres (36,500 hectares) but this in no way discourages them from haunting the barley patch. Although the buffalo are rarely seen from the road in summer, pull over at Mile 241 on the Richardson Highway and scan the country across the Delta River for a possible glimpse.

BELOW: market at the Tanana Valley Fairgrounds.

Beware of collisions.

BELOW: historic
boiler in Eagle.

Landing up at Eagle

After Delta Junction the Richardson becomes the Alaska Highway. Follow this some 110 miles (175 km) to Tetlin Junction and take the rough gravel Taylor Highway for a further 160 miles (255 km) and you will come to **Eagle ㉑**, where the road ends (the road closes in winter and snow isolates the community). This is a popular jumping-off place for Yukon River paddlers, as well as an official stop for river explorers floating from Dawson City. The first city on the American side of the Yukon, Eagle has a post office where river travelers check in with US customs.

Present day Eagle had its beginnings in 1874 when the far-reaching and powerful Northern Commercial Company (NC) stretched its commercial fingers along the Yukon River and established a trading post near here. With the arrival of prospectors overflowing from the 1898 Klondike gold rush at Dawson City, just upriver over the border in Canada, this quiet river bank was transformed into a brazen mining town of 1,700 people. Seized by gold fever, thousands more, digging in every tributary of the Yukon, swept through the territory.

History was being made at the turn of the century: Judge Wickersham built a federal courthouse here in 1900, a major army fort was established, and the Valdez-to-Eagle telegraph line spun out an interesting message in 1905 when Roald Amundsen, passing through after his successful expedition into the Northwest Passage, made his announcement to the world from Eagle.

By 1910 the gold muckers had vanished, trekking after even richer dreams near Fairbanks. They left behind 178 people, about the same population as today. But the buildings still stand and Eagle has undertaken a program to restore many of its fine older structures.

The Eagle Historical Society (tel: 547-2325) conducts a free walking tour which includes **Judge Wickersham's Courthouse**, built by fines he imposed on gamblers and prostitutes in the rowdy mining town. Inside are the judge's desk and an early map of the country constructed of papier-mâché and moose blood. Also open for inspection is US Army **Fort Egbert**, abandoned in 1911.

Map, pages 154–5

Summer visitors will find the basic necessities – laundry, restaurant, lodging, groceries, gas station, airstrip and mechanic shop. For those who are inclined to go further "upriver," a daily commercial cruise motors between Eagle and Dawson City. Make reservations in advance with Gray Line Yukon (tel: 867-993-5599), which also offers a package tour of the area. For information on paddling through the Yukon-Charley Rivers National Preserve, contact the National Park Service Visitor Center, just off 1st Avenue across the airstrip from town (tel: 547-2233).

Railway town

Take State Highway 3, the **George Parks Highway**, 64 miles (103 km) south of Fairbanks and while still in the rolling hills of the Tanana Valley you will reach **Nenana ㉒**. Nenana, an Athabascan word meaning "between two rivers," is situated at the confluence of the Tanana and Nenana rivers. Always one of the main river-freighting centers in Alaska, the town changed with the completion of the Alaska Railroad in 1923.

Older residents of Nenana still remember the stifling hot July day in 1923 when President Warren Harding drove in the golden spike signifying completion of the federally owned railroad.

Constructed in part with excess equipment from the Panama Canal Project, the railroad made headlines again in January 1985 when it was purchased from the US government by the state of Alaska. Shortly thereafter the station was listed on the National Register of Historic Sites, and now incorporates the **Alaska State Railroad Museum** (open daily 8am–6pm; admission free; tel: 832-5500). The train still chugs along at about 50 mph (80 kph) but no longer makes scheduled trips.

Nenana is also the terminus port for tug and barge fleets that still service the villages along the Tanana and Yukon rivers, loaded with supplies, fuel and tons of freight. For a closer inspection of an old tug, visit the refurbished *Taku Chief* behind the **Visitor Information Center** on the corner of A Street and Parks Highway.

Nenana is known far and wide for the **Nenana Ice Classic**, an event that could only be held in the land of snow and ice and cabin fever. Cash prizes are awarded to those who guess the exact time – to the minute – of spring break-up on the Tanana. Break-up is that moment when suddenly there's more water than ice on the river, when massive blocks of ice rip and surge, grind and groan against one another in a spectacular release of winter energy and a special tripod designed for the event tips over.

The Tanana River again becomes the focal point a month or so later with **River Daze**, celebrated during the first weekend in June. One event is the raft race down the Tanana from Fairbanks to Nenana, when par-

BELOW: sturdy back-country ponies.

ticipants create a variety of floating contraptions and enter them as rafts. Anything goes in this race, providing it floats and utilizes only "natural" power.

Off to the gold fields

To drive the **Steese Highway** is to travel with the spirits of the miners who worked the many creek beds prospecting for gold. The road angles to the northeast for 162 miles (260 km) before ending at the Yukon River. Go past the Gold Dredge No. 8 and the viewing point for the trans-Alaska pipeline (*see* page 255), and you will come first to the community of Fox (Mile 11/18 km), an early mining encampment which took its name from a nearby creek. The community is best known now for its excellent spring water. The symmetrical piles of gravel surrounding Fox are the dregs of the mighty earth-eating dredges. The piles lie like great loaves of bread, browned on top and awaiting the next course.

Next stop is the **Monument to Felix Pedro** at Mile 17 (27 km), a modest reminder of the Italian immigrant who was the first to strike it rich in these valleys. Gravel in the creek on the opposite side of the road has been known to show some "color," so you could practice panning here.

The subsequent 3 miles (5 km) of road gradually ascend to **Cleary Summit**, which offers a magnificent panoramic view of the Tanana Valley, the White Mountains and the Alaska Range. Back in 1905, the notorious "Blue Parka Bandit" found this encompassing lookout quite handy for his trade. Charles Hendrickson, engineer-turned-robber and terror of the trails, haunted these granite crags, pinching the pokes of unsuspecting gold miners.

Anyone interested in Alaskan gold rush lore will not want to miss **Fairbanks Creek Road**. Leave the Steese Highway and Cleary Summit and travel south

Hendrickson occasionally tarnished his ignominious reputation with kindness: when he detained an Episcopalian Bishop and his entourage he was persuaded to hand over all the stolen gold.

BELOW: the trans-Alaska pipeline.

along the ridgeline for 8 miles (13 km) to Alder Creek Camp. Beyond this, there's a 1-mile (1.5-km) walk to **Meehan**, an abandoned machine shop area where maintenance was done on mining equipment, and rusted equipment can still be found strewn along the trail.

Fairbanks Creek Camp is an additional 2 miles (3 km) below Meehan. Dredge No. 2 met an untimely end in 1959 along this creek when a deck hand decided to use dynamite to open an ice-blocked hole, and the dredge quickly sank. Fairbanks Creek relinquished many tusks, teeth and bones of Pleistocene mammals during stripping operations. One of the most famous fossils is a well-preserved baby woolly mammoth found in 1949.

Map, pages 154–5

Hot baths for the miners

The old Circle District is not yet devoid of gold or the miners who search for it. Some of them live in **Central ㉓**, a small mining community strung out along the Steese Highway and described by locals as "three miles long and one block wide." An active winter population of only 50 swells to more than 800 during the summer months when miners and vacationers return. Since the addition of a permanent school in 1981, more and more "summer people" are staying on late into fall. Overnight accommodations, camping facilities and general "pit-stop" services are available in the town.

A worthwhile stop is at the **Circle District Historical Society Museum** on the highway (open daily in summer noon–5pm; entrance charge; tel: 520-1893), a museum whose grand opening was celebrated in July 1984. Its displays include pieces of mining equipment, gold nuggets, dog sleds, a period cabin containing authentic artifacts, and examples of some of the hardy alpine wildflowers found on Eagle Summit.

Gold nuggets weren't the only pleasures that warmed the miners' souls during the rush. In 1893 William Greats crept into a small valley for a closer look at the steaming witches' cauldron he had spotted. He must have been a popular fellow for a time, leading colleagues to the mineral springs he'd discovered.

Many areas are abandoned after a gold rush, but never a hot spring. Fortunately, visitors do not have to re-enact the days of old when ice was chipped from tent flaps before they could get into the bathing houses. **Arctic Circle Hot Springs Resort** (tel: 520 5113) has been spruced up and now offers a 1930s hotel refurbished with Victorian decor, an ice cream parlor, family-style restaurant and the Miners' Saloon. The hotel has a rudimentary hostel on the upper floor, as well as basic hotel rooms and cabins, and a camper park with hiking and skiing trails.

But those are places and activities to investigate only after your body has withered beyond recognition and your rubbery legs can no longer propel you to the edge of the open-air pool. There's really nothing quite like dangling from an inner tube in 109°F (43°C) mineral water, completely enveloped in a cloak of mist as the water condenses in the -40°F (-40°C) air.

Scheduled commercial flights are available to the springs resort, but the experience is equally pleasurable after the 130-mile (210-km) trip up the gravel Steese

BELOW: Felix Pedro and partners.

Everyone's dream.

Highway, which is maintained daily during winter, although it is advisable to call ahead for overnight reservations and road conditions (tel: 451-5204). No advance notice is necessary to use the pool.

Road's end

All roads end some place. For the Steese, it's all over at **Circle City** , a tiny community 50 miles (80 km) south of the Arctic Circle, poised along a bend in the Yukon River. In gold rush days Circle had a population of 1,000; today that has dwindled down to about 90.

Once the largest gold mining town on the Yukon, Circle was nearly abandoned after the gold strikes in the Klondike and Fairbanks areas and little now remains to be seen by visitors. Gone are Jack McQuesten's two-story log store, two dozen saloons, eight dance halls, theaters and the music hall that earned Circle City the somewhat exaggerated title of the "Paris of the North." In their places reign a modern-day trading post with a motel, a café, a general store, a bar and a gas station. Rudimentary tourist facilities are geared for summer visitors. Chartered flightseeing trips and boat tours are available, but it's wise to call ahead.

There's usually plenty of waterfront activity in this popular stopping-off place for canoeists and rafters traveling the Yukon River. One popular river trip begins in either Eagle or Circle and terminates at Fort Yukon or farther downstream under the Dalton Highway bridge.

Circle, so named because early miners thought they were camped at the Arctic Circle (although they actually had about another 50 miles (80 km) to go), still offers some activity. Fishwheels smack the water as they turn in the cur-

BELOW: fish camp on the Yukon.

rent, flat-bottomed boats zoom up and down the river and barges still make their way to points upriver. River travelers could easily miss all of this; the "land" in front of Circle is actually an island concealing another channel of the mighty Yukon.

Gamblers gained notoriety in the saloons of boom and bust towns like Circle City. One who went on to national fame was Tex Richard. He was 24 years old in 1895 when he trekked into Circle and found a job in "Square Sam" Bonnifield's gambling saloon. Impressed by the honesty of his boss, for the rest of his life, it is said, he always gambled "as if Sam Bonnifield were looking over his shoulder." Richard's claim to fame was not made in Circle City, however, but a bit later when he built Madison Square Garden in New York City. He was also well-known as a promoter for Jack Dempsey, who became the heavyweight boxing champion of the world in 1919.

To get a real feel for the town, wander upriver to the Pioneer Cemetery and look at some of the weathered gravestones of the early settlers.

Getting into more hot water

Take a right turn at Mile 3 (5 km) on the Steese Highway and you will go rollercoasting through the countryside on Chena Hot Springs Road. This paved beauty, only 56 miles (90 km) long, passes through the middle of the 254,000-acre (103,000-hectare) **Chena River Recreation Area**, and terminates at the gates to the **Chena Hot Springs Resort ㉕** (tel: 452-7867 or 800-478 4681). The closest to Fairbanks of the thermal resorts, and the best developed for the comfort of guests, the place is commercially equipped with all the necessities for extended, year-round visits, and has winter ski trails. But most alluring are

Map, pages 154–5

BELOW: motoring mementos on the Elliott Highway.

Map, pages 154–5

the steaming hot-water pools of Monument Creek Valley, and the indoor swimming and indoor and outdoor soaking facilities.

Blueberries and black gold

The last of the four major highways in the Interior extending out of Fairbanks (five if you count Chena Hot Springs Road) is the **Elliot Highway**, running northwest, and continuing on to the Dalton Highway. The Elliot branches off the Steese 11 miles (18 km) north of Fairbanks and winds through 152 miles (245 km) of gold-mining country trimmed with broad valleys, bubbling creeks, blueberries and poppies, homesteads and mining camps.

Livengood ㉖, near the junction of the Elliot and Dalton highways, once held the "end-of-the-road" position, but the little community experienced an invasion in the mid-1970s when it was transformed from an isolated "mind-your-own-business" neighborhood to a pipeline construction camp.

Three million man-hours, five months of intensive labor, and millions of tons of gravel equal one 416-mile (670-km) service road paralleling one of the most ambitious projects ever undertaken in the North American Arctic – the trans-Alaska pipeline. This service road-cum-state highway, which is officially called the **Dalton Highway** but is often known simply as the "Haul Road," opened up thousands of acres of wilderness territory which can be explored from the comfort of a vehicle. The road is maintained from Livengood to Prudhoe Bay, and although privately owned vehicles used to be allowed only as far as **Disaster Creek** near Dietrich Camp, about 280 miles (450 km) north of Fairbanks and 200 miles (322 km) south of the Arctic Ocean, the whole length of the roadway is now open to the public.

A journey north on the Dalton Highway, above the Arctic Circle, through the land of sheep, bears, wolves and foxes can be the ultimate coup of your trip. Several tour companies offer excursions to the Arctic Circle and Prudhoe Bay. But if you choose to do it alone, beware. Conditions are hazardous; the roadway is rough and dusty in summer and slippery in winter. Because this is primarily a service road, heavily loaded 18-wheelers rule the route. Rental agencies do not allow their cars to be driven up the road.

If you can't resist going, plan it much as you would if you were going on a wilderness camping trip, but remember to take your wallet – automobile towing charges on the highway are very expensive. Service station facilities and emergency communications are available at only two locations, the Yukon River Crossing at Mile 56 (91 km), where you will also find the Yukon Crossing Visitor Center; and Coldfoot at Mile 173.6 (280 km), shortly before you get to Wiseman. For road conditions, tel: 451-2206 or 456-ROAD.

If you feel you can do without the challenge of driving the Dalton Highway, continue to the left on the Elliott Highway when you get to Livengood. This will take you to the Athabascan village of **Minto** on the Tolovana River, and to **Manley Hot Springs Resort**, a good spot if you feel like pampering yourself. Beyond the resort is the little mining center of Manley, where the road runs out. ❑

BELOW: children at Chena Hot Springs.

Yukon villages

What lies beyond Pedro Dome, Cleary Summit and the White Mountains? What is it that the Chena, the Chatanika and the Tanana rivers are all drawn toward? It is, of course, the Yukon River, flowing north of Fairbanks, and seemingly possessing a magnetic force of its own.

If Fairbanks is the heart of the Interior, then the Yukon is surely a life-supporting artery. Not unlike explorers of yesterday, visitors to Fairbanks often feel the urge to soar over the mountain peaks or float with the river current right to its mouth.

Centuries before European explorers spread out over the land, the Yukon River and its many tributaries were a common link in the survival of the nomadic Athabascan tribes living in the Interior. Ironically, the Yukon then provided access to intruders who came up-river in their sternwheelers from St Michael on the Bering Sea to reap the benefits of the fur country and the gold fields.

When explorers, missionaries and fortune hunters penetrated this wilderness in the 19th century, the Athabascans were living as they had for generations, subsisting on salmon, moose or caribou, berries and water birds. They were survivors in a harsh and unmerciful land, still living a semi-nomadic life, but with the arrival of outsiders, they congregated into small communities for better protection against whatever dangers might present themselves.

Scattered along the Yukon are the Athabascan river villages. Dozens of tiny settlements still exist in this inhospitable northern land. The historical perspective of each community varies, but, remarkably, they are part of 20th-century Alaska, while paying silent tributes to the Athabascans of the past.

It would be naive to believe that the villages exist in a totally virgin state, untouched by the modern world. Conversely, it would be presumptuous to assume that they continue to provide a viable existence due only to space-age technology. Generally, villagers maintain a traditional subsistence lifestyle, hunting, fishing, trapping, gardening and gathering berries.

Daily life embraces the rhythm of the seasons, and survival demands adjusting to weather conditions and unpredictable wildlife cycles, just as it has always done.

Elementary schools, many containing modern educational equipment and built and equipped in the 1980s when oil dollars were enriching the state, are a part of every village, and many villages also offer high school education to their young people. Typical village teenagers, carrying the dreams of their ancestors, often find themselves at a crossroad, both personally and culturally.

The village elders, those keepers of the culture, go on dispensing wisdom. And, while many of the benefits of late 20th-century life are enjoyed, village pride seems to have deepened in recent years, as outside influences have pressed into the core of Athabascan strongholds. Almost forgotten dialects now roll easily from the lips of youngsters. Ancient drumbeats and dances are as popular as rock music. The village is a microcosm of contrast, evoking a strong sense of the past as it surges toward the future. ❑

RIGHT: having fun in a Yup'ik village.

NOME AND THE REMOTE WEST

*The cheerful stoicism of Nome, the superb fishing at Unalakleet
and the Museum of the Arctic in Kotzebue are three good
reasons for venturing to the remote west*

Map,
page 276

Alaska
Nome
Anchorage

This remote community has long been known as the city that wouldn't die, although it has had more than enough reason to disappear many times since its founding in 1899. **Nome ** has been burned to the ground; pounded by relentless gales; attacked by flu, diphtheria and other maladies; and almost starved out of existence, yet it has always rebuilt and struggled on.

It was gold, discovered in 1898, that brought men, and later women, to this wind-swept, wave-battered beach on the Seward Peninsula, 75 miles (120 km) or more from the nearest tree. Of all the Alaska gold rush towns, Nome was the largest and the rowdiest. The year 1900 was the big time in Nome. Best estimates put the population in excess of 20,000 people by the end of the summer, but nobody knows for certain.

By the time gold-bearing creeks around the area were discovered, claim jumping and other less-than-ethical mining practices were well advanced in Alaska. Claim-jumping was so rampant that it probably took a dozen years or more before everything was straightened out. By then the boom was dying and Nome had little more than 5,000 residents. Over the years the permanent population has shrunk as low as 500. It has more or less stabilized in recent years at about 3,500 residents.

Nome hosted a whole series of gold rushes, each almost blending into the next. The first gold came the traditional way – it was found in the streams flowing into Norton Sound. The thousands who rushed to Nome set their tents on the beach and explored the nearby gullies, little realizing that all they had to do was sift the sand that was their floor for the precious yellow metal.

The famed black sand beaches of Nome count as the "second" gold rush. Since nobody could legally stake a claim on the beach, a man could work any ground he could stand on near the shoreline. The sands were turned over dozens of times and yielded millions of dollars in gold.

Then geologists pointed out that Nome had more than one beach. Over the centuries, as rivers carried silt to the ocean, the beach line had gradually extended out to sea. The geologists predicted that under the tundra a few yards back from the water, miners would find an ancient beach and, with it, more deposits of gold. And so it was that later years saw yet a third gold rush as ground behind the sea wall was dug and re-dug to extract the precious metal.

Fortune seekers still sift the sands in front of Nome. In the summer of 1984 a Nome resident walking on the beach picked up a gold nugget weighing over an ounce from under a piece of driftwood. Such are the rewards of fresh air and exercise. The beach at Nome is still open to the public. Anyone with a gold pan or a sluice box

PRECEDING PAGES:
Unalakleet from the
air. **LEFT:** dressed up
for winter. **BELOW:**
Eskimo in ivory.

can search for gold along the waterfront, and camping is permitted, too. It's hard, back-breaking work, but then riches have never come easy for miners. Perhaps the only ones who found easy money were the gamblers and the tricksters who made their living relieving miners of their hard-earned gold.

Some shifty characters who learned their crafts in the boom towns of the Wild West converged on Nome as practiced, professional con-artists – men like Wyatt Earp, frontier marshal, who arrived in Nome as a paunchy, 51-year-old saloon keeper (and was frequently at odds with the law).

Yet Nome's gold rush years spawned a hero or two amid the unscrupulous. Shortly after Wyatt Earp arrived, a family named Doolittle moved to the town. One boy, Jimmy, delivered newspapers for the *Nome Nugget*, the oldest continually published newspaper in Alaska. Jimmy grew up to lead "Doolittle's Raiders," the daring group of army pilots who launched their over-sized, over-loaded bombers from the decks of a Navy aircraft carrier in the darkest days of World War II.

Gold can still be found.

Energetic celebrations

The ability to face all comers, whatever the odds, is what makes Nome the rollicking place it is today. Nomites bring a special energy to every project they take on. After all, in western Alaska you sometimes have to make your own fun.

The **Midnight Sun Festival** is a good example. Held on the weekend closest to the solstice (June 21), the two-day festival includes a late-night softball tournament, a street dance, a chicken barbecue, foodstalls (selling reindeer hot dogs and cotton candy) and a dart tournament. The Nome River Raft Race is part of the Midnight Sun Festival, and its only rule seems to be that there are no rules.

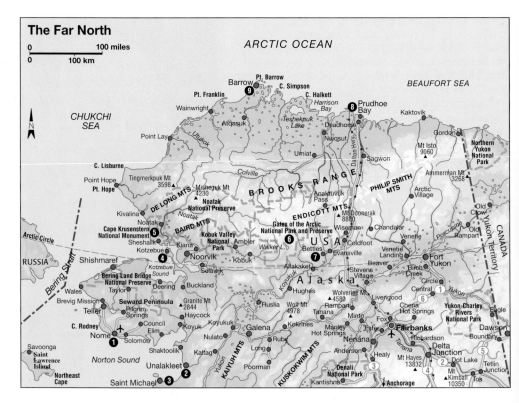

Less than two weeks later, Nome gets ready to party again with the 4th of July celebration. This event includes street games, a big raffle, free ice cream (provided by the fire department) and the Anvil Mountain Run. Runners are required to run up the mountain on the road, but are allowed to take any path they want on the way down; through the tundra is a shorter route, but it's not as smooth going.

As with most civic celebrations, each event has its own parade. There are hardly any spectators because most of the local residents are in the parade. And what would the 4th of July be without fireworks? In the early 1980s Nome's city council wanted to stop such devices within the city limits because of the fire hazard. This particularly affected the mayor of the time, as he was one of the largest fireworks dealers in the area. He solved the problem by setting up his firework stand a few steps outside the city line and gleefully sold all manner of pyrotechnics to the people, who immediately took the goods to their homes in town. Thus there was still plenty of noise, fire and smoke for the 4th of July, and the mayor didn't need to worry about being jailed for breaking the law.

There are advantages to living in a remote frontier town, and they show themselves in many ways. Nome is a close community, with almost anyone available to lend a hand. Consider Christmas. Christmas trees are traditional decorations in local homes just as elsewhere in the United States. The problem with this arises because the last ship of the season usually departs in October, just before Norton Sound freezes. Trees can be flown in, but that's expensive.

However, about 80 miles (130 km) to the east is a convenient forest, and in the weeks before Christmas residents band together and dispatch truck loads of volunteers along a bone-crunching road leading to the forest. The trucks are then filled with small spruce trees, enough to ensure that every household gets one.

Map, page 276

BELOW: light of the midnight sun at Nome.

Native woman in splendid furs.

These aren't the magnificent Douglas firs which are favored in the Lower 48. Instead, they're straggly tundra spruces, but they are adequate for the purpose.

After the holidays, residents take their old trees out to "Nome National Forest" – a stretch of ice outside town – and "plant" them. The trees generally stay there until spring, tended by a self-appointed "ranger" who stands them up when they get blown over, and sometimes visitors to Nome are fooled into thinking there really is a forest here.

The Great Race

After Christmas, there's one more high point in the long winter, the combined Spring Carnival and **Iditarod Trail Sled Dog Race**. The Iditarod commemorates the frantic race to get diphtheria serum to Nome in 1925. The town was teetering on the verge of an epidemic and the only possible way to get the serum through was overland by dog sled. It was taken by train to Nenana and from there experienced mushers ran their sleds and teams in relays, round the clock, to get it to Nome. A trip that normally took a month or more was therefore completed in a matter of days.

Today, the Iditarod is a sporting event billed as "The Last Great Race on Earth." About 65 racers bring their teams to the starting line in Anchorage on the first Saturday in March, conditions permitting. The winners reach Nome about nine days later, having traveled an actual distance of more than 1,100 miles (1,770 km) on the grueling trail. All manner of hostile terrain – and the elements – batter the racers from start to finish.

BELOW: Iditarod team nears Cape Safety.

For example, back in 1985, Susan Butcher, leading the pack a couple of days out of Anchorage, tangled with a moose. Before things were sorted out in the

dark, the moose had stomped and kicked her dog team out of the race. Later the race was halted twice for bad weather. And finally, in an act of considerable courage – or foolhardiness – Libby Riddles, from Teller, a small village north-west of Nome, headed out of a checkpoint into the teeth of a howling gale only a couple of hundred miles from the finish line. No other musher would risk traveling in the storm. But the few miles she made that night before being forced to make camp and sit out the storm gave Riddles the extra edge needed for victory, and she became the first woman to win in the 13-year history of the event.

Also in March is the Bering Sea Ice Golf Classic. Participants dress in wacky outfits for this game, played on artificial grass on top of the ice, next to the "Nome National Forest."

Today Nome is the transportation hub of western Alaska. It has a major airport with jet service to and from Anchorage, Fairbanks and Kotzebue, and provides commuter plane service to every village in the region. Almost everyone touring western Alaska must at least pass through Nome. There is not a lot to do: there's a small museum which concentrates mostly on gold rush memorabilia, and there are the gold dredges just outside town. But if you want an authentic taste of Alaska, Nome will not disappoint you.

Superb fishing

An hour by air southeast of Nome on the eastern edge of Norton Sound is **Unalakleet ❷**, a pleasant Native village with good schools, churches, and prob-ably the best-kept secret in Alaska. The Unalakleet River, which runs through town, supports a large run of king salmon in late June, and the angling is superb. And, unlike most king salmon sport fisheries, bag limits are generous. Six fish

Map, page 276

BELOW: Nome welcomes the winners.

per person per day has been the rule in recent years. Most other major fisheries only allow anglers a single king salmon daily.

Travel agents in Anchorage can set up a stay at a full-service fishing lodge on the Unalakleet River for those who wish to battle the giant salmon. Such a tour is not cheap: $300 to $500 a day or more per person. But a couple of days' fishing in the Unalakleet River when the kings are in is probably the experience of a lifetime for most fishermen.

A western Alaska community that has an interesting history attached to it is **St Michael ❸**, south of Unalakleet on the south of Norton Sound, although there is not a lot to be seen there today. St Michael was the major trans-shipment point for freight going to the Klondike gold fields at the turn of the century. Almost everybody who has read of the Klondike Gold Rush knows about the struggles of the miners to hike the Chilkoot Pass. Less well known are the stories of thousands of miners who reached the same destination by traveling in relative comfort aboard sternwheelers plying the Yukon River. St Michael, not far from the mouth of the Yukon delta, was originally the base for the river steamers. Ocean steamers transferred cargoes bound for Dawson and other upriver points to the river boats at St Michael. Bits and pieces of old river steamers can still be found along the waterfront. Other than the gear miners carried on their backs over the Chilkoot Trail, most of the heavy equipment, food and freight that eventually reached the Klondike gold fields came through St Michael on Alaska's remote western coast.

North of Nome lies **Kotzebue ❹**, a large, predominantly Eskimo community which is served by daily jet service out of Anchorage and Fairbanks. Kotzebue is the headquarters for NANA, one of the regional Native corporations which

BELOW: getting your bearings.

was established in 1971 with the passage of the Alaska Native Claims Settlement Act. That act granted Alaskan Natives nearly $1 billion in cash and title to some 44 million acres (18 million hectares) of land. The money and the ground were divided up by 13 Native corporations formed to manage the sudden wealth. NANA's share was significant and it is now one of the more successful of the corporations. NANA is also actively involved in the reindeer industry. Several other business ventures of a more contemporary nature round out NANA's holdings in industries including mining, oil and tourism. The company is providing jobs to its shareholders and is a significant economic force in western Alaska.

One Kotzebue attraction that shouldn't be missed is the NANA **Museum of the Arctic**. Tours of the museum are arranged primarily for travelers on packages offered by Tour Arctic (tel: 442-3301 or 442 3441; independent travelers can join the tours for a fee). Tours include a one-and-a-half-hour program that is unequaled anywhere in Alaska. It includes story telling, traditional Inupiat dancing and an award-winning slide show. The museum's exhibits include artifacts and traditional art and examples of all the animals indigenous to the region. It is a splendid introduction to the land and its traditional Native culture. Programs are offered twice daily from mid-May through early September. The package also includes a city tour, a visit to the National Park Service office to learn about the wildlife and wilderness areas, and a culture camp demonstration which explains Native culture from both the spiritual and the practical perspectives. Guides take visitors on a walk in the tundra to point out permafrost as well as plants and their traditional uses.

Northeast of Kotzebue NANA also helped develop the Red Dog Mine, a world-class zinc mine that provides hundreds of local jobs, making a tremendous eco-

Map, page 276

BELOW: waterfront at Kotzebue.

Map, page 276

nomic impact on such a sparsely populated area. Cominco, a Canadian-based mining concern, is developing the roads and other infrastructure necessary to support the venture. The state of Alaska guaranteed a $150 million loan in the spring of 1985 for the road system. Zinc deposits are expected to last for 20 years and recoverable quantities of silver, lead and other minerals have been detected in the same area .

But Kotzebue is still traditional. Fishermen tend nets in Kotzebue Sound and nearby streams. Walrus, seal, whale and polar bear hunters still brave the elements in pursuit of their quarries. Kotzebue is a rare combination of the old and the new, and one of the few places where traditional and contemporary lifestyles are blending together in reasonable harmony.

Wilderness adventures

Kotzebue is also the jumping-off point for those seeking wilderness adventure in the **Noatak National Preserve** and the **Kobuk Valley National Park**. Also accessible by charter aircraft from Kotzebue are **Cape Krusenstern National Monument** (*see* page 286) and the **Bering Land Bridge National Preserve**. These remote lands were all set aside as part of the 1980 Alaska National Interest Lands Conservation Act.

The distances involved means that there is no easy or inexpensive way to get to these remote parks and preserves. There are no roads. Charter airplanes from Kotzebue, starting at about $200 an hour (in 1999), are about the only means of access. Check carefully with the National Park Service office in Kotzebue before you go. Activities such as reindeer herding are allowed to take place on portions of these lands, and if you are planning a wilderness trip to seek peace and solitude you won't want to land in the middle of a commercial reindeer drive.

BELOW: red-faced cormorant on the Pribilofs.
RIGHT: Kotzebue kids.

The Pribilof Islands

Three hundred miles (480 km) off the western coast of Alaska lie the **Pribilofs**, the nesting grounds for hundreds of thousands of sea birds of almost 200 different species, and the breeding grounds and summer home of the Pacific fur seals. There's a small hotel in **St Paul** (population about 700) and two small restaurants. Scheduled air service is available from Anchorage to St Paul, and there are package tours, which are certainly the easiest way to visit the islands.

Today, the fishing and tourism industries are being developed as St Paul's main economic supports. Past revenues were generated by the fur seal harvest and government aid. With the ending of this activity, the community was forced to find other means of support. The newly completed harbor is a boon to local fishermen, who had no safe haven for their boats, and is expected to attract new industry.

A trip to Alaska's west coast can be as thrilling as finding gold on the beach, or as daring as competing in the grueling Iditarod sled dog race. The region's residents are fun-loving and hospitable, and unconventional. With a colorful past and a resource-rich future, Alaska's far west teaches you about the traditional way of life, using the language of today. ❏

CAPE KRUSENSTERN

*The remote lands of Cape Krusenstern are only
for the self-sufficient and intrepid traveler,
but the rewards are great*

It's hard to imagine a less likely place for buried treasure. There's nothing particularly conspicuous about **Cape Krusenstern**, no towering mountains, magnificent waterfalls, verdant forests. Only a low, ridged spit with deep furrows, dotted with countless ponds, and bordered by a relentless sea on one side and a large lagoon on the other. Resembling a giant scythe clipping the waves of the Chukchi Sea, Cape Krusenstern stretches into polar waters in northwestern Alaska. Hidden beneath beach ridges on the cape are archeological treasures reaching back at least 4,000 years. This earthbound chronicle of early man in Alaska brought about the establishment of the 560,000-acre (226,600-hectare) **Cape Krusenstern National Monument ❺** in 1980.

Charter planes and boats headquartered in **Kotzebue** take infrequent visitors to the monument, 10 miles (16 km) northwest across Kotzebue Sound at its southern border. The monument lacks visitor services – no public shelters or campgrounds – and receives only about 3,500 visitors a year. The small village of **Kivalina** stretches out along the Chukchi shore north of the monument and to the east of Krusenstern, across the Mulgrave Hills, lies the village of **Noatak**. Kivalina and Noatak have airstrips but most visitors arrive via Kotzebue, which has a jet service from both Anchorage and Fairbanks.

Cape Krusenstern is a bring-your-own-shelter place, and that goes for stove, food and water. Highlands beyond the beaches have freshwater streams, but it's still best to take some. The Krusenstern tableau is waiting, but come prepared to be self-sustaining.

Planes can land on some beaches of the monument, and floatplanes put down on nearby lagoons. Many beach areas are privately owned; visitors should check with monument headquarters staff in Kotzebue for specific locations of private property, as they are not marked. Travelers are free to explore archeological zones, but no digging for artifacts or causing other disturbance is allowed.

Winds sweep almost constantly across the lowlands of Cape Krusenstern. In winter they bring instant freezing to an already cold land. In summer, fog blankets coastal areas, although temperatures are from 40–65°F (4–18°C). Inland, the skies are often clear in June and July, but visitors should always carry raingear and be alert for hypothermia.

Formation of the cape

The cape at Krusenstern didn't always exist. About 10,000 years ago, the coastline angled straight southeast from Point Hope, skirted a small mountain, and turned east. Kotzebue Sound was mostly a giant sandy lowland, not the open waterway it is today. During the Pleistocene Era, from approximately two million to

PRECEDING PAGES:
migrating sandhill
cranes.
BELOW: an
archeological dig.

10,000–15,000 years ago, great ice sheets covered much of the northern hemisphere. These ice masses absorbed water, causing the sea level to recede. As the sea shrank away from the shore, it exposed a land bridge connecting North America and Asia. When the ice sheets melted, the sea level rose once again and covered the land bridge.

Sweeping down the newly aligned coastline, prevailing winds from the northwest propelled waves, which carried bits of gravel in their churning surf, down the beach. When the waves hit the turn where the coastline swung east, they dropped the gravel offshore. Every so often, usually in the spring, the winds shifted to the southwest. Great chunks of ice were driven onshore, but not before the ice scooped up gravel from shallow offshore beds and deposited it on the beach beyond the surf. Ridge after ridge built up on the outer shore of the cape.

Slowly the cape pushed seaward. Hardy beach plants colonized the ridges, their root systems helping to stabilize the gravels. Year after year the birth and death of beach plants built up a thin layer of soil, creating suitable habitat for other plants. Throughout the centuries, a carpet of green followed the shoreline, advancing seaward, until 114 ridges lined an approximately 3-mile (5-km) wide spit. Lt Otto von Kotzebue, sailing with the Imperial Russian Navy, gave geographical recognition to the cape by naming it Krusenstern after the first Russian admiral to circumnavigate the globe in 1803–4.

Arctic archeology

Not until the late 1950s was the significance of the beach ridges correlated with the history of early man in Alaska. Professor J. Louis Giddings, anthropologist and archeologist, unlocked the treasure chest buried in the frozen beach gravels

Map, page 276

BELOW: view of isolated Tunanak.

and began a new chapter in arctic archeology. In 1948 Giddings had uncovered artifacts from the Denbigh Flint people at Cape Denbigh in Norton Sound to the south. These ancient Alaskans left their calling cards – tiny chipped flints – in the soils of prehistoric Alaska about 4,000 years ago. Archeologists view these discoveries as the first from the Arctic Small Tool tradition which eventually spanned the top of the continent from the Bering Sea to Greenland.

At Krusenstern, Giddings probed the ridges back from the shore to discover artifacts related to the succession of early man in northwestern Alaska and probably the entire northern portion of the continent. Laid out in order of their occurrence along the series of beach ridges were the remains of houses or hunting camps for every ancient culture known to northwestern Alaska. Excavations over several years opened the prehistoric record, ridge by ridge, of the ancestors of modern Eskimos and those cultures which preceded them across the land bridge from Asia to arctic North America.

Giddings and his assistants unearthed bits of pottery, ivory and whalebone harpoon heads, snow goggles and other tools of a coastal dwelling lifestyle. Carvings and other decorations on these items pointed to the Thule culture which spread along the northwestern arctic coast about AD 800.

Eventually Giddings came upon artifacts of the Ipiutak people, a highly artistic prehistoric culture dating to about 2,000 years ago. First discovered when archeologists uncovered remnants of a huge village near Point Hope, 100 miles (160 km) to the northwest, the Ipiutaks carved elaborate designs on bone and ivory and fashioned fanciful, seemingly impractical items.

BELOW: a malemute takes a rest.

Moving inland once again, Professor Giddings came upon a more moist habitat. Here pottery decorated with waffle-like rectangles provided the clue to the

early residents of the next series of beaches: the people of the Norton culture.

Earlier in the archeological parade came the Choris people, first discovered on the Choris Peninsula of southern Kotzebue Sound. Identified by their large oval house depressions, they left no signs of permanent houses at Krusenstern. But tiny flakes lying exposed on early beach ridges led scientists to the hearths of temporary hunting camps which were set up by Choris people about 1000 BC. One prized find included a single blade, nearly 7 inches (18 cm) long.

The Old Whalers

Every once in a while the continuity of the archeological record was broken when scientists unearthed artifacts from a culture that did not fit in to the spectrum of early man in northwestern Alaska. One such find was the record of Old Whalers on the beach ridge inland from the Choris remains. These prehistoric people, who lived for a brief time at the cape sometime between 1800 and 1500 BC, relied almost exclusively on the sea for sustenance. Their record indicates a greater use of whales than either preceding or subsequent cultures.

The cape still had more to offer. On the innermost ridges beyond the Old Whalers and adjacent to the lagoon, Giddings came full circle, back to the prehistoric people he first encountered a decade earlier at Cape Denbigh. Beaches a mile and a half from the current Chukchi coast yielded hearths with bits of charcoal, burnt stones and tiny chips – remains of the earliest inhabitants of the beach ridge system, the Denbigh Flint people.

The archeological treasure chest buried in the beach ridges had now been opened, but there remained one final chapter to write. **Ingitkalik Mountain,** whose prehistoric ancestor guarded the Pleistocene coast before the beach ridges

Map, page 276

BELOW: strips of dried salmon for winter.

*An Inupiat woman
making hood trims
from wolf skins.*

formed, rises across the lagoon at the beginning of the benchlands above Cape Krusenstern. At several elevations on the mountain's slopes Giddings found signs of ancient man's presence even older than those of the beach ridges below. Not until excavation of the vertical stratigraphy at the **Onion Portage** site in the Kobuk Valley, east of Kotzebue, were scientists able to confirm that the Palisades findings of the benchlands above Krusenstern were indeed older than any of the artifacts found buried in the beach ridges. Giddings and others had now exposed the archeological treasures of Krusenstern and added to our knowledge of ancient man in Alaska.

The cape today

Each spring, the rivers and streams of Kotzebue basin cleanse themselves when snow melt fills the channels which dump their load into Kotzebue Sound. Whitefish join this migration, leaving their inland wintering grounds and moving into summer feeding areas in coastal estuaries. This annual flooding acts as a catalyst for one of the region's major subsistence hauls.

As the flood waters fan out into Kotzebue Sound, several species of whitefish swarm into sloughs along the Krusenstern coast, fattening throughout the summer in the brackish waters. Local residents congregate at the sloughs each fall when ground swells from the Chukchi Sea push gravel and sand across the channels by which whitefish exit the salt-water areas on their return migration. Residents harvest the fish trapped in the sloughs, to add to their winter staples.

Subsistence controls the lifestyle of Krusenstern residents today as in ancient times. Travelers should take extra care not to disturb fishing nets, boats or other gear on which local residents rely.

BELOW: musk ox hide in Tunanak.

Also crucial is the 6-mile (10-km) flatland at the monument's southern tip – **Sheshalik**, "Place of White Whales." Several families maintain year-round homes at Sheshalik, which is a traditional gathering place for hunters of beluga, the small, white, toothed whale. Life at Sheshalik revolves around stockpiling the meat, fish, berries and greenstuff that see these families through nine months of winter.

When snow and cold blanket the region, families keep busy ice fishing and trapping for small fur-bearers. In spring, marine mammal hunters take to the ice in search of seals. When leads open in the sea ice, belugas become the quarry. For centuries, hunters have gathered at **Sealing Point** on the narrow isthmus separating the Chukchi from the inner lagoons. Returning, their boats loaded with sea mammal carcasses, the hunters portage the isthmus and continue their southerly journey over calm lagoon waters rather than fighting the waves of the open sea.

In May waterfowl return from their winter sojourn and head for Krusenstern where snow melt has weakened the ice and open water spreads early throughout the lagoons. Several species of geese and ducks nest on the ponds, joined by their cousins on stilts, the sandhill cranes.

Later in the summer residents harvest salmonberries, cranberries and blueberries. Women pick greens, preserving some in seal oil for later use. Fish – grayling, Arctic char and whitefish – are hung to dry on wooden racks. Chum salmon are taken for subsistence as well as for the commercial fishery in Kotzebue Sound.

After waterfowl leave in the fall, hunters turn to caribou, ptarmigan and sometimes walrus or – rarely nowadays – bear. Both black and brown bears have been found on the cape; polar bears roam offshore ice in winter and spring. Agile Arctic foxes follow behind these northern barons, ready to inspect any tidbit they leave behind. Onshore, elusive fur-bearers – wolves, wolverines, red foxes, lynx, mink, short-tailed weasels, snowshoe and tundra hare, and Arctic ground squirrels – patrol the tundra. Hunters take moose in low-lying areas or Dall sheep in the Igichuk Hills. A small group of musk ox, descendants of the shaggy mammals which once roamed all arctic North America but were wiped out by hunters in Alaska in the mid-1800s, thunder across the tundra of the Mulgrave Hills.

Other species, generally not part of the subsistence catch, share Krusenstern's bounty. Lesser golden-plovers, western and semipalmated sandpipers, whimbrels, Lapland longspurs and Savannah sparrows add their beauty and song. Arctic and Aleutian terns float gracefully above the tundra, ready to defend their nests from the purposeful forays of glaucous gulls and jaegers. An Asian migrant, the handsome yellow wagtail, builds its nest in tiny cavities in the beach ridges. Overhead, rough-legged hawks soar from their nests in the highlands to hover over the tundra, piercing eyes searching for voles and lemmings.

The ambiance at Krusenstern is understated, but for the curious and the thorough, the history of early man in the north and its modern translation in the subsistence world of local residents are only a step away. ❑

Map, page 276

BELOW: an Arctic tern over Cape Krusenstern.

NATIVE ART AND ARTIFACTS

Items which once had specific purposes are now highly prized as souvenirs, although to the Native people their traditional values are still important

In early times, all Alaska Native art served a particular purpose. The items created had either a practical or a cultural use. For instance, carvers created masks for ceremonies, totem poles to tell the histories of clans, and Chilkat blankets for special dancing, or to present as tokens of esteem.

These days, although much Native art continues to serve traditional purposes, many objects are sold into private hands. Dance fans and masks, for example, are still used in ceremonies today, but they are regularly sold as souvenirs. Often, these sales are a welcome source of income for the villages. Visitors to Alaska eagerly seek ivory scrimshaw, carvings of bone and wood, and baskets woven with colorful grasses or formed from birch bark.

REGIONAL DIFFERENCES

Natives from different parts of Alaska excel in different types of art. Doll-making has been an Eskimo art form for at least 2,000 years. The detailed dolls with carved faces and fur parkas portray Eskimo ways of life, from hunters to berry-pickers and skin sewers. The Athabascans are known for their colorful beadwork, usually flowers created on tanned moose hide, and incorporating porcupine quills and buttons. The Aleuts are masters at making tightly woven grass baskets, often decorated with multicolored embroidery. Some baskets can take up to 15 hours an inch to complete.

◁ **NATIVE DOLLS**
These Yup'ik dolls have faces of moose skin and miniature parkas with wolverine ruffs and beaver mitts.

▷ **SITKA BUILDING**
This Native house in Sitka has been covered with numerous yellow cedar plaques, all carved and painted with different Tlingit designs.

 **MUSK OX MURAL**
This mural decorates the exterior of the Oomingmak Co-Op in Anchorage, a good place to buy articles handmade in villages from the fine, soft musk ox wool called *qiviut*.

▽ **CHILKAT BLANKET**
Chilkat blankets can take over a year to make, and were once highly sought after by Indian nobility. Each told a legend and was used for a special occasion: to cover a body lying in state, or as a gift to an honored guest.

TOTEM POLES: LEGENDS IN WOOD

Totem poles, some as high as 60 ft (18 meters) tall, are one of the most popular examples of Northwest Native woodworking. Figures, or totems, on the poles are comparable to family crests and are used to tell a story, legend or event. The totemic symbols are usually animals, such as bears, eagles or killer whales. Their significance lies in myth – stories passed down through generations about how certain animals may have affected the destiny of ancestors.

Poles could usually be found clustered along the village's shore in front of clan houses or directly on the fronts of private houses, or in cemeteries. According to early accounts of Tlingit life, deceased clan members were cremated and their ashes placed in these poles.

Missionaries and other outsiders contributed to the destruction and neglect of many totem poles. Since the 1930s, many have been restored, some of which now stand in totem parks near villages like Klawock and Saxman and at the Totem Heritage Center in Ketchikan.

△ **CULTURAL SYMBOL**
This totemic symbol is a detail from a pole in the popular Sitka National Historic Park. It is typical of the traditional designs used by the Tlingit people when carving their ceremonial masks, rattles and everyday utensils, each with its own story to tell.

◁ **CEREMONIAL HEADDRESS**
Masks and headdresses such as this one, worn in Sitka, have great symbolic importance, as they portray the relationship of a particular tribe with the spirits, and are worn during special ceremonies.

GATES OF THE ARCTIC

Map, page 276

If you hear the call of the wilderness, the Gates of the Arctic may be the place you are looking for, but plan your trip with care, because you really are on your own

I n 1929, Robert Marshall suggested that all of Alaska north of the Brooks Range should be preserved as wilderness. His vision never came to pass, but the place most dear to Marshall, the central Brooks Range, is preserved in **Gates of the Arctic National Park and Preserve ❻**. In the heart of northern Alaska, the park is 200 miles (320 km) northwest of Fairbanks, and 200 miles south of Barrow, Alaska's largest Eskimo community. No maintained roads or trails exist within the park – no phones, TVs, radios, gas stations, restaurants, stores or hotels. No emergency services are available: no hospitals, first aid stations, ambulances, police or fire stations. There is one permanent ranger station at **Anaktuvuk Pass**, a Native village in the middle of the park. Other park staff operate out of Bettles and the Fairbanks headquarters.

Such wilderness offers a real opportunity to experience freedom from civilization and its attendant trappings – one that only about 2,000 adventurous souls experience each year. When you are liable to meet a bear in 8 million acres (3.2 million hectares) of wilderness, you are on your own. People still freeze and starve to death in remote cabins in the Brooks Range wilderness; months may pass before their bodies are found. If you don't arrange for someone to rescue you, no one will. This experience is called self-reliance – or suicide.

PRECEDING PAGES: a view of Brooks Range. **LEFT:** a cabin in the woods. **BELOW:** lichen rings on a boulder.

A rewarding risk

Yet inherent in the risks are opportunities for wilderness recreation on a grand scale. In the summer, the park provides opportunities for mountaineering, hiking and camping. The lakes, rivers and streams allow for motorboating, rafting, canoeing, kayaking and fishing. Also popular are birding, flightseeing and wildlife viewing.

Fall activities include blueberry and cranberry picking, and hunting for bear, caribou, moose, ducks, geese, rabbits and ptarmigan. In winter, the park is quiet. The sun drops below the horizon in November and doesn't surface again until February. The temperature can drop to -70°F (-57°C). Between February and April the sun returns and a few hardy adventurers use the park for cross-country skiing, dog sledding and snowshoeing.

The Gates of the Arctic area is personalized by the Athabascan Indians and several Eskimo cultures. The lifestyles of trappers, homesteaders and others who live in isolated cabins add color and character. Visitors, flogging past a Native fish camp, may see orange-red salmon strips drying on birch poles or a fish net bobbing with the flow of the river. They may even encounter a trapper's secluded log home with a snow-machine outside, traps and a bearskin hanging from the cabin walls. But people are rarely seen. The area population is less than one person per 5,000 acres (2,000 hectares).

Gateway to Gates

Gates of the Arctic National Park and Preserve is remote, pristine wilderness. The meaning of "remote" becomes immediately evident when trying to get here. **Bettles ❼** is the gateway to Gates. You can take a scheduled flight from Fairbanks to this friendly little outpost, then hire an air taxi. Bettles also provides visitors to Gates with potential outfitters, guides and a lodge. From here, any number of trips are possible into the park, but they all cost quite a lot. If you want to cut costs it's sensible to travel in a group. A trip for six from Bettles can cost less than half what it costs for two. Compare services to prices and ask for references. Reputable guides will have names of people to contact who have taken their trips. The steep price of visiting Gates of the Arctic National Park can be an advantage if you like solitude, for few people make their way in. It's a place that requires time, money and the ability to face a challenge.

If you are short of money but have the time and the physical stamina you can backpack the many miles to the park, after driving along the **Dalton Highway**. Check in at Fairbanks for road conditions on the Highway (the Alaska Department of Transportation, Road Maintenance, tel: 456-ROAD or 451-2206). The road is rough gravel, very narrow and dominated by commercial trucks. Most local people refuse to take cars over the road, preferring vehicles with stronger suspension systems. Gear to deal with breakdowns and multiple flat tires is essential. Only two places sell gas (or anything else) on the road: the truckstop at the Yukon River Bridge and the truck stop at Coldfoot. The road is open for more than 400 miles (645 km) to Prudhoe Bay.

Fairbanks is also a recommended stop for maps, information and supplies. The **Alaska Public Lands Information Center** (250 Cushman Street, tel: 456-

Coldfoot was given its name by Klondike gold miners who, having traveled so far north, got "cold feet" in both senses of the words.

BELOW: a beaver takes an alder branch home.

0527) has a complete list of air services, commercial services, information books and maps. Information is also available directly from the National Park Service, the Alaska Department of Fish and Game, the Department of Transportation, the Alaska State Troopers and the State Department of Tourism.

Fairbanks is generally the last stop to shop for supplies, as well. Since all fuel must be flown in, many communities have erratic or non-existent fuel supplies; camp stove fuel is not allowed on regularly scheduled airlines. Villages are often not equipped with facilities for visitors, so travelers should have adequate food supplies and should have arranged return transportation in advance.

The Dalton Highway winds through wild and beautiful wilderness and nears the Gates' vicinity at **Coldfoot**, approximately 250 miles (400 km) north of Fairbanks. In early September, when the birch leaves are golden in the hills and the weather is sunny and dry, the drive alone is worth the trip. A stop at the **Coldfoot Services Truckstop** is a must for any visitor. In the lodge-style dining hall restaurant, meals are eaten on oilcloth-covered tables with wooden benches, mining camp-style. Motel rooms are available. A summer visitor center at Coldfoot is operated jointly by the National Park Service and other federal agencies. Another visitor center is located at the Yukon River Bridge (open in summer only; tel: 678-5209).

Trips and trails

The most easily accessed trail into the park is in **Wiseman**, 15 miles (24 km) north of Coldfoot. Wiseman is a turn-of-the-century mining community. Its weathered buildings are still home to a small group of miners. The road from Dalton Highway to Wiseman extends on to several trails that enter the park. The

Map, page 276

TIP

The arctic summer provides 24-hour daylight, so if you are taking photographs – a very popular activity in the park – you won't need a flash.

BELOW: post office at Coldfoot.

Nolan-Wiseman Creek Trail goes through the historic mining area of the park to the Glacier River. Another popular trail follows the Hammond River north from Wiseman.

The most popular Gates of the Arctic trip is to the north fork of the Koyukuk River, where the peaks, **Frigid Craigs** and **Boreal Mountain**, stand guard. They are the climax of a backpacking trip that starts at **Summit Lake** and ends at **Chimney Lake**; a trip that averages 10 days. Another favored excursion involves flightseeing out of the village of Bettles.

Float trips – and combination backpacking/float trips – can be arranged throughout the park. Or seek fish-filled **Walker Lake**, a blue jewel nestled in the deep forested hills in the southern part of the park. Winter cross-country ski trips, dog sled rides and ice fishing are also available at Walker Lake. A few private cabins are the only places where a visitor can sleep indoors in the park.

*Hiding from
mosquitoes.*

If you want solitude and isolation you would be better off avoiding favored places, such as the north fork of the Koyukuk and the Gates of the Arctic peaks area. Customized trips to unnamed valleys are available for those who want to vacation alone.

Sport-hunting is only allowed in the park's preserve portion and non-Alaskans must have a guide if they want to hunt for certain big game animals. A guide familiar with local conditions is recommended even if not actually required. Some game can be taken only by permit. Contact the Alaska Department of Fish and Game for specifics (tel: 459-7306 or 459-7206).

BELOW: canoeing in
Gates of the Arctic.

As well as being home to bear and game, Gates is also host to hordes of mosquitoes. During certain times of the year, wilderness travelers can only survive the ever-present swarm of bugs by keeping their entire body, including their

hands, completely covered, and wearing a headnet. Always carry a good mosquito repellent, preferably one with a high DEET concentration, and a finely screened tent. Another wilderness creature that inhabits Gates is *Giardia lamblia*, a microscopic water organism that causes "beaver fever," an unpleasant intestinal disorder. The best prevention is to boil all drinking water or use chemical disinfectants such as iodine or chlorine. This applies to all wilderness areas of Alaska.

June and July are the wettest months. Thunderstorms are frequent occurrences. Rain has been known to start in mid-August and not stop until it turns to snow in September. Temperatures range from -70°F (-57°C) to 92°F (32°C). Snow may fall in any month of the year. The average summer temperature ranges from freezing to 85°F (29°C), prime hypothermia (body-chilling) conditions. Wool clothing keeps you warm and dry, and hiking boots are needed to survive in wet, rocky and soggy conditions.

Anyone who wants to visit the Gates needs to do considerable research: topographical maps are a must, and problems must be anticipated and planned for. Hundreds of miles from the nearest tree is *not* the place to learn how to start a fire without wood!

Avoid the tragic wilderness experiences. People have drowned sleeping on sandbars; others have found that a gentle stream can become a raging whitewater river in a matter of hours in a downpour. Three to 10 days' leeway should be allowed for water level changes if any river or creek crossings are involved. The Gates of the Arctic is no place to live by the clock and, although offering a rare encounter with nature, the park requires some careful planning and outdoors experience. ❑

Map, page 276

BELOW: fortified supply hut known as a "*cache*".

THE NORTH SLOPE

Stand on the edge of the continent and bask in the midnight sun in the most remote part of Alaska

Map, page 276

Bush pilots on Alaska's north coast have little use for aerial charts, because there are few usable landmarks that can be depicted on a map to aid a pilot in this world of myriad tiny lakes and meandering rivers. Pilots usually plot their positions by counting the number of rivers crossed from a known starting point. Rivers flow from south to north on the North Slope, a vaguely defined but huge chunk of territory that includes everything north of the summit of the Brooks Range. Once a pilot locates a particular river by flying east or west, he turns inland toward terrain with more features, the treeless northern side of the mountains about 100 miles (160 km) to the south.

Most people fly bush planes or helicopters in these latitudes. There are no roads between communities and few means of overland travel of any kind except snow-machines and, very occasionally, dog sleds in the winter. Constant fog is a hazard: a 1,500-ft (458-meter) thick cloud of mist blankets the north coast of Alaska many days of the year. It often stretches inland for about 20 miles (32 km); most of the airports are hidden in the fog. Helicopter pilots, who rarely fly on instruments, roar along at 120 mph (200 kph) through the perpetual mist.

Hidden riches

Stark, trackless beauty and the undisturbed miracles of nature surround you on the North Slope. Aircrews forced down in the northern Brooks Range may have to survive for several days on only their wits and the gear they have aboard the aircraft. A gun is handy in these circumstances for killing food animals or defending themselves against marauding bears.

But there are lighter moments. A sack lunch on a 6,000-ft (1,830-meter) ridge overlooking miles of unexplored territory could be one of them. Standing on the low northern edge of the continent and seeing Native villagers land a bowhead whale might be another. These moments, and more, do exist.

Almost every stone or fossil is a clue to the varying layers of rock underlying the flat coastal plain, a clue that can lead to the eventual discovery of oil. And every clue is zealously guarded by the company that finds it, for finding and developing oil is the name of the game on the North Slope. Initial explorations by geologists are just the first move by the players.

Alaska's economy floats on an ocean of black gold, most of it pumped from beneath the tundra on the North Slope. Oil generates 85 percent of the state government's income and provides a living for a large transient population of oil-industry workers who live on the Arctic coast.

Prudhoe Bay ❽ is a working person's world, visited by few tourists. Several hundred people live and work at

PRECEDING PAGES: oil production at Prudhoe Bay. **LEFT:** pipeline welder on the North Slope. **BELOW:** an oil company worker.

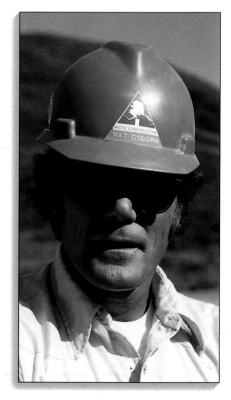

the industrial facility – there are no schools, no public roads and few entertainment facilities. The work-day is 12 hours long, seven days a week. The pace, though, is temporary. After two or three weeks on the job, workers fly to Anchorage, Fairbanks or even Dallas, Texas, for a week or sometimes two of vacation. It's not uncommon for a worker on the slope to make $75,000 a year for only 26 actual weeks on the job.

The larger oil companies house and feed their personnel, at no expense to employees. Living quarters usually include a library, a gymnasium with an indoor track, weights room, game rooms and satellite television, but they tend to be quiet places where the workers settle into a routine – and there is little time for more than working, sleeping and eating.

Many Slope transient workers see nothing more than the inside of the housing building, work station and air terminal. For them, Prudhoe Bay is the latest example of US technology transplanted into a frozen wilderness. Little outside their doors interests them; it's only frozen tundra and fog. Frozen it may be for most of the year, but some people have called Alaska's Arctic coast home for centuries, and have managed to scrape a living there. For some workers on the Slope, on the other hand, their few hours of unscheduled time are a rare opportunity for photographing summer wildlife, such as migrating caribou or birds, or winter's northern lights.

Tour companies offer flights to the Prudhoe Bay oilfields, often with a return by bus over 500 miles (800 km) of gravel road to Fairbanks. A fixed fee provides a bed for the two-night trip, meals at a North Slope dining facility, and the round-trip air fare. Four-hour tours of the oilfields round out the arrangement. It is also possible to take a one-day package, flying both ways. Visitors are usu-

Helicopter pilots sometimes joke that the only navigational hazards on this flat, fog-shrouded terrain are caribou who have a habit of standing up unexpectedly.

BELOW: snow-machining through the sun fog.

ally impressed by the neatness of the facility and how little the buildings seem to disturb the landscape. The silver slash of the trans-Alaska oil pipeline originates here, then winds south toward the Brooks Range. Seeing all this, you realize that here beats the heart that pumps black gold, the life blood of Alaska's contemporary economy.

Map, page 276

North Slope Native life

West of Prudhoe Bay and east of Barrow, **Nuiqsut** is geographically placed between oil and tradition. Unlike most northern communities, it is several miles inland from the coast, at the apex of the Colville River delta, about 60 miles (100 km) from Prudhoe. Inupiat men still hunt whales off the coast (although regulations now strictly limit the number of whales they may take each year), as well as polar bears and seals.

Although most still lead a traditional lifestyle of hunting and gathering, a few jobs are available, mostly in government-run organizations. But for those who still venture onto the frozen sea in search of food and skins, their safety is less in the hands of chance these days. If they are late returning to their modern frame houses in the village, one quick telephone call launches a helicopter to search the coastline near the delta's mouth.

On the continent's edge

Located to the west and just south of Point Barrow, the northernmost tip of North America, **Barrow** ❾ is the largest Eskimo settlement in Alaska. It is the headquarters of the Arctic Slope Regional Corporation, a Native corporation formed to manage the huge sums of money and vast tracts of land deeded to Alaska

BELOW: Inupiat children in the street at Barrow.

**Map,
page 276**

TIP

Taking a package tour is worthwhile. Staying at the Top of the World Hotel in Barrow can otherwise be expensive during the months of the midnight sun.

BELOW: Native woman with an *ulu*.
RIGHT: aerial view of Barrow icepack.

Native groups by the Alaska Native Claims Settlement Act of 1971. When that legislation was approved by the US Congress, Barrow and other key Native villages in Alaska instantly became corporate centers, modern enclaves of big business in a traditional land. Barrow today stands as the ultimate contrast between tradition and technology.

Skin whaling boats are still used for the spring hunt. Modern aluminum craft are used for the fall hunt. Whaling is now very strictly regulated, but captains teach their sons the secrets of harpooning and landing the bowhead whale, more as a means of keeping the culture alive than as a necessary tool of survival.

The opportunity to see an ancient culture and its traditions lure some visitors to Barrow, but most come to see the midnight sun, which does not set from mid-May to early August, and for a chance to stand momentarily on the continent's northern edge. For many visitors the most vivid memory of their Barrow trip is the brief moment they stood on the sand at the tip of the continent. It's only a windswept stretch of dark-sand beach, often shrouded in fog, and usually littered with ice, but it is the edge of the continent.

For winter visitors, the northern lights are another attraction, but they are equally apparent in Fairbanks, which is a great deal more accessible than Barrow.

Most people come here as part of a package tour. Travel agencies offer overnight trips to Barrow from Anchorage and Fairbanks for an all-in charge which covers a hotel room, a few local tours and the use of a parka. Contact Alaska Airlines, tel: (800) 468-2248 for details.

The package tours and independent visitors alike stop at **Pepe's North of the Border Restaurant**, Barrow's most famous eating house, which serves typical American-Mexican food. Others may squeamishly try a bite of *muktuk* (whale blubber), or perhaps a piece of seal meat. But these local delicacies are available only sporadically and those visitors who like to live on the culinary edge may have to search for them.

Eskimo lore

It is perhaps unfortunate that most trips to Barrow are so brief. Inupiat culture is varied and ancient, but it is difficult and time-consuming for an outsider to gain a detailed knowledge of it. And, although English is spoken by most Inupiats (except for the very old), traditional behavior may be confusing and interfere with communication. For example, Inupiats are not being impolite when they fail to respond immediately to a question or acknowledge a statement. It is simply not their custom to do so, but outsiders may find their long pauses uncomfortable. Saying thank you is also not customary: traditionally, Inupiat people will simply return a favor – and expect no thanks from the recipient.

Perhaps the best advice for tourists is to assume a slower-paced style of speaking and behaving, a pace which is more attuned to the traditional lifestyles of the region, and to remember that the Inupiat people live not by the clock but by the change of seasons. Changing one's behavior takes a conscious effort, and may be difficult at first, but a journey to the North Slope is an opportunity to live, albeit briefly, in a different way and experience an unfamiliar culture. ❑

INSIGHT GUIDES

TRAVEL TIPS

New *Insight Maps*

Maps in Insight Guides are tailored to complement the text. But when you're on the road you sometimes need the big picture that only a large-scale map can provide. This new range of durable Insight Fleximaps has been designed to meet just that need.

Detailed, clear cartography
makes the comprehensive route and city maps easy to follow, highlights all the major tourist sites and provides valuable motoring information plus a full index.

Informative and easy to use
with additional text and photographs covering a destination's top 10 essential sites, plus useful addresses, facts about the destination and handy tips on getting around.

Laminated finish
allows you to mark your route on the map using a non-permanent marker pen, and wipe it off. It makes the maps more durable and easier to fold than traditional maps.

The first titles
cover many popular destinations. They include Algarve, Amsterdam, Bangkok, California, Cyprus, Dominican Republic, Florence, Hong Kong, Ireland, London, Mallorca, Paris, Prague, Rome, San Francisco, Sydney, Thailand, Tuscany, USA Southwest, Venice, and Vienna.

※ INSIGHT GUIDES
The world's largest collection of visual travel guides

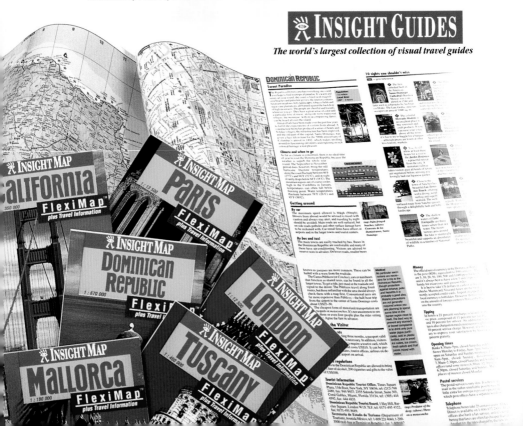

CONTENTS

Getting Acquainted

Capital: Juneau.
Area: 586,000 sq. miles (1,430,000 sq. km).
Population: 621,400, of which 42 percent live in the Anchorage area. There is a population of some 104,100 indigenous people, about half of whom are Eskimos.
Religion: A mixture of all the religions represented in the rest of the United States, plus a strong Russian Orthodox influence in the south.
Time Zone: Alaska Standard Time (Pacific Standard Time minus 1 hour; Eastern Standard Time minus 5 hours; GMT minus 10 hours). The Aleutian Chain and St Lawrence Island are in the Hawaii-Aleutian Time Zone, which is 1 hour earlier.
Dialing Code: US international code (1) + 907.
Weights and Measures: Imperial.
Electricity: 110/120 volts.
Highest mountain: Mount McKinley (20,320 ft/6,196 meters).
Northernmost point: Point Barrow.
Largest lake: Lake Iliamna (1,100 sq. miles/2,850 sq. km).
State Song: *Alaska's Flag.*
Nickname: The Last Frontier.
State Flower: Forget-me-not.
State Fish: King (chinook) Salmon.
State Bird: Willow Ptarmigan (pronounced tar-mi-gun).
State Tree: Sitka Spruce.
State Sport: Dog mushing.

Climate

Alaska's vastness defies attempts to categorize its climate. For convenience, however, the state can be divided into five regions about which some climatic generalizations can be made.

Southeast: This is Alaska's Panhandle, a narrow ribbon of mountains and islands extending along the western edge of British Columbia. Wet and mild are the best terms to describe its climate. Certain communities in the region can receive more than 200 inches (5 meters) of precipitation annually. On rare, sunny days in summer, high temperatures might reach the mid-70°F (21°C) range. High 40s (4°C) to mid 60s (15°C) are the summer norms, under cloudy skies. Winter temperatures rarely fall much below freezing. Skagway and Haines are usually drier and cooler in winter.

Southcentral: Anchorage and most of the gulf coast comprise this part of Alaska. Coastal communities are frequently as wet as southeastern cities, but the amount of rainfall lessens considerably just a short distance inland. Anchorage occasionally has summer highs in the 80s (26°C) but the 60s (15°C) and low 70s (21°C) are more common.

Interior: The broad expanse of inland Alaska, loosely centered on Fairbanks, gets an average of 10 inches (25 cm) of moisture annually. Summer temperatures have reached 100°F (37°C) on occasions; 70s and 80s (21°C and 26°C) temperatures are common, with typical winter lows to -40°F (-40°C).

Arctic Coast: This is a loosely described region encompassing most of Alaska's northern fringe and the west coast as far south as Kotzebue. High winds are common, and average temperatures are too cool to permit trees to grow. Near Nome, summer temperatures can climb into the 60s (15°C), but the high 30s (3°C) and 40s (4°C) are more common. Winter temperatures, though extreme, are never as low as some Interior temperatures. This is also an extremely dry area, receiving only minimal amounts of moisture every year. Barrow, for example, receives just 4.7 inches (11.5 cm) of precipitation annually.

Southwest & The Aleutians: The Aleutian Islands are justly known for some of the most miserable weather on earth. High winds (williwaws) can rise without warning and smash through the islands at speeds of 100 mph (165 kph). Heavy fog is common, as are rain and cool temperatures. The southwestern mainland is the meeting point for Aleutian weather and Interior weather, and often experiences unsettled conditions, frequently accompanied by high winds.

Temperatures

Average Daily High Temperatures

Farenheit			Centigrade		
CITY	JANUARY	JULY	CITY	JANUARY	JULY
Anchorage	21.4°	65.2°	Anchorage	-6°	18.3°
Barrow	-7.4°	45°	Barrow	-22°	7.2°
Cold Bay	33.1°	55.1°	Cold Bay	0.5°	12.7°
Fairbanks	-1.6°	72°	Fairbanks	-18°	22.2°
Juneau	29.4°	63.9°	Juneau	-1.7°	17.6°
Kodiak	35°	60.5°	Kodiak	-1.6°	15.7°
Nome	14.7°	57.7°	Nome	-10°	14.1°

Planning the Trip

What To Bring

Visitors entering Alaska from anywhere other than a US port of embarkation will proceed through US customs. Canadian citizens entering from the Western Hemisphere do not need a visa or a passport. All other foreign visitors must have passports and the necessary documents.

When packing for Alaska, remember you are traveling north. While Alaskans may describe the climate as warm in the summer, those from warmer climates find even the summer chilly. No matter what part of the state you are visiting, bring along a warm coat and a synthetic pile or fleece jacket. A wool sweater, hat and mittens are also necessities.

Layering clothing is the best way to stay warm. While you may be able to run around in shirt sleeves on a warm summer day, the evenings often require a sweater or light jacket. Tour companies sometimes furnish specialty items such as parkas for overnight trips to Barrow, Kotzebue, Prudhoe Bay and other colder areas.

The key for fashion in Alaska is casual and practical. Suits and evening dresses are rarely necessary except for special occasions. Jeans or casual trousers, flannel shirts and comfortable shoes are much more common. Pants are perfectly acceptable for women year-round and in almost any social situation. Dress for comfort. Alaska is not a place where residents wear the latest haute couture. Since you will probably do a lot of walking, be sure to wear good walking shoes. And don't buy them right before your trip. Make sure they are broken in before you leave.

No matter where you visit in Alaska, you are likely to run into periods of rain, so good quality rainwear is recommended.

If your travel plans include flying to a remote area in a small plane, take – and wear – durable warm clothing; survival gear is required for cross-country flights in small planes. Air services and charter flight operators normally carry sufficient survival gear as required by law; it's up to passengers to dress appropriately.

Currency

Travelers' checks in US dollars are advised to ease problems in dealing with the currency. National banks in Alaska's major cities – Anchorage, Fairbanks and Juneau – can convert foreign currency at the prevailing exchange rate. Outside of these metropolitan areas the opportunities to convert foreign money are dramatically reduced. Automatic Teller Machines (ATMs) can be found in just about every town on the road system.

There is no state sales tax in Alaska. However, different boroughs and municipalities across the state may impose a sales tax on all or some goods and services. If uncertain as to whether or not there is a local sales tax, ask any cashier or sales clerk.

Getting There

By Air
At one time Anchorage was a primary refueling stop for international passenger carriers flying over the North Pole on intercontinental flights. But with the opening of Russian air space to commercial traffic after the Cold War, and with new long-range jumbo jets, the international passenger airlines make fewer stops in Anchorage.

Nonetheless, Anchorage is still heavily used for international cargo flights; the US courier company Federal Express, for example, uses Anchorage as a major package handling hub.

International air carriers offering passenger service to Anchorage include: British Airways, China Airlines (Taiwan), Korean Airlines, Alaska Airlines (eastern Russia) and Aeroflot (Moscow). In summer, there are numerous charter flights from Asia and Europe.

US domestic passenger carriers providing service from the Lower 48 states are: Alaska Airlines, Continental, Delta, Reno Air, Northwest and United. Several smaller airlines fly within Alaska itself, including Alaska, Era Aviation, Peninsula and Reeve Aleutian Airways.

Besides Anchorage, connections from Seattle are available for Ketchikan, Sitka, Wrangell, Petersburg, Juneau, Cordova and Fairbanks.

By Sea
Many visitors arrive in Alaska via cruise-ship. This is a luxurious and exciting way to come to Alaska. Cruise-ships sail through the spectacular Inside Passage arriving at Skagway, Ketchikan, Sitka, Juneau, Misty Fjord, Valdez, Seward and Anchorage. Around a dozen cruise lines serve Alaska, with several small vessels offering excursions. Cruises normally start from Vancouver, BC and San Francisco, with a few voyages leaving Seattle.

Cruise lines normally operate between May and September.

They offer a variety of travel options including round-trip or one-way cruises, and cruises which are sold as part of a package tour. Such tours may also include air, rail and/or motorcoach transportation within Alaska.

For further information about cruise options and to make reservations, contact a travel agent.

Marine Highway

Another popular option for cruising the Inside Passage is to go via the **Alaska Marine Highway** system. This state ferry system carries both vehicles and passengers. It operates year-round, but summer service is more frequent.

Passengers and vehicles board in Bellingham, Washington or Prince Rupert in British Columbia, Canada. Southeastern ports of call include Ketchikan, Wrangell, Petersburg, Sitka, Juneau, Haines and Skagway.

The system also serves South Central Alaska, where ferries port in Kodiak, Homer, Seldovia, Seward, Valdez, Cordova, Whittier and, in the Aleutians, Dutch Harbor.

Vessels feature food service, a sightseeing solarium and staterooms. Passengers can also sleep in the public lounge or on deck. During the summer Forest Service naturalists offer interpretive programs on the larger ferries. Reservations should be made at least six months in advance. Bookings are accepted starting in December.

For current information and reservations contact: Alaska Marine Highway, PO Box 25535, Juneau, Alaska 99802, tel: (907) 465-3941 or (800) 642-0066.

Some of the most popular cruise lines serving Alaska include: Cunard Line, Princess Cruises, Royal Caribbean Line and Westours/Holland America Line.

By Rail

There is no rail service directly to Alaska from the US. However, the Alaska Railroad provides passenger service within the state. It connects Anchorage with Fairbanks to the north and with Whittier and Seward to the south.

For more information, contact: Alaska Railroad, PO Box 1-07500, Anchorage, Alaska 99510-7500; tel: (907) 265-2494 or toll free (800) 544-0552. The railroad offers a variety of packages to destinations like Denali National Park, Fairbanks and Seward with cruises on Prince William Sound. One-day trips are also available to Talkeetna.

By Road

Traveling the Alaska Highway is a great adventure. However, because of the great distance, it can only be considered by visitors with plenty of time.

By Bus: Bus service and motorcoach tours are available to Alaska by way of the Alaska Highway. From Seattle, Washington, Greyhound connects with Canadian Greyhound Coachways, offering service to Whitehorse in the Yukon Territory, Canada. In Whitehorse, tours can be arranged to Alaska and other Yukon destinations. Several companies offer motorcoach tours between the continental United States and Alaska. For more information, contact a travel agent.

By Car: The new improvements to the Alaska Highway have made driving enjoyable and safe, but distance may be a drawback. It is 1,520 miles (2,445 km) from Dawson Creek, BC to Fairbanks.

For more information about driving the Alaska highways, refer to *The Milepost* (*All-the-North Guide*), published by Alaska Northwest Publishing Company, and *Alaska Yukon & British Columbia Travel Guide*, published by Alaska Travel Guide. Each gives a detailed description of the highway system and is updated annually. A free state-published brochure on the Alaska highways can be obtained through the Alaska Division of Tourism, PO Box 110801, Juneau, Alaska 99811, tel: (907) 465–2010.

Tour Operators

Alaska Rainforest Tours. Wilderness, adventure, wildlife watching and cultural tours for the independent traveler seeking quality, knowledge and the unusual in Alaska's rainforest. 1813 Shell Simmons Drive, Juneau, AK 99801, tel: (907) 463-3466, e-mail: artour@alaska.net.

Alaska Up Close. Customized eco-tours planned for independent travelers to Southeast Alaska. PO Box 32666, Juneau, AK 99803, tel: (907) 789-9544; website: http://www.wetpage.com/upclose.

Alaska Village Tours, Inc. Culturally rich rural Alaska tours led by local villagers with intimate understanding of subsistence lifestyle and Native culture. 1577 C St., Suite 304, Anchorage, AK 99501, tel: (907) 274-5400.

Arctic Village Tours. Cultural and wilderness tours into the Venetie Indian Reserve and Arctic National Wildlife Refuge. PO Box 82896, Fairbanks, AK 99708, tel: (907) 479-4648.

Athabascan Cultural Journeys. Four-day journeys into the world of the Athabascan Natives, sharing their culture and traditions at wilderness camps. PO Box 10, Huslia, AK 99746, tel: (907) 829-2261 or (800) 423-0094.

Bear Tribal House. Tlingit tribal house of the Bear on Shakes Island. Nine totems and community house open for cruise ships during summer and by appointment year-round. PO Box 253, Wrangell, AK 99929, tel: (907) 874-3747.

Camp Alaska Tours. Unique camping tours through Alaska, British Columbia and the Yukon. Travel is in small groups on itineraries ranging from six to 22 days with opportunities for scenic flights, cruises, hiking and rafting. Tours depart May through September. PO Box 872247, Wasilla, AK 99687, tel: (907) 376-9438 or (800) 376-9438.

Custom Tours of Kodiak. One- or two-day tours of Kodiak Island, including a city/backcountry road safari to remote villages for fishing, sightseeing and bear watching. PO Box 985, Kodiak, AK 99615, tel: (907) 486-4997.

El Dorado Gold Camp. Two tours daily, including a narrow-gauge train ride and gold panning. 1975 Discovery Dr., Fairbanks, AK 99709, tel: (907) 479-7613.

Far North Tours. Exclusive tours and charters throughout the state. PO Box 102873, Anchorage, AK 99510, tel: (907) 272-7480 or (800) 478-7480. e-mail: farnorthqk@aol.com

Frontier Excursions. Tours, shuttles and charters include Skagway, White Pass, Yukon and Dyea. Also shuttle service to Chilkoot trailhead.

e-mail: fronteir@ptialaska.net PO Box 543, Skagway, AK 99840, tel: (907) 983-2512.

Island Terrific Tours. Full one-day guided motor tour of scenic historic Kodiak and nearby attractions. PO Box 3001, Kodiak, AK 99615, tel: (907) 486-4777.

Kenai Fjords Tours. Explore Kenai Fjords National Park and the Chiswell Islands bird rookeries aboard large, comfortable excursion boats. Day trips, meals and overnight stays at an island wilderness lodge are available. 513 W. 4th Ave., Anchorage, AK 99501, tel: (907) 276-6249 (800) 478-8068; website: http:// www.kenaifjords.com.

Klondike Tours. Historic Skagway tours, helicopter flightseeing onto glaciers, freshwater fly fishing and salt-water charters available. PO Box 320, Skagway, AK 99840, tel: (907) 983-2075, (888) 983-2075.

New Directions Charters. Escorted tours by motorcoach to destinations such as Anchorage, Valdez, Fairbanks and Denali, plus glacier cruises. 32852 Five Mile Rd., Livonia, MI 48154, tel: (313) 261-1995 or (800) 343-3242.

Nome Tour and Marketing. Guided tours of gold rush city include gold panning and a sled dog demonstration. PO Box 430, Nome, AK 99762, tel: (907) 443-2323/2651.

US Travel Ecotourism opportunities throughout the state, including river rafting the Matanuska River and Arctic tours in Barrow. 1590 Financial Dr., Wasilla, AK 99654,

tel: (907) 373-1212. email: mwheeler@ustravelak.com website:http//www.ustravelak.c om

Sitka Tours. During ferry port stop or a day in Sitka, visit Sitka totem park, Sitka National Historical Park, Sheldon Jackson Museum and Russian Cathedral. PO Box 1000, Sitka, AK 99835, tel: (907) 747-8443.

Skagway Street Car Company. Take an historical tour of the city in a vintage touring car from the 1930s with guides dressed in turn-of-the-century attire. PO Box 400, Skagway, AK 99840 tel: (907) 983-2908.

Southeast Tours. Two-and-a-half-hour land tours include the Skagway Overlook, a Gold Rush cemetery and the US-Canadian border. Harbor cruises fishing charters, river float trips, horseback riding and dogsledding are also available. PO Box 637, Skagway, AK 99840, tel: (907) 983-2990.

Tour Arctic. Guided sightseeing, traditional Eskimo cultural activities, midnight sun and Arctic tundra tours in and around Kotzebue. PO Box 49, Kotzebue, AK 99752, tel: (907) 442-3301.

Trans-Arctic Circle Treks. Highway treks in Alaska, including the Dalton Highway between Fairbanks and Prudhoe Bay. 4825 Glasgow Dr., Fairbanks, AK 99709, tel: (907) 479-5451, fax (US only) (800) 479-8908.

Tundra Tours. Experience Inupiat Eskimo culture, the Arctic Ocean and the midnight sun. Summertime at the northernmost point in America. Cultural program includes Eskimo arts and crafts. PO Box 189, Barrow,

AK 99723,
tel: (907) 852-3900 or
(800) 882-8478.

Van Go Custom Tours.
Visit Native villages.
PO Box 81914,
Fairbanks, AK 99708,
tel: (907) 235-5431.

Viking Travel, Inc.
Bookings on Luxury and Explorer
class cruise ships, ferries and
cruise tour itineraries available.
Individual trip planning.
101 N. Nordic, PO Box 787,
Petersburg, AK 99833,
tel: (800) 327-2571 or
(907) 772-3818.

**White Pass & Yukon Route
Railroad.** Built 1898–1900
during the Klondike Gold Rush,
the railroad takes passengers on
day excursions past sheer rock
cliffs and through solid granite
tunnels to White Pass Summit.
PO Box 435-B, Skagway,
AK 99840,
tel: (907) 983-2217,
(800) 343-7373;
e-mail: info@whitepass.net
website: http://
www.whitepassrailroad.com

World Express Tours.
Travel agency and custom trip
planner organizes an array of
Alaska tours and adventure
programs including executive
and private charters, fishing
packages, rafting and sailing
programs, independent
car/motorhome packages,
mountaineering and hiking trips.
200 W. 34th Avenue, Suite 412,
Anchorage, AK 99503,
tel: (800) 544-2235;
website: http://
worldexpresstour.com.

Yukon River Tours.
The Koyukon Athabascans of
Stevens Village invite you to
experience and understand the
natural world and learn Native
customs.
214 Second Ave.,
Fairbanks, AK 99701,
tel: (907) 452-7162.

Cruises

Alaska Cruises.
Cruises to Misty Fjords National
Monument and on the Ketchikan
harbor. Also available, kayaker
transportation.
PO Box 7814, Ketchikan,
AK 99901,
tel: (907) 225-6044,
(800) 228-1905;
website: http://
www.ptialaska.net/~akcruise.

**Alaska Glacier Bay Tours and
Cruises.** Operates day boat and
small-ship cruises to the glaciers
and wildlife of Glacier Bay
National Park.
520 Pike St., Suite 1400,
Seattle, WA 98101,
tel: (206) 623-2417,
(800) 451-5952;
website: http://
www.glacierbaytours.com.

**Alaska Sightseeing/
Cruise West.**
Small-ship cruises on the Inside
Passage and Prince William
Sound with multi-day
motorcoach tours to Denali,
Anchorage, gold rush sites and
other destinations.
2401 Fourth Avenue,
Suite 700, Seattle, WA 98121,
tel: (206) 441-8687 or
(800) 426-7702.

Central Charters.
Wildlife tour aboard classic yacht
Danny J across Kachemak Bay
to Halibut Cove's artist
community and other custom
tours.
4241 Homer Spit Road,
Homer, AK 99603,
tel: (907) 235-7847 or
(800) 478-7847.

Frontier Adventures.
Personalized trips aboard your
own private 50-ft (15-meter)
yacht. Fishing, sightseeing,
whale watching, cruising the
Inside Passage, glacier cruises
and kayak-support trips
available. By the day or week,
maximum six guests.
PO Box 32731, Juneau,
AK 99803,
tel and fax: (907) 789-0539.

**Holland America-Westours,
Gray Line of Alaska.**
One-day and extended air, day
boat, railroad, and motorcoach
tours and cruises covering the
entire state available for
individuals and groups.
300 Elliott Ave. W.,
Seattle, WA 98119,
tel: (800) 628-2449.

Phillips' Cruises and Tours.
Six-hour, 110-mile (180-km)
cruise within protected waters of
Prince William Sound. See
whales, seals, sea otters,
porpoises, bird rookeries and as
many as 26 glaciers in College
and Harriman fjords.
519 W. Fourth Avenue, Suite
100, Anchorage, AK 99501,
tel: (907) 276-8023 or
(800) 544-0529;
website:
http//www.26glaciers.com

Portage Glacier Cruises.
Take a one-hour cruise to the
face of Alaska's most-visited
glacier on the *Ptarmigan*.
Offered through Gray Line of
Alaska.
745 W. 4th Ave, Suite 200,
Anchorage, AK 99501,
tel: (907) 283-2983.

Princess Cruises & Tours.
Alaska vacations combine Gulf
of Alaska and Inside Passage
cruises, tours aboard the
Princess Love Boats and land
tour packages.
2815 2nd Ave., Suite 400,
Seattle, WA 98121,
tel: (206) 728-4202,
(800) 835-8907.

**Prince William Sound Cruises
and Tours.**
Formerly known as Stan
Stephens Cruises, offers daily
Columbia Glacier Cruises, or
stays at their tent camp on
Growler Island, near Columbia
Glacier. Also runs trips from
Anchorage through Whittier
across the sound to Valdez.
PO Box 1297, Valdez,
AK 99686,
tel: (907) 835-4731 or
(800) 992-1297;
e-mail: ssc@alaska.net.

website:
www.princewilliamsound.com
Rainbow Tours.
On the boardwalk at Homer Spit.
Two- to six-hour boat tours
including natural history tour to
Peterson Bay and Gull Island
Bird Rookery. Hotel
accommodation in Seldovia can
be arranged. Group rates.
PO Box 1526, Homer,
AK 99603,
tel: (907) 235-7272.

Adventure Tours

Adventure Alaska Tours.
Wilderness and land excursions
include sightseeing tours, dog
sledding and bed-and-breakfast
inns. Specializes in small
groups.
PO Box 64,
Hope, AK 99605;
tel: (907) 782-3730,
(800) 365-7057,
fax: (907) 782-3725.

Alaska Adventures Unlimited.
Sport-fishing charters.
PO Box 6244,
Sitka, AK 99835,
tel: (907) 747-5576
**Alaska Passages Adventure
Cruises**.
Fishing, whale-watching,
kayaking, photography and
charters for research
expeditions.
PO Box 213,
Petersburg, AK 99833,
tel: (907) 772-3967.
Alaska Wildland Adventures.
Nationally recognized natural
history and ecotourism operator
offers outdoor-oriented trips of
varying lengths for a variety of
ages to Denali, Kenai Fjords,
Kenai River fishing and
elsewhere.
PO Box 389,
Girdwood, AK 99587,
tel: (907) 783-2928 or
(800) 334-8730;
e-mail: wildland@alaska.net.

Arctic Treks.
Wilderness backpacking and
rafting in the Brooks Range. Two-
week combination trips and
seven- to ten-day base camp
hiking trips in Gates of the Arctic
and remote Arctic National
Wildlife Refuge. Recognized
outfitters and guides used for all
programs.
PO Box 73452, Fairbanks, AK
99707,
tel: (907) 455-6502;
website: http://
www.gorp.com/arctreks.
Great Alaska Safaris.
Small-group safaris include
Denali, bear-viewing, fishing
and glaciers.
HC1 Box 218,
Sterling, AK 99672,
tel: (907) 262-4515 or
(800) 544-2261.
Log Cabin Resort and RV Park
Log cabins, campgrounds and
log house with suites. RV
hookups, rustic beach cabins

Fishing Tours

**Alaska Customized
Sportfishing/Viking Travel**.
Itineraries feature quality lodges
and guided fishing in wilderness
settings.
101 N. Nordic, PO Box 787,
Petersburg, AK 99833,
tel: (800) 327-2571 or
(907) 772-3818.
Alaska Dream Charters.
Come to Sitka Sound for king or
silver salmon and halibut fishing.
713 Katlian Ave,
Sitka, AK 99835,
tel: (907) 747-8611
Alaska Fish and Trail Unlimited.
Backpacking, fishing, river rafting
and wildlife photography in the
Brooks Range.
1177 Shypoke Drive, Fairbanks,
AK 99709,
tel: (907) 479-7630.
Website: http://
www2.polarnet.com/~aktrails.
Alaska Fishing Adventure.
Four-day/three-night guided
fishing package and sightseeing

in Misty Fjords. Excellent rates,
food and accommodations.
326 Front Street,
Ketchikan, AK 99901,
tel: (907) 225-9423,
(800) 275-9423.
Great Alaska Fish Camp.
Deluxe adventure lodge and
wilderness bear-viewing camp on
the Kenai river. Fish the world's
largest salmon, halibut and
rainbow trout. Retreat facilities.
33881 Sterling Hwy,
Sterling, AK 99672,
tel: (907) 262-4515 or
(800) 544-2261.
**Juneau Sportfishing and
Sightseeing**.
Complete fishing service
represents a fleet of 40 charter
boats. Includes bait, tackle,
license, lunch and
transportation. Charter by day,
week or month on lakes, rivers
or ocean; also whale-watching.
PO Box 20438,
Juneau, AK 99802,

tel: (907) 586-1887;
website: http://
www.alaska.net/~suparna.
Sea Hunter Charters.
Sport-fishing, hunting and
sightseeing in Prince William
Sound. Minimum four-day
trips.Food and tackle provided.
PO Box 621, Eagle River,
AK99577,
tel: (907) 694-2229.
Silver Fox Charters.
Sport-fishing for halibut in
Kachemek Bay. Radio-equipped
fiberform boats, maximum six
per boat. Gear and bait
furnished.
PO Box 402,
Homer, AK 99603,
tel: (907) 235-8792 or
(800) 478-8792.
Sportfishing Alaska. Fishery
biologist creates personalized
fishing vacations.
1401 Shore Drive, Anchorage,
AK99515-3206, tel: (907) 344-
8674.

with modern kitchens and baths. Outboards, skiffs, canoes for fishing in rivers, lakes and saltwater for salmon or halibut. Licensed charters. Canoeing, hiking, bird- and whale-watching, and photography.
PO Box 54, Klawock,
AK 99925,
tel: (907) 755-2205 or
(800) 544-2205.

Nunivak Island Guide Service.
Wilderness trips include beach-combing, sport-fishing, musk ox sport hunting and wildlife viewing on the Nunivak National Wildlife Range.
PO Box 31, Mekoryuk,
AK 99630,
tel: (907) 827-8213,
(888) 223-2289.

Sourdough Outfitters.
Guided and unguided wilderness trips in the Brooks Range. The oldest outfitting business in the Arctic offers canoe, raft and kayak trips, and backpacking throughout the Brooks Range; plus dog sled, cross-country ski and snow-machine trips; raft and canoe rentals.
PO Box 90,
Bettles, AK 99726,
tel: (907) 692-5252;
website: http://
www.sourdoughoutfitters.com

Travel Wild Expeditions.
Natural history tours and wildlife viewing, photography and scenery in Katmei, Denali National Park and the Inside Passage.
PO Box 1637, Vashon Island,
WA 98070,
tel: (206) 463-5362 or
(800) 368-0077,
fax: (206) 463-5484.

Wilderness Alaska.
Brooks Range backpacking and river trips. Customized and scheduled trips throughout the Brooks Range, and sea kayaking trips in Prince William Sound. Special focus on wilderness skills and field biology unique to the high Arctic.
PO Box 113063,
Anchorage, AK 99511,

tel: (907) 345-3567.

Wilderness Alaska-Mexico.
Guided backpacking, kayaking and rafting adventures in the Arctic National Wildlife Refuge, Gates of the Arctic and Arrigetch Peaks areas and on the Noatak and Kobuk rivers.
1231 Sundance Loop,
Fairbanks, AK 99709,
tel: (907) 479-8203.

Kayaking/River Trips

ABEC's **Alaska Adventures**.
Wilderness adventures on the rivers of Alaska. Rafting, kayaking and canoeing trips ranging from wild water to relaxing float trips. Specializes in the Brooks Range.
1550 Alpine Vista Court,
Fairbanks, AK 99712,
tel: (907) 457-8907;
fax: (907) 457-6689.
email: abec@polarnet.com.

Alaska Discovery Wilderness Adventures.
Wilderness tours by raft, kayak, and canoe. Also one-day bear-watching at Pack Creek. Completely outfitted expeditions into Glacier Bay, Admiralty Island, Hubbard Glacier and all of Southeast Alaska. Also expeditions to the Noatak River in the Gates of the Arctic National Park and the Kongaut River in the Arctic National Wildlife Refuge. Group size limited.
5449 Shaune Dr., Ste. 4
Juneau, AK 99801,
tel: (907) 780-6226 or
(800) 586-1911;
website: http://
www.akdiscovery.com

Alaska Outback Expeditions.
Explore the Patterson or Stikine rivers or LeConte Glacier by raft, sea kayak or boat. Whale-watching in Glacier Bay and all-Alaska wilderness/wildlife itineraries also available.
101 N. Nordic, PO Box 787,
Petersburg, AK 99833,
tel: (800) 327-2571 or
(907) 772-3818.

Alaska Rivers Company.
Scenic or whitewater raft trips and float fishing on the upper Kenai River.
PO Box 827, Cooper Landing, AK 99572,
tel: (907) 595-1226.

Alaska Whitewater.
One-day and extended raft trips in the Alaska wilderness; also raft rentals.
PO Box 142294,
Anchorage, AK 99514,
tel: (907) 337-7238 or
(800) 337-7238.

Auk Ta Shaa Discovery.
Half-day and full-day guided float in large rubber rafts and kayak trips. Mixture of rapids and calm water; for all ages.
76 Egan Drive,
Juneau, AK 99801,
tel: (907) 586-8687 or (800) 820-2628.

Chilkat Guides.
Half-day river cruise in the heart of the Chilkat Bald Eagle Preserve and upper Chilkat River. Snack included. Multi-day raft trips also available.
PO Box 170,
Haines, AK 99827,
tel: (907) 766-2491.

Coastal Kayaking and Custom Adventures Worldwide.
Kayak in Kenai Fjords National Park, Prince William Sound and Resurrection Bay. Year-round trips available all over the world.
414 K Street,
Anchorage, AK 99501,
tel: (907) 258-3866,
(800) 288-3134;
website: http://
www. alaskan.com/kayak.

Denali Raft Adventures.
Two-hour, four-hour, full-day and overnight raft trips. Mild water or whitewater, oared or paddle boats, on the Nenana River, which forms the eastern border of Denali National Park.
Drawer 190, Denali National Park, AK 99755,
tel: (907) 683-2234.

Keystone Raft and Kayak Adventures, Inc.
Wilderness whitewater

adventures, fishing and camping. Raft trips from two hours to two weeks. Kayak support trips and class III, IV and V kayak excursions. PO Box 1486, Valdez, AK 99686, tel: (907) 835-2606 or (800) 328-8460, website: http://www.alaskawhitewater.com.

McKinley Raft Tours.
Float the western boundary of Denali National Park on the Nenana River. Great whitewater, beautiful scenery and wildlife viewing. Mid-May through mid-September.
PO Box 138, Denali National Park, AK 99755, tel: (907) 683-2392.
fax: (907) 683-2581.
website: http://www.AlaskaOne.com/mbtours.

Ouzel Expeditions.
Guided river float trips in western AK and Brooks Range. Fishing trips, scenic float trips on whitewater and calm rivers. Superb fishing for salmon, grayling and trout. Custom-tailored tours.
PO Box 935, Girdwood, AK 99587, tel: (907) 783-2216 or (800) 825-8196.

Rock Rest Adventures.
Guided canoeing and sea kayaking adventures using low-impact camping methods. Emphasizing natural history interpretation and conservation. 747 Rock Rest Rd., Pittsboro, NC 27312; tel: (919) 542-5502.
Website: http://www.minspring.com/~rockrest.

Southeast Exposure.
Guided sea-kayaking trips through local waters, Misty Fjords National Monument or Barrier Islands. Rental, instruction and sales.
PO Box 9143, Ketchikan, AK 99901, tel: (907) 225-8829.

Tongass Kayak Adventures/Viking Travel.

Day trips, base camps and week-long sea-kayak explorations on Alaska's Inside Passage.
101 N. Nordic, PO Box 787, Petersburg, AK 99833, tel: (907) 772-4600.

Worldwide Adventures
Float Alaska's spectacular rivers, hike remote wilderness areas and view wildlife.
PO Box 220204, Anchorage, AK 99522, tel: (907) 349-2964.

Yukon River Tours.
River charters into Arctic National Wildlife Refuge via Porcupine River. Cruise the mighty Yukon River from Circle City to Fort Yukon. Native Alaskan guides and owners.
PO Box 221, Fort Yukon, AK 99740, tel: (907) 452-7162 or tel: (0800) 820-2628.

Hiking Tours

Alaska-Denali Guiding.
Five- to eight-day wilderness hiking trips, 24-day Denali expeditions and other climbs within Denali National Park. Hiking and cross-country skiing.
PO Box 566, Talkeetna, AK 99676, tel: (907) 733-2649
Website: http://www.alaska.net/~adg/.

Skiing Tours

Alyeska Resort.
Year-round resort 40 miles (64 km) southeast of Anchorage on Seward Highway. Six chair lifts and tram, night skiing, condominium accommodation and luxury hotel with convention facilities, restaurant, lounge, swimming pool, exercise room and hot tub with a view of the mountain. There's also a day lodge, ski school, alpine and telemark skiing, ski rental and repair, ski shops and ice skating; dog sledding and sleigh rides can be arranged. Summer sightseeing tram lift ride.

Biking Tours

Alaskan Bicycle Adventures.
Fully supported bike tours of Alaska and Canada's Yukon Territory. Packages include meals, lodging, support van, bicycle rental, Alaska Railroad, glacier cruises, river rafting and canoeing.
907E. Dowling Rd., No 29, Anchorage, AK 99518, tel: (907) 243-2329 or (800) 770-7242;
website: http://www.alaskabike.com

Sockeye Cycle Co.
Tours range from two hours to nine days around Haines, Skagway and the Yukon. Full-service shop offers mountain bike sales, repairs and rentals.
PO Box 829, Haines, AK 99827, tel: (907) 766-2869 in Haines or (907) 983-2851 in Skagway.

1000 Arlberg Avenue, PO Box 249, Girdwood, AK 99587, tel: (907) 754-1111 or (800) 880-3880.

Eaglecrest Ski Area.
Twelve miles (19 km) from downtown Juneau, there's a base lodge, food service, rental shop, ski school, mountain facilities, two chairlifts, one surface lift and mountain-top warming hut. Winter offers 640 acres (259 hectares) of alpine/nordic skiing and 40 acres (16 hectares) of snow-making (where machines produce snow during periods of low snowfall). Bus service weekends and holidays only.
155 S. Seward, Juneau, AK 99801, tel: (907) 586-5284.

Special Interest

Alaska Hunting & Fishing Ventures.
Charters for halibut and salmon. Guided hunts for big game. Overnight fishing trips include

tackle, bait and fish cleaning.
PO Box 813,
Homer, AK 99603,
tel: (907) 235-7427.
Alaska Outdoor Services.
Guided fishing trips.
PO Box 1066,
Soldotna, AK 99669,
tel: (907) 262 4589 or
(888) 434-7425,
fax: (907) 262-4042.
Alaska Sled Dog Racing Association.
During winter months, sled dog races are held every Saturday and Sunday at Tudor Road race track. Teams from all over AK and the world gather for these events. Spectators are very welcome.
PO Box 110569, Anchorage, AK 99510-0569,
tel: (907) 562-2235.
Alaska Wilderness Sailing and Kayaking
Owners Jim and Nancy Lethcoe, authors of two guide books on Prince William Sound, offer half-day and custom kayak trips from Growler Island near Columbia Glacier. They also run custom sailing trips.
PO Box 1313,
Valdez, AK 99686,
tel: (907) 835-5175
website:
http://alaskawilderness.com
Center for Alaskan Coastal Studies.
Environmental education and research field trips studying the marine and coastal ecosystems of Kachemak Bay; beach and coastal rainforest studies.
PO Box 2225,
Homer, AK 99603,
tel: (907) 235-6667.
Crow Creek Mine.
Historic gold mining building with artifacts near bird wood, now on National Register of Historic Places. Open to tourists to pan for gold – equipment supplied and gold guaranteed. Gold also on sale in shop. Overnight camping. Groups of up to 200 people.
Tel: (907) 278-8060.

Dig Afognak
Koniag native-owned business offers six-day professionally led archeological digs at remote sites on Kodiak Island.
215 Mission Road,
Kodiak, AK 99615
tel: (907) 486-6014 or (800) 770-6104.
Eclipse Alaska.
Personalized guiding service for professional photographers, videographers and film-makers in Southeast Alaska and the Alaska Chilkat Bald Eagle Preserve. Reservations required.
310–16 Main St. Box 689,
Haines, AK 99827-0689,
tel: (907) 766-2670.
Joseph Van Os Photo Safaris.
Wildlife photography tours for beginners to professionals.
PO Box 655,
Vashon Island, WA 98070,
tel: (206) 463-5383,
fax: (206) 463-5484.
Website: http://www.photosafaris.com.
Sound Sailing.
Sail the protected waters of Southeast Alaska. Watch eagles soar, whales breach and icebergs calve from fully equipped 42-ft (13-meter) sailboats.
231 Raft Island Drive E.,
Gig Harbor, WA 98335,
tel: (253) 265-3972.
Tak Outfitters.
Horse pack trips in the rugged Kenai mountains.
PO Box 66,
Moose Pass, AK 99631,
tel and fax: (907) 288-3640.
Wilderness Birding Adventures.
Bird-watching throughout the state, especially in the Brooks Range and Bering Strait.
PO Box 103747,
Anchorage, AK 99510-3747,
tel: (907) 694-7442.

Tourist Information

Anchorage Convention and Visitors Bureau,
524 W. 4th Ave.,

Vacation Planner

One of Alaska's major industries is tourism, so the visitor will find information easily accessible. To help in trip preparation, the Alaska State Division of Tourism annually publishes the Alaska Vacation Planner. It is a booklet crammed with facts about Alaska and a directory of where to stay, eat and tour. To obtain a free copy write to the Alaska Division of Tourism, PO Box 110801,
Juneau, Alaska 99811,
tel: (907) 465-2012;
fax: (907) 465-5442.
Most communities also have visitor information centers and local chambers of commerce which provide specific details on their areas. Write for advance or call in information can be received in advance by writing or in person when visiting the area.

Anchorage, AK 99501,
tel: (907) 276-4118,
fax: (907) 278-5559.
Fairbanks Visitor Information Center,
550 First Ave.,
Fairbanks, AK 99701,
tel: (907) 456-5774 or (800) 327-5774.
Haines Visitor Center,
PO Box 530,
Haines, AK, 99827,
tel: (907) 766-2234 or (800) 458-3579,
fax: (907) 766-3155;
website: http://www.haines.AK.us
Juneau Visitor and Convention Center,
134 Third St.,
Juneau, AK 99801,
tel: (907) 586-2201.
Kodiak Island Convention and Visitors Bureau,
100 Marine Way,
Kodiak, AK 99615,
tel: (907) 486-4782.

**Kenai Visitors and
Cultural Center,**
11471 Kenai Spur Highway,
Kenai, AK 99611,
tel: (907) 283-1991.
Ketchikan Visitors Bureau,
131 Front St.,
Ketchikan, AK 99901,
tel: (907) 225-6166,
(800) 770-3300,
fax: (907) 225-4250;
website: http://www.ktn.net
**Mat-Su Convention
and Visitors Bureau,**
HC01 Box 6166J-21,
Palmer, AK 99645,
tel: (907) 746-5000.
**Nome Convention
and Visitors Bureau,**
PO Box 240,
Nome, AK 99762,
tel: (907) 443-5535;
website: http://
www.nomealaska.org
**Petersburg Visitor
Information Center,**
PO Box 649,
Petersburg, AK 99833,
tel: (907) 772-4636.
**Sitka Convention
and Visitors Bureau,**
PO Box 1226,
Sitka, AK 99835,
tel: (907) 747-5940;
website: http://
www.sitka.org
**Skagway Convention and
Visitors Bureau,**
PO Box 415,
Skagway, AK 99840,
tel: (907) 983-2854,
(888) 762-1898;
website: http://
www.skagway.org
**Southeast Alaska
Tourism Council,**
PO Box 20710,
Juneau, AK 99802,
tel: (907) 586-4777 or
(800) 423-0568.
**Valdez Convention and
Visitors Bureau,**
PO Box 1603,
Valdez, AK 99686,
tel: (907) 835-2984 or
(800) 770-5954;
website: http://
www.alaska.net/~valdezak

Wrangell Visitor Center,
PO Box 49,
Wrangell, AK 99929,
tel: (907) 874-3901 or
(800) 367-9745.

Chambers of Commerce

**Anchorage Chamber
of Commerce,**
441 W. Fifth Ave., #300,
Anchorage, AK 99501,
tel: (907) 272-2401;
website: http://
www.anchoragechamber.org
**Anchor Point Chamber
of Commerce,**
PO Box 610,
Anchor Point, AK 99556
tel: (907) 235-2600.
website: http://xyz.net/~apcoc
Barrow Chamber of Commerce,
PO Box 629,
Barrow, AK 99723
tel: (907) 852-5211.
Bethel Chamber of Commerce,
PO Box 329,
Bethel, AK 99559
tel: (907) 543-2911.
**Cordova Chamber of
Commerce,**
PO Box 99,
Cordova, AK 99574,
tel: (907) 424-7260.
**Delta Junction Chamber
of Commerce,**
PO Box 987,
Delta Junction, AK 99737,
tel: (907) 895-5068.
**Greater Fairbanks
Chamber of Commerce,**
250 Cushman St., Suite 2D,
Fairbanks, AK 99701-4665,
tel: (907) 452-1105,
fax (907) 456-6968.
**Greater Ketchikan
Chamber of Commerce,**
PO Box 5957,
Ketchikan, AK 99901,
tel: (907) 225-3184,
fax: (907) 225-3187.
**Greater Palmer Chamber of
Commerce & Visitor Center,**
PO Box 45,
Palmer, AK 99645,
tel: (907) 745-2880.
Haines Chamber of Commerce,
PO Box 1449,

Haines, AK 99827,
tel: (907) 766-2202,
fax: (907) 766-2271.
Homer Chamber of Commerce,
PO Box 541,
Homer, AK 99603,
tel: (907) 235-7740 or
(907) 235-5300;
website: http://
www.homeralaska.org
Juneau Chamber of Commerce,
3100 Channel Drive, 300,
Juneau,
AK 99801,
tel: (907) 463-3488.
website: http://
ptialaska.net/~juneau
Kenai Chamber of Commerce,
402 Overland,
Kenai, AK 99611,
tel: (907) 283-7989.
website:
http://ptialasta.net/~juneau
Kodiak Chamber of Commerce,
PO Box 1485,
Kodiak, AK 99615,
tel: (907) 486-5557;
website: http://
www.kodiak.org
**Petersburg Chamber of
Commerce**
PO Box 649,
Petersburg, AK 99833,
tel: (907) 772-3626;
website: http://
www.petersburg.org
**Seldovia Chamber
of Commerce,**
Drawer F,
Seldovia, AK 99663,
tel: (907) 234-7612.
Seward Chamber of Commerce,
PO Box 749,
Seward, AK 99664,
tel: (907) 224-8051.
website:
http://seward.net/chamber
**Greater Sitka Chamber
of Commerce,**
PO Box 638,
Sitka, AK 99835,
tel: (907) 747-8604.
**Greater Soldotna
Chamber of Commerce,**
44790 Sterling Highway,
Soldotna, AK 99669,
tel: (907) 262-1337;
website: http://

Dog Mushing

Dog mushing is the state sport and sled dog races are held throughout much of the state in the winter. The best known race is the internationally acclaimed **Iditarod Trail Sled Dog Race** (tel: 907 376-5155). It starts on the first Saturday in March from Anchorage. The trail covers more than 1,100 miles (1,770 km) to Nome, crossing vast tracts of wilderness and some of the most rugged country on the continent. Generally mushers arrive in Nome within two weeks; the current record is nine days. Other sled dog races are held in Fairbanks, Tok, Delta Junction and Nome.

www.soldotnachamber.com
**Wrangell Chamber
of Commerce**,
PO Box 49,
Wrangell, AK 99929,
tel: (907) 874-3901.
website:
http://www.wrangell.com

Special Events

Public Holidays & Festivals
Alaska celebrates all the traditional and official US holidays. In addition, there are many unusual festivals occurring year-round within the state. Some are created purely for amusement, while others are part of the cultural heritage.

Winter festivals are popular in Alaska. The largest is the **Fur Rendezvous**, held in Anchorage. It starts on the second Friday in February and lasts 10 days with more than 150 events. A highlight of the event is the **World Championship Sprint Sled Dog Race**. Homer also celebrates a winter carnival in February and the **North Pole Winter Carnival** is held in March and in Valdez the World Extreme

Skiing Championship draws the world's most daring skiers. It's held the last week of march or early April.

For a rare opportunity to observe the rich Native culture, visitors can attend the **Savoonga Walrus Festival** held on St Lawrence Island in May. This is not a tourist event, it is traditionally Eskimo. In June, Nalukataq (**Whaling Feast**) is celebrated in Barrow by the Eskimo community.

Other festivals are held tongue in cheek and for pure fun. Swimmers take to the icy waters of the Bering Sea in Nome for the annual **Polar Bear Swim** in May and locals join in the **Moose Dropping Festival** held in Talkeetna in July.

Dates change annually, so make sure you have a current schedule from the Alaska Division of Tourism, PO Box 110801, Juneau, AK 99811, tel: (907) 465-2010.

Annual Events

(National holidays in bold)
January
New Year's Day (1st)
Martin Luther King's Birthday (15th)
Klondike 300 Sled Dog Race, Big Lake
Knik 200 Sled Dog Race, Knik
Polar Bear Jump Off Festival, Seward
Russian New Year and Masquerade Ball, Kodiak

Willow Winter Carnival, Willow

February
President's Day (3rd Monday)
(formerly Lincoln/Washington's birthday)
Cordova Ice Worm Festival, Cordova
Festival of the North, Ketchikan
Fur Rendezvous, Anchorage
Gold Rush Classic Snowmachine Race, Wasilla to Nome
Tent City Festival, Wrangell
Winterfest, King Salmon and Naknek
Yukon Quest International Sled Dog Race, Fairbanks to Whitehorse

March
Seward's Day (last Monday)
Alaska Folk Festival, Juneau
Bering Sea Ice Golf Classic, Nome
Nenana Ice Classic Tripod Weekend, Nenana
Iditarod Basketball Tournament, Nome
Iditarod Trail Sled Dog Race, Anchorage to Nome
North Pole Winter Carnival and International Sled Dog Race, North Pole
Pillar Mountain Golf Classic, Kodiak
Winter Carnival, Fairbanks
Winter Carnival, Valdez
World Ice Art Championships, Fairbanks

April
Alyeska Spring Carnival, Girdwood

Eskimo-Indian Olympics

In July, the **World Eskimo-Indian Olympics** are held in Fairbanks. Eskimos compete in 25 different events requiring the strength, speed and endurance that they have been practising for generations. These games help keep the people both physically and mentally fit.

Events include the One-Foot-High Kick, which involves the contestant hopping in the air, kicking a target and landing on the same foot. The Arm Pull is a display of strength using the same muscles that are needed to haul in seals or whales – contestants lock arms facing each other, then try to make the other straighten his arm.

(*See Insight on Eskimo-Indian Olympics, page 256.*)

Arctic Man Ski & Sno-go Classic,
Mile 196 Richardson Highway
Copper River Shorebird Festival,
Cordova

May
Annual Dart Tournament and
Golf Classic, Copper Valley
Kodiak Crab Festival, Kodiak
Little Norway Festival,
Petersburg
Polar Bear Swim, Nome
Shorebird and Wooden Boat
Festival, Homer

June
Alaska Mardi Gras, Haines
Alaska Run for Women,
Anchorage
All-Alaska Logging
Championship, Sitka
Colony Days, Palmer
Dyea to Dawson Race
Kenai River Festival, Kenai
Mayor's Midnight Sun Marathon,
Anchorage
Midnight Sun Festival and
Softball Tournament, Nome
Midnight Sun Run, Fairbanks
Sitka Summer Music Festival,
Sitka
Summer Solstice, Statewide

July
Independence Day (4th)
Bear Paw Festival,
Chugiak/Eagle River
Big Lake Regatta, Big Lake
Fairbanks Summer Arts Festival,
Fairbanks
Girdwood Forest Faire, Girdwood
Golden Days, Fairbanks
Moose Dropping Festival,
Talkeetna
Mount Marathon Race, Seward
Soapy Smith's Wake, Skagway
Stewart/Hyder International
Rodeo, Stewart, Hyder
World Eskimo-Indian Olympics,
Fairbanks

August
Alaska State Fair, Palmer
Bald Eagle Music Festival &
Triathalon, Haines
Blueberry Arts Festival,
Ketchikan
Kenai Peninsula State Fair,

Ninilchik
Southeast Alaska State Fair,
Haines
State Fair and Rodeo, Kodiak
Tanana Valley State Fair,
Fairbanks
Tundra Valley Golf Classic,
Unalaska

September
Labor Day (1st Monday)
Equinox Marathon, Fairbanks
Klondike Trail of '98 Road Relay,
Skagway and Whitehorse
Kodiak State Fair and Rodeo,
Kodiak
Seward Silver Salmon Run,
Seward

October
Alaska Day (3rd Monday)
Alaska Day Festival, Sitka
Oktoberfest, Anchorage
Seafood Fest and Humpy 500
Go-Cart Race, Petersburg

November
Veterans' Day (2nd Monday)
Thanksgiving (4th Thursday)
Athabascan Fiddling Festival,
Fairbanks
Community Christmas Festival,
Cordova
Festival of Lights, Ketchikan
Great Alaska Shootout,
Anchorage

December
Christmas (25th)
Bachelor Society
Ball/Wilderness Women's
Contest, Talkeetna
Colony Christmas Celebration,
Palmer
Harbor Stars Boat Parade,
Kodiak
Northern Lights Invitational
basketball tournament,
Anchorage

Practical Tips

Security & Crime

Alaska is not crime-ridden, but
occasional outbursts of violence
are not unknown. Basic common
sense should be followed by all
visitors – it is better to be safe
than sorry.

Leave large amounts of
money, travelers checks, jewelry
and other valuables in the hotel
safe. Don't flaunt your money in
public or display other valuables
which could encourage a thief.
Be careful where you leave
packages, handbags and your
luggage.

Sexual assault rates are quite
high and women should not
travel alone in secluded areas
(such as wooded bike paths),
near bars or other potentially
troublesome areas. Use
common sense and avoid
dubious areas of town.

Anchorage, Fairbanks,
Juneau, Homer and Seward have
their own police departments
and most villages have public
safety officers. The Alaska State
Troopers are a professional
police force and respond to calls
in most outlying areas.

Dialing 911 will put you in
touch with a dispatcher capable
of providing the required
emergency service (police, fire
or ambulance). Be specific as to
the nature of your problem and
your location, but remember that
Alaska's vast size may mean
that help is several miles away.

Medical Services

Two major hospitals serve the
general public in Anchorage, one

in Fairbanks and another in Juneau. Additionally, there is a Native hospital in Anchorage run by the federal government. Treatment there is free for anyone who is one-quarter or more American Indian, Eskimo or Aleut. There is also a hospital on Elmendorf Air Force Base, in Anchorage, that serves military personnel and their families.

Like hospital costs all over the United States, fees in the public hospitals are terribly high. A trip to the emergency room due to an accident or serious illness can easily cost $1,000 or more. However, provisions can be made for indigent patients.

The major hospitals provide 24-hour emergency room service. Treatment is thorough and professional. Non-emergency medical care can be obtained in a doctor's office or in one of several medical clinics throughout Alaska.

Clinics typically are staffed by some combination of physicians, nurses. health aids and, occasionally, dentists. Most routine problems can be handled at a clinic. Appointments, scheduled in advance, are preferred, but walk-in patients can usually be accommodated if they are willing to wait.

Alaska Regional Hospital,
2801 DeBarr Rd., Anchorage,
tel: (907) 276-1131.
Providence Medical Center,
3200 Providence Dr.,
Anchorage,
tel: (907) 562-2211.
Alaska Native Medical Center,
4315 Diplomacy Dr., Anchorage,
tel: (907) 563-2662.
Fairbanks Memorial Hospital,
1650 Cowles, Fairbanks,
tel: (907) 452-8181.
Bartlett Regional Hospital,
3260 Hospital Dr., Juneau,
tel: (907) 586-2611.

Pharmacies

Prescription drugs can normally be purchased at hospitals and medical clinics throughout Alaska, as well as in drugstores and grocery stores with pharmacies. If you require prescription medication after hours, most hospital or clinic emergency rooms can supply enough to meet requirements until the next business day.

Business Hours

Government offices are normally open from 8am to 4.30pm Monday through Friday, with banks generally open from 10am to 5pm and, in some cases, during limited hours on Saturday. Except for necessary public services, most government offices and businesses are closed on public holidays. Retailers, especially in peak summer months, are the exception and are often open seven days a week with hours well into the evening.

Tipping

Tipping for service is pretty similar to the rest of the world. Airport skycaps usually receive $1 for the first bag and 50 cents for each additional bag. (Don't expect skycap service outside of Anchorage.) Similar tips are appropriate for bellhops in the larger hotels.

Waiters and waitresses normally receive about 15 percent of the bill. Tipping as high as 20 percent for restaurant service shows you thought the attention excellent in all respects. Tips are inappropriate in most fast-food restaurants and cafeterias. Bartenders should get 10 to 15 percent of the bill depending on the quality of service. If service is shoddy or the person performing the service is ill-mannered, no tip is necessary.

Media

Alaskans are kept informed by a mix of local newspapers (ranging from serious broadsheets to gossip rags), television networks and radio stations.

Newspapers

The three major daily newspapers published in Alaska are the *Juneau Empire*, the *Anchorage Daily News* and the *Fairbanks Daily News-Miner*.

Many smaller communities also put out newspapers and, in most cases, are not afraid to tackle important or controversial local issues. For native issues, the *Tundra Drums* (Bethel) is a good source of information and editorials.

Bookstores and variety stores normally have one or more of the major dailies available for sale. In large cities, Seattle newspapers, the *New York Times* and the *Wall Street Journal* are normally available in bookstores and large grocery stores.

Radio & Television

Some commercial radio stations in Alaska are still used to pass on messages to residents living in the bush. Regularly scheduled times are set aside for transmitting everything from messages of endearment to doctors' appointments.

The major radio networks have affiliates in all the larger cities, and most towns or villages of any consequence will have a locally-owned radio station. Quality varies from excellent to horrible.

The vast majority of radio programs are broadcast in English, though many of the public stations also offer a limited number of programs in Spanish, Russian or the Native dialect that is spoken in a particular village or region.

Only Anchorage has enough stations to affiliate actively with the four major television networks. These are CBS, Channel 11; ABC, Channel 13; NBC, Channel 2; and Fox Network, Channel 4. Other major cities will have one station or more, loosely affiliated with one of the networks, but usually offering a spread of programs from all three of the major networks along with a variety of locally produced shows. Public television (or "educational" television) is available in most of the state.

Again, the vast majority of television programs are transmitted in English, although a number of local or regional shows may be broadcast in the area's Native dialect. Most of these programs are on public television.

In the last few years, with the growing use of satellite communications equipment, even the most rural areas have gained access to television through the Alaska Rural Communications Services (ARCS).

Telecommunications

Telephones and Telegrams

Public telephones can be found almost everywhere – hotel lobbies, stores, restaurants, bars, etc. Local calls cost from 15 to 25 cents.

Check the directory or dial 411 for local numbers. Information on telephone listings anywhere in the state can be obtained by dialing 1-907-555-1212. Information for other states and Canada can be obtained by dialing 1, followed by the appropriate three-digit area code and then 555-1212. The three-digit area code for all telephone exchanges within Alaska is 907.

To send a telegram via Western Union, call toll free, tel: (800) 325-6000.

Cell phones can be used in most major communities, such as Barrow, Fairbanks, Tok, Valdez, Anchorage , Cordova, Juneau and Whittier. Check with your cell phone provider before arriving in Alaska.

Getting Around

By Air

The secret to conquering Alaska's vastness is air travel. Commuter airlines and charter aircraft services are everywhere. More often than not, even the most remote cabins in the wilderness have some sort of airstrip nearby, or a stretch of hard-packed sand on a river bar to serve as a landing strip.

Per capita, six times as many Alaskans have a pilot's license as do residents of the rest of the country.

Charter aircraft are available for those who don't wish to wait for regular, scheduled flights to remote destinations, or for those who wish to go into the middle of the wilderness.

Costs typically range from $230 to $350 an hour (flight time) to charter a pilot and plane that can carry three to seven passengers, depending on the amount of baggage. If you're traveling with a large group, it's even possible to charter a vintage DC-3, a twin-engine plane capable of hauling large loads for long distances. Also check local air taxi operators for charter and commuter service to Alaskan communities.

Following is a list of many of the carriers offering scheduled intrastate air service. Interline service is available to most rural Alaska points: check with carriers.

ANCHORAGE

It is best to consult the Anchorage *Yellow Pages* for an

Postal Services

Every community in Alaska, no matter how remote, has some sort of mail service. Cities and towns of sufficient size have one or more facilities with regular hours, usually Monday through Friday from 8.30am to 4.30pm. In Anchorage, the main post office near the international airport is open 24 hours a day, 365 days a year.

Small, remote communities only open the post office window when the mail plane arrives.

Meeting the mail plane is often a social occasion in these isolated communities. The postal service can be daily, or it can be much more infrequent. Flights may also be subject to the whims of the weather.

Stamps can be purchased at all postal facilities, at many grocery stores and from vending machines in Alaska's larger cities. Generally speaking the postal service throughout the state performs reasonably efficiently.

If travel plans include an extended stay in any particular community, mail can be addressed to you at that post office, care of general delivery. You will have to go in person to collect your mail.

extensive listing of those airlines operating out of the state's largest city. The ones listed here are just a few of the key players.

Major Carriers

Alaska Airlines
tel: (800) 426-0333
Delta Airlines
tel: (800) 221-1212
Northwest Airlines
tel: (800) 225-2525
Reno Air
tel: (800) 736-6247
Local Carriers
ERA Aviation
tel: (800) 866-8394
Air Taxis
Alaska Air Taxi
tel: (907) 243 3944
Alaska Bush Carrier Inc.
tel: (907) 243-3127
Regal Air
tel: (907) 243-8535

FAIRBAMKS
Major Carriers
Alaska Airlines
tel: (800) 426-0333
Reno Air
tel: (800) 736-6247
Delta
tel: (800) 221-1212
Northwest
tel: (800) 225-2525
Local Carriers
Air North (Canada)
tel: (907) 474-3999
Frontier Flying
tel: (907) 474-0014
Larry's Flying Service
tel: (907) 474-9169
Tanana Air Service
tel: (907) 474-0301

Air Travel

Virtually every community that merits mention on the map is served by an air carrier. Most cities with a population exceeding 1,000 serve as a base for one or more commuter airline. If you know where you want to go, there's a pilot somewhere in Alaska who is prepared to take you.

Warbelow's Air
tel: (907) 474-0518
Wright's Air Service
tel: (907) 474-0502
HAINES
Local Carriers
Haines Airways
tel: (907) 766-2646
L.A.B Flying Service
tel: (800) 426-0543
Wings of Alaska
tel: (907) 766-2030

HOMER
Local Carriers
ERA Aviation
tel: (800) 866-8394
Homer Air
tel: (907) 235-8591

JUNEAU
Major Carrier
Alaska Airlines
tel: (800) 866-8394
Local Carriers
Haines Airways
tel: (907) 789-2336
L.A.B. Flying Service
tel: (800) 426-0543
Loken Aviation
tel: (907) 789-3331
Wings of Alaska
tel: (907) 789-0790
Helicopter Services
Costal Helicopters
tel: (907) 789-5600
ERA Aviation
tel: (907) 586-2030
Temsco Helicopters
tel: (907) 789-9501

KENAI
Local Carriers
ERA Aviation
tel: (800) 866-8394
Yute Air
tel: (907) 283-7757 or
(888) 359-9883

KETCHIKAN
Major Carrier
Alaska Airlines
tel: (800) 426-0333
Local Carriers
Ketchikan Air Service
tel: (907) 225-6608
Promech Air
tel: (907) 225-3845

Taquan Air
tel: (800) 770-8800

KODIAK
Major Carrier
Alaska Airlines
tel: (800) 426-0333
Local Carriers
ERA Aviation
tel: (800) 866-8394
PenAir
tel: (800) 448-4226

NOME
Major Carrier
Alaska Airlines
tel: (800) 426-0333
Local Carriers
Bering Air
tel: (907) 443-5464
Cape Smythe Air
tel: (907) 443-2414
Frontier Flying
tel: (907) 474-0014
Yute Air
tel: (907) 283-7757

PETERSBURG
Major Carrier
Alaska Airlines
tel: (800) 426-0333
Local Carriers
L.A.B Flying Service
tel: (800) 426-0543
Taquan Air
tel: (800) 770-8800

SEWARD
Local Carrier
ERA Aviation
tel: (800) 866-8394

SITKA
Major Carrier
Alaska Airlines
tel: (800) 426-0333
Local Carriers
L.A.B. Flying Service
tel: (800) 426-0543
Mountain Aviation
tel: (907) 966-2288
Taquan Air
tel: (907) 747-8636 or
(800) 770-8800

SKAGWAY
Local Carrier
L.A.B Flying Service

Railroads

In addition to the Alaska Railroad, which offers travel between Seward and Fairbanks, there is one other railroad in operation – the White Pass & Yukon Route, out of Skagway. Service was discontinued for a few years, but the railroad is now back in operation. The ride is a must for visitors to Skagway.

This historic railway was started in the days of the mad rush to the Klondike in 1898.

Passenger cars, some of which are authentic 1890s models, are pulled for the first part of all trips by an authentic steam engine. Some of the longer excursions have steam power the whole way. On clear days, the ride is breathtaking as the train climbs along the gray rock cliffs and travels over a trestle which spans a gorge over a narrow box canyon, finishing at the top of the treeless alpine pass that was once the

gateway to the gold fields.

Take the summit excursion to White Pass or scheduled through service to Fraser, BC, where passengers connect with a motorcoach to Whitehorse, Yukon Territory.

For more information, contact White Pass & Yukon Route, PO Box 435-B, Skagway, AK, 99840, tel: (907) 983-2217 or (800) 343-7373; website: http:// www.whitepassrailroad.com

tel: (800) 426-0543
Skagway Sir Service
tel: (907) 983-2218
Wings of Alaska
tel: (907) 983-2442

VALDEZ
Local Carrier
Alaska Aerial Tours
(in Anchorage)
tel: (907) 248-6898
ERA Aviation
tel: (800) 866-8394
Ketchum Air Service
tel: (800) 433-9114

WRANGELL
Major Carrier
Alaska Airlines
tel: (800) 426-0333
Local Carriers
Sunrise Aviation
tel: (907) 874-2319
Taquan Air
tel: (800) 770-8800
Temsco Helicopter
tel: (907) 874-2010

Water Transportation

Besides sailing from Seattle to southeastern Alaska, the Alaska Marine Highway operates several vehicle and passenger ferries on the gulf coast. Seward, Homer, and Whittier on the Kenai Peninsula are connected to the Prince William Sound communities of Valdez and Cordova via the ferries. It's

also possible to sail from Homer to Kodiak Island and onward to several Aleutian destinations. Check at the ferry office near the harbor if you're in any of the towns along the route, or get information in advance from the Alaska Marine Highway, PO Box 25535, Juneau, AK 99802, tel: (907) 465-3941 or toll free (800) 642-0066.

Public Transportation

Most communities with any road system at all will have some form of taxi service. Taxis are nice for getting around town, but can be extremely expensive for long distances.

Private Transportation

Most major US car rental companies have offices in Alaska's larger cities and virtually all of them have a booth at Anchorage International Airport. Generally, you have to be at least 21 years old, possess a valid driver's licence and have a major credit card (Visa, MasterCard, American Express or Diner's Club) before being able to rent a car.

Shopping around with smaller companies such as Rent-A-Wreck or Rent-A-Dent can often save you money, although the automobile you get may not be

anything to brag about.

Package deals including transportation to Alaska, accommodations and a car are available from most travel agencies. Check with a travel agent if you are interested in a combination price which is probably cheaper than arranging everything yourself.

Recreational Vehicle Rentals

Renting an RV camper has become increasingly popular. There are dozens of businesses offering this service.

A & M RV Center
tel: (907) 279-5508 or (800) 478-4678
website: http//www.goRV.com
Alaskan Adventures RV
tel: (907) 344-2072 or (800) 676-8911
ABC Motorhome & RV
tel: (907) 279-2000 or (800) 421-7456
website: http://www.alaskan.com/abcmotorhomes/

Motoring Advisories

The speed limit on most Alaska highways is 55 mph (88 km), although speeds of up to 65 mph (104 km) are allowed on some portions. Speed limits are lower within cities, in residential areas and especially near schools. Obey posted speed limits and you should have few problems.

A right turn is permitted against a red light unless otherwise posted, but only after you stop long enough to confirm there is no traffic with which you will interfere. All drivers in both directions are required to stop for a school bus with its warning lights operating. Drivers may not proceed around or past a school bus until the lights have been turned off.

Drivers in Alaska will see a lot of hitchhikers; it's a popular form of travel for college students and others. You pick up hitchhikers at your own risk.

Prudence dictates that you slow your speed during the winter months. Highways in Alaska are not the best in the world, and in combination with ice and snow, can be treacherous.

Where to Stay

Hotels & Motels

Accommodations in Alaska vary greatly. Larger communities offer a range of hotels, with luxury accommodations of an international standard available. Bed-and-breakfasts are also very popular across the state, with many offering outstanding service. In the very smallest communities, facilities may be mediocre or non-existent. Regardless of where you stay, the prices are likely to seem high, especially during peak summer months.

During 1997 and 1998, Anchorage experienced a boom in hotel construction, with new facilities built near the airport, downtown, midtown and on the east side. Many of the new hotels offer relatively lower rates but with few extras, such as full-service restaurants or conference facilities.

Rates given here are for standard double rooms during peak summer months. Rates during the off-season are considerably lower.

For more information about bed-and-breakfast accommodations, write **Alaska Private Lodgings/ Stay With A Friend**, 704 W. 2nd Avenue, Anchorage, AK 99501, tel: (907) 258-1717.

The Alaska Division of Tourism has an extensive list of accommodations throughout the state in the Alaska Vacation Planner. For this free booklet contact Alaska Division of Tourism, PO Box 110801, Juneau, AK 99811, tel: (907) 465-2010.

ANCHORAGE

Best Western Barratt Inn, 4616 Spenard Rd, Anchorage, AK 99503, tel: (907) 243-3131. Near Spenard Lake; 217 rooms. There are four buildings in this complex; ask for the most recently renovated. Restaurant, lounge, laundry, travel services. $$$

Comfort Inn Ship Creek, 111 Ship Creek Ave., Anchorage, AK 99501, tel: (907) 277-6887, or toll free (800) 362-6887. Just north of downtown right across from the railroad tracks; 100 rooms in various configurations, some with kitchens. $$$

Hillside Motel and RV Park, 2150 Gambell St., Anchorage, AK 99503, tel: (907) 258-6006. Offers budget rooms with microwave ovens and refrigerators and is near midtown shopping malls, 24-hour restaurants and a movie theater; 26 rooms. $–$$

Hilton Anchorage Hotel, 500 W. 3rd Ave., Anchorage, AK 99501, Tel: (907) 272-7411 or (800) 245-2527. Downtown Anchorage; 591 rooms, recently renovated, which include data ports and voice mail. Two restaurant/lounges, gift shops, travel office. $$$$

Holiday Inn Anchorage/Downtown , 239 W. 4th Ave., Anchorage, AK 99501. tel: 800-holiday. tel: (907) 279-8671 Completely renovated by new owners in 1998; 251 rooms. Pools, restaurant, lounge, exercise room, laundry. $$$

Hotel Captain Cook, 5th Avenue and K St, Anchorage, AK 99501,

tel: (907) 276-6000 or toll free (800) 843-1950.
Among Anchorage's finest; offers rooms with either mountain or inlet views; 547 rooms. Restaurants, lounges, coffee shop, several gift shops, athletic club with pool. $$$$

Inlet Tower Suites,
1200 L St.,
Anchorage, AK 99501,
tel: (907) 276-0110 or (800) 544-0786.
Condo-style rooms with fully equipped kitchens six blocks south of downtown; 180 suites. Saunas, beauty salon, laundromat. $$–$$$

The Northern Lights Hotel,
598 W. Northern Lights Blvd.,
Anchorage, AK 99503,
tel: (907) 561-5200.
In midtown; 148 rooms. Restaurant, brew pub with satellite and sports TV. $$$

Regal Alaskan Hotel,
4800 Spenard Rd.,
Anchorage, AK 99517,
tel: (907) 243-2300 (800) 544-0784.
Near airport on scenic Lake Spenard where float planes come and go; 248 rooms. Recently remodeled with rustic lodge motif. Lobby sports stone fireplace and trophy heads, two restaurants, lounge, patio, gift shop, exercise room. $$$$

Sheraton Anchorage,
401 E. 6th Ave.,
Anchorage, AK 99501,
tel: (907) 276-8700 (800) 325-3535.
Downtown luxury hotel with acres of cream-colored marble and winding jade staircase; 375 rooms. Restaurant, lounge, café, in-house nightly entertainment. $$$$

Snowshoe Inn,
826 K St.,
Anchorage, AK 99501,
tel: (907) 258-7669.
Family run hotel within walking distance of the downtown sights; 16 rooms. All rooms have TVs, VCRs, phones, refrigerators and microwave ovens. $$

Voyager Hotel,
501 K St., Anchorage, AK 99501, tel: (907) 277-9501 or (800) 247-9070.
A favorite with business travelers as all rooms have fully equipped kitchens, queen beds, voice mail and data ports; 38 rooms. Walking distance to downtown shops, restaurants, entertainment. $$$

Westmark Anchorage,
720 W. Fifth Ave.,
Anchorage, Alaska 99501,
tel: (907) 276-7676 or (800) 544-0970.
Dark teak furniture in rooms, which are done in blues and mauve; 200 rooms. Each has its own balcony. $$$

BARROW
Barrow Airport Inn,
1815 Momegana St., PO Box 933, Barrow, AK 99723,
tel: (907) 852-2525.
A homey atmosphere across the street from the airport. 14 rooms, all with refrigerators and microwave ovens, 9 with kitchenettes. $$$

Top of the World Hotel,
1200 Agvik St., PO Box 189, Barrow, AK 99723,
tel: (907) 852-3900 or (800) 882-8478.
The town's main accommodation and center of activities; 50 rooms with refrigerators. Adjoining restaurant. $$$

BETHEL
Kuskokwim Inn,
PO Box 888, Bethel, AK 99559,
tel: (907) 543-2207,
fax: (907) 543-2828.
39 rooms with private baths; restaurant. $$

COPPER CENTER
Copper Center Lodge,
Drawer J, Copper Center, AK 99573, tel: (907) 822-3245.
An historic log structure with an unspoiled country atmosphere. Meals available. $

Price Guide

Summer Standard Double

$	up to $89
$$	$90 to $124
$$$	$125 to $199
$$$$	$200-plus

CORDOVA
Reluctant Fisherman Inn,
401 Railroad Ave., PO Box 150, Cordova, AK 99574,
tel: (907) 424-3272.
41 comfortable rooms overlooking the boat harbor. Common areas are lavishly decorated in a style reflecting the town's mining history. Restaurant, lounge, gift shop, travel agency, car rental. $$$

DELTA JUNCTION
Alaska 7 Motel,
3548 Richardson Highway, PO Box 1115, Delta Junction, AK 99737,
tel: (907) 895-4848.
16 budget rooms for highway travelers which have been recently renovated. $

Kelly's Country Inn,
PO Box 849, Delta Junction, AK 99737,
tel: (907) 895-4667.
In the town center, 21 rooms, each with its own style. $

DENALI NATIONAL PARK
Camp Denali,
PO Box 67,
Denali National Park,
AK 99755,
tel: (907) 683-2290.
17 cabins without bath in the Kantishna area. Prices include all meals and a unique, highly acclaimed program of naturalist-led activities deep within the park. $$$$

Denali Backcountry Lodge,
PO Box 189,
Denali National Park,
AK 99755,
tel: (907) 683-2594 or (800) 841-0692.
30 cabins beside a creek in the

Kantishna area. Meals and outdoor guided activities at the edge of the park are included. $$$$

Denali National Park Hotel, Mile 1.5 Denali National Park Road, PO Box 87, Denali National Park, AK 99755. For reservations, contact Denali Park Resorts, 241 Ship Creek Ave., Anchorage, AK 99501, tel: (907) 272-7275 or (800) 276-7234.
The only hotel inside the park, located just inside the boundary; 100 standard rooms. Facilities include a theater for films and nature talks, restaurants, gift shop, tours. $$$

Denali Princess Lodge, Mile 238.5 George Parks Highway, PO Box 110, Denali National Park, AK 99755, tel: (800) 426-0500
280 rooms and suites, with spacious common areas, off the highway. Spas, gift shops, dining room, lounge, café, tour desk. . $$$

Denali Riverview Inn, Mile 238.4 George Parks Highway, PO Box 49, Denali National Park, AK 99755, tel: (907) 683-2663.
Overlooking the Nenana River, 12 rooms with refrigerators. $$$

Denali Park Resorts Chalets, Mile 238.5 George Parks Highway.
For reservations, contact Denali Park Resorts, 241 Ship Creek Ave., Anchorage, AK 99501, tel: (907) 276-7234 or (800) 276-7234.
288 rooms with charming rustic furniture in various buildings connected by a shuttle bus. Restaurant, lounge and wilderness adventures available. $$$

DILLINGHAM
Bristol Inn, 104 Main St.,PO Box 330, Dillingham, AK 99576,

tel: (907) 842-2240 or (800) 764-9704; fax: (907) 842-3340.
30 rooms with private baths, cable and phone, some with kitchenettes. Freezer and laundry facilities available. $$$

Dillingham Hotel, 429 Second Ave.,PO Box 550, Dillingham, AK 99576, tel: (907) 842-5316, fax: (907) 842-5666.
right in the heart of town, this was the first hotel built in Dillingham; 30 rooms, some with private bath. Refurbished in the mid-1970s. $$

DUTCH HARBOR
The Grand Aleutian Hotel, 498 Salmon Way, PO Box 921169, Dutch Harbor, AK 99692, tel: (907) 581-3844 or (800) 891-1194.
Built in 1993, was opened amid great fanfare; 106 rooms. This beautiful hotel has two restaurants and, with views of Margaret Bay. $$$

Price Guide

Summer Standard Double
$	up to $89
$$	$90 to $124
$$$	$125 to $199
$$$$	$200-plus

FAIRBANKS
Bridgewater Hotel, 723 1st Ave., Fairbanks, AK 99701, tel: (907) 452-6661.
A concrete structure on the banks of the Chena River, 89 rooms. Basement dining facilities, cocktail lounge. $$$

Captain Bartlett Inn, 1411 Airport Way, Fairbanks, AK 99701, tel: (907) 452-1888.
Located on a main commercial road, the inn tries for a rustic roadhouse atmosphere. Restaurant. $$$

Chena Hot Springs Resort, Chena Hot Springs Rd., PO Box 73440, Fairbanks, AK 99707, tel: (907) 452-7867 or (800) 478-4681
In a wilderness setting, 59 miles (95 km) from Fairbanks; 47 rooms, 10 cabins. Year-round resort with swimming in mineral hot springs. $$

Fairbanks Princess Hotel, 4477 Pikes Landing Rd., Fairbanks, AK 99701, tel: (907) 455-4477 or (800) 426-0500.
Located in a wooded area on the banks of the Chena River near the airport; 200 rooms. Restaurants, lounge, live entertainment, gift shop. $$$$

Golden North Motel, 4888 Old Airport Way, Fairbanks, AK 99701, tel: (907) 479-6201 or (800) 447-1910 in the US and (800) 478-1910 in Canada.
Near shopping malls and airport; 62 budget rooms. $

Regency Fairbanks Hotel, 95 Tenth Ave., Fairbanks, AK 99701, tel: (907) 452-3200 or (800) 348-1340.
129 rooms, all with kitchens. Dining room, lounge, gift shop. $$$

Sophie Station Hotel, 1717 University Ave., Fairbanks, AK 99709, tel: (907) 479-3650 or (800) 528-4916.
Elegant, all-suite hotel with 147 units. Gift shop, restaurant and lounge. $$$

Wedgewood Resort, 212 Wedgewood Drive, Fairbanks, AK 99701, tel: (907) 452-1442 or (800) 528-4916.
440 rooms. Some are fully furnished condo-style one-bedroom apartments, others are recently built luxury hotel rooms. $$$

Westmark Fairbanks Hotel,
813 Noble St.,
Fairbanks, AK 99701,
tel: (907) 456-7722 or (800)
544-0970.
Website: http://
Westmarkhotels.com
Newly remodelled and
conveniently located downtown
around a large courtyard; 240
rooms. Restaurant and lounge.
$$$

GIRDWOOD
**The Westin Alyeska Prince
Hotel/Alyeska Resort**,
1000 Arlberg Avenue,
PO Box 249,
Girdwood, AK 99587,
tel: (907) 754-1111 or (800)
880-3880.
Year-round luxury resort 40
miles (64 km) southeast of
Anchorage on Seward Highway.
Six chair lifts and tram, night
skiing, condominium
accommodations, convention
facilities, restaurant, lounge,
swimming pool, exercise room
and hot tub with a view of the
mountain. There's also a day
lodge, ski school, alpine and
telemark skiing, ski rental and
repair, ski shops and ice
skating; dog sledding and sleigh
rides can be arranged. Summer
sightseeing tram lift ride.
Price $$–$$$$.

GLACIER BAY/GUSTAVUS
Glacier Bay Lodge,
520 Pike St., Ste 1610,
Seattle, WA 98101,
tel: (206) 623-2417 or (800)
451-5952.
Only hotel within the park,
situated above the dock where
day boats begin trips to the
glaciers; 55 rooms. Dining room
and gift shop. $$$
Gustavus Inn
PO Box 60,
Gustavus, AK 99826,
tel: (907) 697-2254 or (800)
649-5220.
A luxurious country inn near
Glacier Bay National Park
offering all-inclusive packages

for fishing, whale-watching, sea-
kayaking and other activities; 11
rooms. Prices inclusive of family-
style meals. $$$$

GLENNALLEN
New Caribou Hotel,
Glennallen, AK 99588,
Mile 187 Glenn Highway,
PO Box 329,
tel: (907) 822-3302.
Has various room configurations
– the 27 rooms in the trailer-like
annex in front of the main
building are clean but spartan
with shared bath; 48 nicely
furnished rooms in main building
cost more. Restaurant and gift
shop next door. $–$$.

HAINES
Captain's Choice Motel,
PO Box 392,
Haines, AK 99827,
tel: (907) 766-3111 or (800)
247-7153 outside Alaska, (800)
478-2345 in Alaska and
Canada.
Centrally located overlooking
Portage Cove and Chilkoot Inlet;
40 rooms. Car rental. $$
Hotel Halsingland,
PO Box 1589,
Haines, AK 99827,
tel: (907) 766-2000 or(800)
542-6363.
An historic Fort William Seward
building facing the parade
grounds; 50 rooms. Cocktail
lounge, restaurant featuring
locally caught seafood, car
rental and activity desk.
$$
Mountain View Motel,
within walking distance of
downtown and Fort William
Seward; 9 budget rooms.
PO Box 62,
Haines, AK 99827,
tel: (907) 766-2900. $
HOMER
Bay View Inn,
PO Box 804,
Homer, AK 99603,
tel: (907) 235-8485.
12 basic rooms, six with
kitchens, plus a guest cottage,
with magnificent views of the

Kachemak Bay. $$
Driftwood Inn,
135 W. Bunnell,
Homer, AK 99603,
tel: (907) 235-8019 or (800)
478-8019.
One block from Bishop's Beach;
21 rooms (some with shared
bath). Clean and cozy, with
common sitting room and eating
area – serve-yourself cold
breakfast if desired. 22 RV hook-
ups. $–$$$
Heritage Hotel,
147 E. Pioneer Ave.,
Homer, AK 99603,
tel: (907) 235-7787.
Downtown; 32 standard rooms.
Large, comfortable lobby with
free coffee. Within walking
distance of restaurants,
shopping and entertainment.
$
Land's End Hotel and RV Park,
4786 Homer Spit Rd.,
Homer, AK 99603,
tel: (907) 235-2500.
61 rooms in a variety of sizes,
half with views of the bay. Full-
service restaurant specializing in
fresh seafood, gift shop.
$$–$$$
Ocean Shores Motel,
3500 Crittenden Dr.,
Homer, AK 99603,
tel: (907) 235-7775 or (800)
770-7775.
Three blocks from downtown in
wooded residential area; two
new buildings completed in
1996 and 1997 with spacious
rooms, bay view and private
beach. $$

JUNEAU
Best Western Country Lane Inn,
9300 Glacier Highway,
Juneau, AK 99801,
tel: (907) 789-5005 or (800)
528-1234.
Near the airport and Mendenhall
Glacier; 55 rooms.
$$
Driftwood Lodge,
435 Willoughby,
Juneau, AK 99801,
tel: (907) 586-2280 or (800)
544-2239.

Downtown; 62 rooms, many with kitchenettes and apartment-style floor-plans. Laundry facilities, 24-hour airport shuttle. $

Inn at the Waterfront,
455 South Franklin St.,
Juneau, AK 99801,
tel: (907) 586-2050
Near the cruise ship dock; 21 small rooms. Fine dining in the Summit Restaurant. $

Super 8 Motel,
2295 Trout St.,
Juneau, AK 99801,
tel: (907) 789-4858 or (800) 800-8000.
Near the airport; 75 rooms. Freezers available, 24-hour airport and ferry shuttle. $$

The Baranof Hotel,
127 North Franklin St.,
Juneau, AK 99801,
tel: (907) 586-2660 or (800) 544-0970.
Nine story art deco structure; 193 rooms. Coffee shop, lounge, restaurant – all popular with politicians and state employees. $$$

The Breakwater,
1711 Glacier Ave.,
Juneau, AK 99802,
tel: (907) 586-6303 or (800) 544-2250.
Overlooking the small boat harbor; 40 rooms, some with balconies. Restaurant, lounge, gift shop. $$

Westmark Juneau,
51 West Egan Dr.,
PO Box 20929,
Juneau, AK 99802,
tel: (907) 586-6900, or (800) 544-0970.
Downtown on the waterfront; 104 rooms and suites. Lounge, restaurant. $$$

KATMAI

Brooks Lodge,
For reservations contact:
Katmailand Inc.
4125 Aircraft Dr.,
Anchorage, AK 99502,
tel: (907) 243-5448 or (800) 544-0551.

Only accommodations within the park, on the Naknek Lake and Brooks River; 16 rustic rooms/cabins. Main lodge, restaurant, sportfishing and bear-viewing. $$$$

Grosvenor Lodge,
Katmailand Inc.
4125 Aircraft Dr.,
Anchorage, AK 99502,
tel: (907) 243-5448 or (800) 544-0551.
3- to 7-night packages available, including everything from air fare to rods and waders for sport fishing. $$$$

Katmai Wilderness Lodge,
Contact PO Box 4332,
Kodiak, AK 99615,
tel: (907) 486-8767 or (800) 488-8767.
3 bedrooms and 3 bathrooms. Bear-viewing, glacier trekking, fishing, photography, kayaking. $950 per person includes air fare from Kodiak and gourmet meals. $$$$

KENAI PENINSULA

Price Guide	
Summer Standard Double	
$	up to $89
$$	$90 to $124
$$$	$125 to $199
$$$$	$200-plus

Gwin's Lodge,
Mile 52 Sterling Highway,
HC64 Box 50,
Cooper Landing, AK 99572,
tel: (907) 595-1266.
Half a mile (1 km) from Russian River fisheries; 6 rustic cabins each with bath; 2 more modest fishermen's cabins. $$

Kenai Merit Inn,
260 South Willow, Kenai, AK 99611,
tel: (907) 283-6131 or (800) 227-6131.
Downtown Kenai; 60 rooms. Walking distance to shops and restaurants; fishing packages available. $

Kenai Princess Lodge,
PO Box 676,

Cooper Landing, AK 99572,
tel: (907) 595-1425 or (800) 426-0500.
70-room luxury resort hotel near Cooper Landing overlooking Kenai River. Built cabin-style, with path from main lodge to four-unit log cabins. Restaurant, lounge, spa. $$$

Sunrise Inn,
Mile 45 Sterling Highway,
Cooper Landing, AK 99572,
tel: (907) 595-1222.
On Kenai Lake, 10 units each with TV and private bath. Restaurant. $$

KETCHIKAN

Gilmore Hotel,
326 Front St.,
Ketchikan, AK 99901,
tel: (907) 225-9423.
Downtown on the waterfront ; 30 rooms. Restaurant. $

Ingersoll Hotel,
303 Mission St.,
Ketchikan, AK 99901,
tel: (907) 225-2124 or ●
(800) 478-2124.
Walking distance to downtown sights; 58 rooms. $$

Super 8 Motel,
2151 Sea Level Dr.,
Ketchikan, AK 99901,
tel: (907) 225-9088 or (800) 800-8000.
Situated ear a shopping mall between ferry terminal and downtown; 82 rooms. Shuttle service and freezers available. $

Westmark Cape Fox Lodge,
800 Venetia Way,
Ketchikan, AK 99901,
tel: (907) 255-8001 or (800) 544-0970
Located above downtown Ketchikan and Tongass Narrows, access is by scenic tram from downtown; 72 rooms. Dining room, lounge, meeting and banquet facilities. $$$

KING SALMON

Quinnat Landing Hotel,
PO Box 418,
King Salmon, AK 99613,
tel: (907) 246-3000 or (800) 770-FISH.

overlooking Naknek River; 48
rooms. Restaurant, lounge,
sportfishing, bear-viewing; 32-ft
(10-meter) enclosed jet boat to
Brooks Falls and Katmai.
Price:$$$

KODIAK
Buskin River Inn,
1395 Airport Way,
Kodiak, AK 99615,
tel: (907) 487-2700 or (800)
544-2202.
Located near the airport; 50
rooms (some with voice mail and
data ports). Salmon fishing on
nearby river, restaurant and
lounge. $$.
Kodiak Bed and Breakfast,
308 Cope St.,
Kodiak, AK 99615,
tel: (907) 486-5367.
Overlooking the boat harbor; 2
rooms with shared bath.
$
Northland Ranch Resort,
PO Box 2376
Kodiak, AK 99615,
tel: (907) 486-5578.
Hunting accommodations on a
cattle, quarterhorse and buffalo
ranch; 14 rooms. Restaurant,
lounge, fishing, hunting, hiking,
horseback riding. $$$$
Kodiak Inn,
236 W. Rezanof Dr.,
Kodiak, AK 99615,
tel: (907) 486-5712 or (800)
544-0970 or
(888) 563-4254.
In town center above the
waterfront; 81 rooms. Lounge,
restaurant. $$$

KOTZEBUE
Nullagvik Hotel,
Shore Ave. and Tundra Way.
PO Box 336,
Kotzebue, AK 99752,
tel: (907) 442-3331.
Overlooking Kotzebue Sound; 80
rooms. Restaurants. $$$

NOME
Nugget Inn,
PO Box 430,
Nome, AK 99762,
tel: (907) 443-2323.

47 rooms with private baths.
Restaurant, lounge.
Front Street and Bering.
$$

PALMER AREA
Hatcher Pass Lodge,
Mile 17.5 Hatcher Pass Rd.,
PO Box 763,
Palmer, AK 99645,
tel: (907) 745-5897.
60 miles (96 km) northeast of
Anchorage; 9 modern cabins
each with chemical toilet. Meals,
bar, entertainment, sauna,
cross-country skiing. $$.
Sheep Mountain Lodge,
Mile 113 Glenn Highway.
HC03 Box 8490,
Palmer, AK 99645,
tel: (907) 745-5121.
10 cabins with bath and shower.
Restaurant, hot tub, sauna.
$$
Valley Hotel,
606 S. Alaska,
Palmer, AK 99645,
tel: (907) 745-3330.
Downtown near visitor center.
30-room hotel was built in 1948.
24-hour restaurant, cocktail
lounge. $
Colony Inn,
325 Elmwood (check-in handled
at the neighboring Valley Hotel –
see address above);
tel: (907) 745-3330.
Lovingly restored historic
building with large downstairs
sitting area; 12 guest rooms
decorated with quilts and
antique reproductions.
Restaurant . Price $

PETERSBURG
Narrows Inn,
PO Box 1048,
Petersburg, AK 99833,
tel: (907) 772-4284 or (800)
665-8433.
Across from ferry terminal, 22
budget rooms (some with
kitchenettes). $
Scandia House,
110 Nordic Dr.,
PO Box 689,
Petersburg, AK 99833,
tel: (907) 772-4281 or (800)

722-5006.
Downtown hotel rebuilt in 1995;
33 rooms. Car, bike and boat
rental. $$
Tides Inn,
307 N. First St.,
PO Box 1048,
Petersburg, AK 99833,
tel: (907) 772-4288 or (800)
665-8433.
Downtown, 47 rooms (some with
kitchenettes). $

SELDOVIA
Boardwalk Hotel,
PO Box 72,
Seldovia, AK 99663,
tel: (907) 234-7816.
On the waterfront with view of
water or mountains; 14 rooms.
Sun-lit parlor with wood stove
and coffee service. $
Across the Bay
Tent and Breakfast,
PO Box 112054,
Anchorage, AK 99511 (winter);
tel: (907) 345-2571
Red Mountain, Box RDO, Homer,
Alaska 99603 (summer);
tel: (907) 235-3633.
Sturdy wall tents with twin beds.
Hearty meals served at main
house, bike and kayak rentals.
Access is by water taxi from
Homer. $

SEWARD
Best Western Hotel Seward,
221 Fifth Ave., PO Box 670,
Seward, AK 99664,
tel: (907) 224-2378 or (800)
528-1234.
Downtown; 38 rooms – some
with bay views, all with
refrigerators. Free shuttle to
airport, railroad depot and
harbor. $$$–$$$$
Breeze Inn Motel,
1306 Seward Highway;
PO Box 2147,
Seward, AK 99664,
tel: (907) 224-5237.
On the main road into town right
in the small boat harbor; 86
rooms (20 built in 1997).
Restaurant, lounge, espresso
and gift shops. $$

Marina Hotel,
Mile 1 Seward Highway,
PO Box 1134,
Seward, AK 99664,
tel: (907) 224-5518.
Across from the boat harbor, one
mile from downtown; 18 rooms.
$$

Seward Windsong Lodge,
Mile 6 Exit Glacier Road,
PO Box 221011,
Anchorage, AK 99522,
tel: (907) 245-0200 or (800)
208-0200.
Forested setting near the banks
of Resurrection River; 24 rooms
have either mountain or river
view. Another 24 rooms and a
full-service restaurant are
scheduled to open in 1998.
$$$

SITKA
Potlatch Motel,
713 Katlian St.,
Sitka, AK 99835,
tel: (907) 747-8611.
About a mile from the downtown
sights; 32 standard rooms with
kitchen suites. Launderette. $$

Sitka Hotel,
118 Lincoln St.,
Sitka, AK 99835,
tel: (907) 747-3288.
Downtown; 60 budget rooms,
some with shared bathrooms. $

Westmark Shee Atika,
330 Seward St.,
Sitka, AK 99835,
tel: (907) 747-6241, (800) 544-
0970.
Overlooking the Crescent Harbor
waterfront; 98 rooms.
Restaurant; lounge. $$$

SKAGWAY
Gold Rush Lodge,
6th Ave. and Alaskan St.,
PO Box 514, Skagway, AK
99840, tel: (907) 983-2831.
within walking distance of
historical sites; 12 rooms.
$

Golden North Hotel,
Third Ave. and Broadway,
PO Box 343,
Skagway, AK 99840,
tel: (907) 983-2451.

Downtown, 31-room historic
hotel, with gold rush-era
antiques; dining room, pub. $

Skagway Inn
Bed and Breakfast,
Seventh Ave. and Broadway,
PO Box 500,
Skagway, AK 99840,
tel: (907) 983-2289.
12 rooms with 6 hallway baths.
$$

Westmark Inn Skagway,
Third and Spring Streets,
PO Box 515,
Skagway, AK 99840,
tel: (907) 983-6000 or (800)
544-0970.
Near stores and attractions; 212
rooms. Mostly serving package
tour passengers; restaurant and
lounge. $$$

Wind Valley Lodge,
22nd Ave. and State St.,
PO Box 354,
Skagway, AK 99840,
tel: (907) 983-2236.
15 blocks from the historic
sights; 30 rooms. $

SOLDOTNA
Goodnight Inn,
44715 Sterling Highway,
Soldotna, AK 99669,
tel: (907) 262-4584.
33 rooms of various sizes and
configurations, with one
kitchenette. Restaurant, lounge.
$$

Kenai River Lodge,
393 Riverside Dr.,
Soldotna, AK 99669,
tel: (907) 262-4292.
Overlooking the famous Kenai
River; all 25 rooms have coffee
pots and TVs. Excellent
sportfishing. $

Soldotna Inn,
35041 Spur Highway,
Soldotna, AK 99669,
tel: (907) 262-9169.
28 modern rooms, most with
refrigerators, some with
kitchenettes. Restaurant,
lounge. $$

TALKEETNA
Swiss-Alaska Inn,
PO Box 565,

Talkeetna, AK 99676;
tel: (907) 733-2424.
Family-run with 20 rooooms, 8 of
them newly built and decorated
in bright, floral motif.
Restaurant. East Talkeetna by
the boat launch. $–$$

TOK
Westmark Inn-Tok,
Mile 1315 Alaska Highway,
PO Box 130,
Tok, AK, 99780,
tel: (907) 883-5174 or (800)
554-0970.
72 standard rooms in buildings
connected by boardwalks.
Restaurant, gift shop. $$

Young's Motel,
P.O. Box 482,
Tok, AK,
tel: (907) 883-4411.
Along the Alaska Highway behind
the area's most popular
restaurant, Fast Eddie's; 43
rooms in one-story buildings. $

VALDEZ
Village Inn,
PO Box 365,
Valdez, AK 99686
tel: (907) 835-4445
Conveniently located downtown;
79 rooms, views of surrounding
mountains and Valdez Arm. $$

Westmark Valdez Hotel,
105 Fidalgo,
Valdez, AK 99686
tel: (907) 835-4391 or (800)
544-0970
Located right on the harbour in
downtown Valdez. $$$

Bed & Breakfast

The following list gives the
central reservations
organizations in the main towns.
They will help you find
recommended B&B
accommodation.

ANCHORAGE
Bed & Breakfast Association
Hotline
P.O.Box 242623
Anchorage, AK 99524,
tel: (888) 584-5147 or (907)
272-4429.

Alaska Available Bed & Breakfast Reservation Services
3800 Delwood Place,
Anchorage, AK 99504-4429,
Tel: (907) 337-3414.
FAIRBANKS
Fairbanks Association of Bed & Breakfasts
P.O.Box 7334,
Fairbanks, AK 99707-3334
tel: (907) 456-5774 or (800) 327-5774.
Bed & Breakfast Reservation System
P.O.Box 711131,
Fairbanks, AK 99707,
tel: (907) 479-8165 or (800) 770-8165.
HOMER
Central Charters
4241 Homer Spit Road,
Homer, AK 99603,
tel: (907) 235-7847 or (800) 478-7847.
JUNEAU
Alaska Bed & Breakfast Association
369 S. Franklin St., Suite 200
Juneau, AK 99801,
tel: (907) 586-2959.
KETCHIKAN
Ketchikan Reservation Service
412 D-1 Loop Road,
Ketchikan, AK 99901
tel: (907) 247-5337 or (800) 987-5337.
KODIAK
Visitors' Information Center
100 Marine Way,
Kodiak, AK 99615,
tel: (907) 486-4782.
VALDEZ
One Call Does It All
P.O.Box 2197,
Valze, AK 99686,
tel: (907) 835-4988.

Public Use Cabins

For a totally Alaskan experience, visitors can stay in remote wilderness cabins maintained by the US Forest Service or Alaska State Parks. The cabins are accessible by trails, boat or chartered air service (arranged by the renter). There are over 200 cabins scattered throughout the Tongass and Chugach National Forest in Southeast and Southcentral Alaska. They are located in beautiful, remote areas and give visitors a chance to experience the great outdoors on their own, but they are very basic. Averaging 12 x 14 ft (3.7x 4.3 meters), they lack running water and electricity. They are equipped with a table and oil- or wood burning stove for heat. Wooden bunks without mattresses are provided and outhouses are located a few steps away. Cabins on a lake often have an aluminum boat or skiff available.

Renters are expected to bring their own food, stoves, cooking utensils and bedding, and to take out their garbage and replace any of the fire wood they burn. Often outfitters and air charter operators will help with the gear needed for a cabin stay. The cost of rentals is low (around $35 to $50 a night), but getting there can be quite expensive.

For more information on Forest Service cabins, write to the Alaska Public Lands Information Center, 605 W. Fourth Avenue, Suite 105, Anchorage, AK 99501, tel: (907) 271-2599 or Tongass National Forest, Centennial Hall, 101 Egan Drive, Juneau, AK 99801, tel: (907) 586-8751. For reservations, call the National Recreation Reservation Center, tel: (800) 280-2267 or write to the center at P.O. Box 900, Cumberland, MD, 21502-0900. You can reserve cabins up to 180 days in advance, using a Visa, MasterCard or Discover card. Information is also available on the web at http://www.nrrc.com.
For State Park Cabins write: Department of Natural Resources, 3601 C St., Suite 200, Anchorage, AK, 99503-5929 or tel: (907) 269-8400. web:http://www.dnr.state.ak.us/parks/directory.html

Campgrounds

Federal, state, municipal and private campgrounds dot the landscape in Alaska. They can vary from barely organized tent sites to full hook-up recreational vehicle parking sites. As a general rule, there are usually one or more campgrounds nearby if you are anywhere along the road system.

Most campgrounds, whether state, federal or private, charge fees for overnight use. Daily rates vary from $10 at rustic sites to more than $20 for full hook-up sites in private campgrounds. All the campgrounds remain open during the summer months only.

State and federal (Bureau of Land Management, National Park Service, National Forest Service) campgrounds generally provide water, picnic tables, fire pits, pit toilets, a parking space and space for tents or recreational vehicles (noon to noon). Generally, registration is self-service at a kiosk at the campground entrance, but sometimes a volunteer campground host is on duty.

The best sources for listings of public and private campgrounds are *The Milepost*, available from Alaska Northwest Publishing Co., the *Alaska Vacation Planner*, and the state map and *Campground Guide* available from the Alaska State Division of Tourism, PO Box 110801, Juneau, AK 99802 or (907) 465-2010. Both are updated annually.

Guidance, maps and publications are available in person from the Alaska Public Lands Information Centers in Anchorage, Fairbanks, Tok and Ketchikan. (See Public Parks & Lands.)

Where to Eat

What To Eat

All Alaskan cities offer a variety of dining options. Once out of the city, however, food ranges from great home cooking to rather bland and poor fare. One thing that is consistent wherever you go, however, is that prices are high. The rationale behind this is that virtually all food products must be flown in and staff costs are also high. Keep this in mind when planning your food budgets.

Many Alaskan restaurants serve truly outstanding seafood. Both Alaska King and Dungeness crab are often on the menu when in season. Other shellfish, such as local shrimp, scallops, mussels and oysters, are also often available, as are fresh salmon and halibut.

Fast-food chains can be found in larger communities, as can ethnic restaurants serving Thai, Vietnamese and Mexican fare in particular.

You can ask the locals for a recommendation, but we provide a small selection of suggestions below.

Restaurants

ANCHORAGE
Club Paris
417 W. 5th Ave.,
tel: (907) 277-6332.
The bar up front is dark, smokey and characterful and a favorite haunt of long-time Alaskans; the steaks and prime rib served in the back are big, tender and flavorful.
$$$–$$$$

City Market
13th Avenue & I Street,
tel: (907) 274-9797.
Offers espresso, fresh breads, pastries and gourmet pizzas served with trendy urban chic; also several hot entrées served cafeteria style. $

L'Aroma Bakery & Deli
3700 Old Seward Highway, tel: (907) 562-9797.
Sister operation to the above; same style and range of food, minus the hot dishes. $

Lucky Wishbone
1033 E. 5th Ave.,
tel: (907) 272-3454.
This is a great chicken and burger joint that is popular with all sorts of people from local lawyers and oil executives to cabbies and mechanics. The homemade shakes are rich and creamy. $

Marx Brothers' Café
627 W. 3rd Ave.,
tel: (907) 278-2133.
Innovative fine dining and an extensive wine list can be found at this little frame house on a downtown bluff. Built in 1916 and attractively renovated by the café's owners, it is one of Anchorage's finest restaurants and worthy of a special occasion. $$$$

Moose's Tooth Pub and Pizzeria
3300 Old Seward Hwy,
tel: (907) 258-2537.
This brew pub and pizzeria offers handcrafted ales and gourmet pizzas with with a great range of toppings, such as artichoke hearts, feta cheese and spinach. $$–$$$

Sack's Café
625 W. 5th Ave.,
tel: (907) 276-3546.
This popular urban café offers interesting combinations of ingredients all carefully prepared – such as Mediterranean chicken with feta cheese over pasta. It is especially popular at lunchtime and also for dinner before the theater or for a long and lazy Sunday brunch. $$$$

Price Guide

Prices based on a main course for one:
$=under $13, $$=$13–18, $$$=$18–25, $$$$=$25+

FAIRBANKS
Gambardella's Italian Café
706 Second Ave.,
tel: (907) 456-3417.
Southern Italian cuisine, including its famous lasagna, is served indoors on white table cloths or outside on a garden terrace. $$

The Pump House Restaurant and Saloon
1.3 Mile Chena Pump Rd,
tel: (907) 479-8452.
Steak and seafood in large dining rooms set within an historic gold mining building on the banks of the Chena River. Tables on a deck over the water are available. $$$

Thai House
526 Fifth Ave.,
tel: (907) 452-6123
A Thai family serves their national cuisine in a simple storefront restaurant. $

Drinking Notes

The legal age for purchasing and consuming alcoholic drinks is 21 – make sure you carry adequate identification. Alcohol is sold or served in specific liquor stores, lounges and restaurants licensed by the state. A number of small communities in rural Alaska have completely banned the importation, sale and consumption of alcoholic drinks – and they take it seriously. You could be arrested, fined, jailed or deported for violating these local ordinances. Before traveling to a remote destination, make sure you are familiar with the local liquor laws.

**Two Rivers Lodge/
Tuscan Gardens**
4968 Chena Hot Springs Rd.,
tel: (907) 488-6815.
Inside the log roadhouse, a
menu of excellent steak and
seafood is served in a relatively
formal setting. Outside, on the
deck over the duck pond,
inexpensive, casual meals are
cooked in a Tuscan brick oven.
$$–$$$

HOMER
Café Cups
162 W. Pioneer Ave.,
tel: (907) 235-8330.
Locals and visitors alike crowd
into this cozy dining room for
coffee and conversation in the
morning or later in the day for
fresh pasta, local seafood and
an eclectic, but reasonably
priced, wine selection. $$
Homestead Restaurant
Mile 8.2, East End Rd.,
tel: (907) 235-8723.
This former log roadhouse
specializes in steak, prime rib
and seasonal seafood creatively
prepared with garlic, citrus
fruits, macadamia nuts or spicy
ethnic sauces. $$$$
Saltry in Halibut Cove
4241 Homer Spit Rd.,
tel: (907) 235-7847.
Located across Kachemak Bay
in Halibut Cove. Serves local
seafood as sushi or in curries
and pastas. A wide selection of
imported beers is available.
Take the *Danny J* ferry from the
Homer Spit boardwalk through
Central Charters. $$$$

JUNEAU
Armadillo Tex-Mex Café
431 S. Franklin St.,
tel: (907) 586-1880.
This small storefront near the
cruise ship dock is famous
among locals for southwestern-
style food that customers order
at the counter. $
Douglas Café
916 Third St., Douglas Island,
tel: (907) 364-3307
A bright, casual café, popular for

hearty breakfasts, but also
serving dinners drawing on many
styles of cuisine. $$
**Fiddlehead Restaurant
and Bakery**
429 Willoughby Ave.,
tel: (907) 586-3150.
Upstairs, eclectic and creative
fine dining; downstairs, a
reasonably priced café with
healthy ingredients, wholewheat
breads and local seafood. The
owners published a popular cook
book.Reservations are
recommended if you want to
dine upstairs. $$–$$$
The Hangar
2 Marine Way,
tel: (907) 586-5018.
Popular local bar and grill
situated in a former aircraft
hangar on a water-front dock. It
has big windows for a great view
and more than two dozen
varieties of beer on tap. $$$
The Summit Restaurant
455 S. Franklin St.,
tel: (907) 586-2050
Continental cuisine, steak and
local seafood in an intimate
waterfront dining room with only
nine tables. Reservations
recommended. $$$

SKAGWAY
Oliva's at the Skagway Inn
Seventh Ave. and Broadway,
tel: (907) 983-2289.
Fine dining featuring fresh
Alaska seafood and local fresh
produce. Victorian bed &
breakfast. Reservations
required. $$

Wildlife

Parks & Preserves

With eight national parks (many
with attached preserves), four
national monuments, three
separate national preserves, 16
wildlife refuges, 25 wild and
scenic rivers and 12 designated
federal wilderness, Alaska holds
more land in the public trust
than any other state. National
park rangers, US Fish and
Wildlife Service personnel and
US Forest Service rangers patrol
these vast acreages on foot,
from airplanes, in canoes,
jetboats, outboard motor boats
and ocean cruisers, and by
vehicle.
   Several of the state's
wilderness areas and refuges
are extremely remote, expensive
and difficult to get to and
provide few, if any, visitor
amenities. The information
listed here is, therefore, limited
to those commonly visited and
with specific activities or
attractions.
**Alaska Public Lands
Information Center,**
 605 W. Fourth Ave.,
Anchorage, AK 99501,
tel: (907) 271-2737.
**US Fish and Wildlife Service
Alaska Regional Office,**
1011 East Tudor Rd.,
Anchorage, AK 99503,
tel: (907) 786-3309.
**Admiralty Island National
Monument**
Southeastern Alaskan island
located 15 miles (25 km) west of
Juneau across Stephens
Passage. Primary access is by
boat or floatplane from Juneau,

but wheeled planes are allowed to land on beaches. Mountainous terrain in coastal rainforest. Size: about 900,000 acres (364,500 hectares). Contact: Forest Service Info. Center, 101 Egan Dr., Juneau, AK 99801. tel: (907) 586-8806.

Alaska Chilkat Bald Eagle Preserve
Approximately 20 miles (32 km) from Haines on the Haines Highway. Winter feeding ground for thousands of bald eagles, when it holds the largest concentration of these birds in the world – the best viewing is in November, December and January.
Contact: Haines Visitor Information Center, PO Box 530, Haines, AK 99827, tel: (907) 766-2234 or (800) 458-3578. website: http://www.haines.alaska

Alaska Maritime National Wildlife Refuge
Scattered coastal units from southeastern Alaska all the way around to the west coast, including the Aleutian Islands. Marine mammals and marine birds, including 50 million nesting seabirds. Size: approximately 4,500,000 acres (1,822,500 hectares). Contact: 2355 Kachemak Bay Dr. Suite 101, Homer, AK 99603, tel: (907) 235-6546.

Alaska Peninsula National Wildlife Refuge
Alaska Peninsula in southwestern Alaska features salmon, brown/grizzly bears, moose, caribou, wolves and wolverines, rolling tundra, towering mountains and active volcanoes. Excellent big-game hunting. Size: 3.5 million acres (1,417,500 hectares). Contact: PO Box 277, King Salmon, AK 99613, tel: (907) 246-3339.

Arctic National Wildlife Refuge
Extreme northeastern region of Alaska bordering Canada, which is home to the Porcupine

Caribou herd. (160,000-plus animals), Dall sheep, polar bears on the coast, grizzly bears, wolves, wolverine, black bears, musk ox, 140 species of birds and spectacular plant life. Excellent hiking. Size: 8,894,624 acres (3,602,323 hectares). Contact: 101 12th Ave., PO Box 20, Fairbanks, AK 99701, tel: (907) 456-0250.

Denali National Park and Preserve
One of Alaska's most popular tourist destinations, with an average 350,000 visitors a year, it is also home to Mount McKinley, at 20,320 feet (6,195 meters), the highest peak in North America. Attractions include mountain climbing and wildlife tours (Dall sheep, grizzlies, moose and caribou are some of the species seen frequently). Located 140 (225 km) miles south of Fairbanks, 220 miles (354 km) north of Anchorage, on Parks Highway. Size: approximately 6 million acres (2.42 million hectares).

For shuttle bus reservations, contact Denali Park Resorts VTS, 241 W. Ship Creek Avenue, Anchorage, AK 99501, tel: (907) 272-7275 or (800) 622-7275.

For park entry reservations, applications must be made 30 days in advance, providing the name and age of each passenger, dates and times of their travel, and a credit card number with its expiration date. Contact: P.O. Box 9, McKinley Park, AK 99755, tel: (907) 276-7234, (907) 683-2294 or (800) 276-7234. website: http://www.nps.gov/dena

At least 40 percent of ticket seats are released for early reservation, the rest are on sale two days before date of travel.

Endicott River Wilderness
Located on the west side of Lynn Canal, about 45 miles (72 km) northwest of Juneau, its western

edge bounds the eastern border of Glacier Bay National Park. Size: 94,000 acres (38,070 hectares). Contact: US Forest Service, Chatham Area, Tongass National Forest, 201 Katlian, Suite 109. Sitka, AK 99835. tel: (907) 747-6671.

Gates of the Arctic National Park and Preserve
The peaks and valleys of the central Brooks Range, north and south of the continental divide, lie within the 8.4 million acres (3.4 million hectares) of the park and preserve, 200 miles (322 km) northwest of Fairbanks. The most convenient access is by air with scheduled service from Fairbanks to Bettles, 40 miles (64 km) south of the park. Hire charter aircraft in Bettles for flightseeing or drop off in the park.
Contact: P.O. Box 74680, Fairbanks, AK 99707; tel: (907) 456-0281. website: http://www.nps.gov/gaar

Glacier Bay National Park and Preserve
Located 50 miles (80 km) northwest of Juneau at the northern end of Alaska's Panhandle, Glacier Bay is an ever-changing wilderness of tidewater glaciers, marine mammals and northern birds. Size: 3,328,000 acres (1,347,840 hectares). Contact: P.O. Box 140, Gustavus, AK 99826; tel: (907) 697-2230. website: http://www.nps.gov/glba

Izembak National Wildlife Refuge
At the tip of Alaska Peninsula in southwestern Alaska, on Bering Sea. Outstanding birding and wildlife viewing, including caribou. Access is usually from Cold Bay. Size: 320,893 acres (129,962 hectares). Contact: P.O. Box 127, Cold Bay, AK 99571; tel: (907) 532-2445.

Info on Refuges

For information on any – or all of the National Wildlife Refuges – contact: US Fish and Wildlife Service, Regional Office, 1011 E. Tudor Rd., Anchorage, Alaska 99503.

Katmai National Park and Preserve

Initially set aside in 1918 as a national monument to protect the Valley of 10,000 Smokes created by a massive volcanic eruption in 1912. Excellent fishing and brown bear-viewing. Size: approximately 4 million acres (1.6 hectares) on the Alaska Peninsula, approximately 250 miles (400km) southwest of Anchorage.
Contact: P.O. Box 7, King Salmon, AK 99613,
tel: (907) 246-3305.
website:
http://www.nps.gov/katm

Kenai Fjords National Park

Boat or floatplane charters from Seward, on the Kenai Peninsula, 130 road miles (210 km) south of Anchorage, are the usual means of access. Features the Harding Icefield, one of the major ice caps in the United States. Abundant wildlife and marine mammal viewing. Size: 567,000 acres (229,635 hectares).
Contact: PO Box 1727, Seward, AK 99664,
tel: (907) 224-2132 or (907) 224-3175
website:
http//www.nps.gov/ketj

Kenai National Wildlife Refuge

Kenai Peninsula across Turnagain Arm south of Anchorage. Spruce and birch forests with hundreds of lakes make this prime moose habitat. Size: about 2 million acres (810,000 hectares).
Contact: P.O. Box 2139, Soldotna, AK 99669; tel: (907) 262-7021.

Kobuk Valley National Park

This western Brooks Range park is 350 miles (563 km) northwest of Fairbanks and 75 miles (120 km) west of Kotzebue. Great Kobuk Sand Dunes cover 25 sq miles (40 sq km). Canoe, kayak and raft trips are the primary recreational opportunities. Size: 1.7 million acres (692,550 hectares).
Contact: P.O. Box 1029, Kotzebue, AK 99752,
tel: (907) 442-3890.

Kodiak National Wildlife Refuge

Kodiak and Afognak islands southwest of Anchorage. Excellent hunting, as well as wildlife viewing, rafting and camping amid spruce forests. Size: 1,865,000 acres (754,325 hectares).
Contact: 1390 Buskin River Rd., Kodiak, AK 99615, tel: (907) 487-2600.

Lake Clark National Park and Preserve

Across Cook Inlet from Anchorage, the Lake Clark area has long been favored by outdoorsmen. Fishing and hiking are major recreational opportunities. Size: approximately 4 million acres (1.6 million hectares).
Contact: 4230 University Dr., Anchorage, AK 99508,
tel: (907) 781-2218.
website:
http://www.nps.gov.lacl

Misty Fjords National Monument

About 22 air miles (35 km) from Ketchikan, near the southern tip of Alaska's Panhandle. Wet, scenic region of steep mountains descending into deep fjords. Floatplane or boat access only. Size: nearly 2.3 million acres (1 million hectares).
Contact: US Forest Service 3031 Tongass Ave., Federal Building, Ketchikan, AK 99901.
tel: (907) 225-2148.

Noatak National Preserve

Just a few miles north of Kotzebue, this northwestern Alaska preserve has no road access. Flights from Kotzebue are the normal means of getting to the area. Fantastic float trip opportunities. Size: 6.5 million acres (2.6 million hectares).
Contact: P.O. Box 1029, Kotzebue, AK 99752,
tel: (907) 442-3890.

Petersburg Creek-Duncan Salt Chuck Wilderness

Kupreanof Island across Wrangell Narrows from Petersburg in southeastern Alaska. Size: 50,000 acres (20,250 hectares).
Contact: Tongass National Forest, PO Box 309, Petersburg, AK 99833,
tel: (907) 785-3341.

Russel Fjord Wilderness.

Heavily glaciated fjord about 25 miles (40 km) northeast of Yakutat. Size: 307,000 acres (124,355 hectares).
Contact: US Forest Service, P.O. Box 1980, Sitka, AK 99835,
tel: (907) 747-6671.

Selawik National Wildlife Refuge

Northwestern Alaska about 360 miles (580 km) northwest of Fairbanks. Home to caribou and waterfowl. Recreational activities include river floating, sportfishing and hunting. Size: 2 million acres (810,000 hectares).
Contact: P.O. Box 270, Kotzebue, AK 99752, tel: (907) 442-3799.

Sitka National Historical Park

The site of the 1804 Battle of Sitka between Tlingits and Russians. Located in a woodland setting with a collection of totem poles and an interpretive center for Russian and Native history. Ask for directions.
Contact: National Park Service, Sitka National Historical Park 106 Metlakat la St., Sitka, AK 99835
tel: (907) 747-6281

South Prince of Wales Wilderness

Approximately 40 air miles (64 km) southwest of Ketchikan on Prince of Wales Island. Size:

97,000 acres (39,285 hectares).
Contact: US Forest Service, Ketchikan Area, Tongass National Forest, Federal Building, Ketchikan, AK 99901, tel: (907) 225-2148.

Stikine-LeConte Wilderness
Southeastern Alaska mainland, a short distance north of Wrangell. Boats capable of navigating the Stikine River are the most common means of access. Size: 443,000 acres (179,415 hectares).
Contact: US Forest Service, Stikine Area, Tongass National Forest, PO Box 309, Petersburg, AK 99833, tel: (907) 785-3341.

Tetlin National Wildlife Refuge.
South side of Alaska Highway at the Canadian border. Waterfowl, moose, caribou, black bears and wolves. Two lakeshore campgrounds; duck, caribou and moose hunting. Size: 700,000 acres (283,500 hectares).
Contact: PO Box 779, Tok, AK 99780, tel: (907) 883-5312.

Tracy Arm-Fords Terror Wilderness
Southeastern Alaska between Tracy Arm and Endicott Arm, bordered on the east by Canada. Access is by boat. Size: 656,000 acres (265,680 hectares).
Contact: US Forest Service, Chatham Area, Tongass National Forest, P.O. Box 1980, Sitka, AK 99835.

Wrangell-St Elias National Park and Preserve
Wrangell-St Elias occupies the southeast corner of the mainland, tucked against the Canadian border. This huge park/preserve is the largest in Alaska, and totals more than 12.3 million acres (5 million hectares). Portions of the road system either enter the park/preserve or pass close to it. Access is by air from Glennallen.
Contact: National Park Service,

P.O. Box 439, Glennallen, AK 99573, tel: (907) 822-5234.
website: http://www.nps.gov/wrst

Yukon-Charley Rivers National Preserve
Includes a portion of the Yukon River near Eagle, 325 road miles (523 km) northeast of Fairbanks by road. Also accessible by road is Circle, outside the western boundary, about 140 road miles (225 km) from Fairbanks. Home to gold rush relics, bear, Dall sheep, moose and a population of peregrine falcons. Size: 1.7 million acres (5 million hectares).
Contact: National Park Service, P.O. Box 74718, Fairbanks, AK 99707, tel: (907) 456-0281.
website: http://www.nps.gov/yuch

Yukon Delta National Wildlife Refuge
Deltas of the Yukon and Kuskokwim rivers in southwestern Alaska. Plenty of waterfowl and seabirds – 170 species seen in the area and 136 species known to breed here, plus moose, caribou, brown bear and wolves. Fishing, hunting and back country recreation are excellent. Size: 19.6 million acres (700,000 hectares).
Contact: P.O. Box 346, Bethel, AK 99559, tel: (907) 543-3151.

Culture

Music/Dance/Drama

Communities across Alaska have much to offer in the way of entertainment, although many of the major performing groups take the summer off to prepare for their regular fall and winter seasons. Your best bet is to check with local information centers or scan local newspapers to find out what's playing in the communities you plan to visit.

Days of '98 Show.
Good family fun for all. Spend an evening gambling with phoney money. See the gold rush history of Skagway unfold on the stage of the 250-seat theater. Shows nightly mid-May through mid-September. Matinees for cruise-ships. Tickets at the door.
P.O. Box 1897, Skagway, AK 99840-0215, tel: (907) 983-2545.

Fairbanks Summer Arts Festival.
Two weeks of workshops, rehearsals, performances and concerts with studies in music, dance, theater, opera, ice skating and visual arts in July and August – an arts camp for adults.
P.O. Box 80845, Fairbanks, AK 99708, tel: (907) 479-8869.

Kodiak Alutiiq Dancers.
Daily summer performances of traditional Alutiiq songs and dances; cultural demonstrations and Native arts and crafts.
P.O. Box 1974, Kodiak, AK 99615, tel: (907) 486-4449.

New Archangel Dancers.
Folk dances from various parts of Russia. Performances timed to docking of cruise ship or by special arrangement.
P.O. Box 1687,
Sitka, AK 99835.

Northern Lights Photo Symphony Theatre
A spectacular multi-image show of the Northern Lights accompanied by a symphony on a 34-ft (10-meter) screen.
P.O. Box 65,
Denali Park, AK 99755,
tel: (907) 683-4000.

Crown of Lights Northern Lights Show.
LeRoy Zimmerman's award-winning Northern Lights show, "The Crown of Light," at Ester Gold Camp Historic District is a spectacular blend of Northern Lights photography and symphonic music.
P.O. Box 109,
Ester, AK 99725,
tel: (907) 479-2500 or (800) 676-6925.

Pier One Theatre.
Local talent lights up an intimate stage in a "come-as-you-are" warehouse on the Homer Spit. Dance, drama, musicals. Seasonal service, Memorial Day through Labor Day.
P.O. Box 894,
Homer, AK 99603,
tel: (907) 235-7333.

Anchorage Museum of History and Art
During the summer months the museum regularly features visiting Native dancing groups.
121 W. 7th Ave
Anchorage, AK 99501
tel: (907) 343-4326

Alaska Native Heritage Center
A new center that opened in 1999 featuring Native dancers, demonstrating artists, and story tellers. On the Glen Highway near Muldoon Road in Anchorage.
tel: (907) 330-8000 or (800) 315-6608
website:
http://www.alaskanative.net

Shopping

What To Buy

Many rare crafts and products are available to buy throughout the state. Popular items include gold nugget and jade jewelry. Don't expect a bargain, but do expect quality goods. Gold nugget jewelry is a speciality and makes a wonderful Alaskan souvenir or gift. Jade is found locally in Alaska, in carvings as well as jewelry. Jade stones come in various shades of green, brown, black, yellow, white and red.

Alaska also is home to many wonderful artists whose works can be purchased at local galleries and shops. Their works are generally inspired by the beauty of the land. In addition to works of art and jewelry, look for seal oil candles, carved wooden totem poles, canned food products and clothing.

Native crafts are abundant and include items carved from walrus ivory, soapstone and jade. Scrimshawed ivory – scenes are etched on the ivory – is an authentic handicraft.

Visitors who wish to take ivory to a country other than the United States must obtain an export permit from the US Fish and Wildlife Service. Be sure to ask about restrictions when your purchase is made.

Alaska Native women make some of the most intricately woven baskets in the world. Materials used for the baskets include beachgrass, birch bark and whale baleen. These items have become very popular over the years and command a high price, some selling for several hundred dollars. They also make beaded slippers from seal skin and wolf hair. Unusual porcupine quill earrings are affordable and attractive.

There are two ways to ensure you're buying authentic goods. If an item was manufactured in Alaska, the tag features a polar bear and the words, "Made in Alaska." Authentic Native-made products show a silver hand with the designation "Native Handicraft."

Museum and major hotels have gift shops selling Alaskan products, ivory carvings, and the like. If you are visiting rural areas, don't buy from shops in larger communities until you've had a chance to investigate local offerings. Although opportunities to pick up bargains from the actual producers have declined markedly in recent years, it's occasionally possible to strike a good deal in the villages. If you find nothing in the villages that appeals to you, the stores in larger cities are likely to have what you're looking for.

Alaska is still sufficiently folksy for many of the most interesting places to shop to be "Mom and Pop" operations. Your best bet for finding such establishments is to wander slowly through whatever town you're in and take time to check even the most rundown looking stores. Ivory, Native crafts, novelties, and just about anything is available if you look hard enough.

Shopping Areas

The suburban shopping mall has come to Alaska's larger cities to stay. Smaller communities also are beginning to establish mini-malls of their own.

ANCHORAGE
Fourth Avenue is still the most popular place to shop, with a variety of stores. In recent years,

Arts & Crafts

Beautiful arts and crafts can be found throughout the state, with individual regions specializing in particular crafts and art forms – for example, birch bark baskets in the southeast, skin sewing in the Interior and ivory carving farther north. Browse in museum gift shops, most of which have an excellent range of goods, or ask locals what's available and where. Because of its size, Anchorage has a huge selection of items for sale. Among the specialist outlets are:

Oomingmak Musk Ox Producers' Co-op.
Exquisite garments hand-knit in traditional patterns by Eskimo villagers from the rare wool, *qiviut*, combed from the Arctic musk ox as he sheds each spring. A unique northern gift. For information and brochures, contact: Oomingmak Musk Ox Producers' Co-op, 604 H St., Anchorage, AK 99501, tel: (907) 272-9225.

Alaska Native Medical Center Includes a gift shop that specializes in native crafts and works of art. Excellent selection of beaded slippers, carvings, baskets and more. Open limited hours, so call first.
4315 Diplomacy Dr., Anchorage, AK 99508, tel: (907) 563-2662.

however, it seems that the majority have become souvenir shops, popular with tourists.
Anchorage Fifth Avenue Mall, 320 W. Fifth Ave., includes Nordstrom and J.C. Penney department stores, Eddie Bauer outdoor clothing and several specialty shops, including The Body Shop and the Gap.
Dimond Center, located at the corner of Dimond Boulevard and the Old Seward Highway in south Anchorage, is the largest mall in Alaska. Besides major department and chain stores there are a variety of smaller shops. An ice rink is located at the southern end, in addition to several fast-food restaurants and a multi-screen movie theater.
Northway Mall, on the Glenn Highway just northeast of downtown Anchorage, has a department store, chain grocery store and lots of smaller shops. Two large discount stores are located to the east of the mall, which is easily spotted as you drive into town from the north.

FAIRBANKS
The main downtown shopping district runs along Cushman Avenue.
Bentley Mall, on the corner of College Road and the Old Steese Highway, is Fairbanks' largest. That and other local malls were an outgrowth of the building boom of the mid-1970s.

Duty Free

Duty free goods are available in the International Terminal of Anchorage Airport for purchase by passengers embarking on flights to foreign destinations.

Sport

Participant Sports

See under the appropriate headings on pages 314–20 for operators and outfitters for the activity of your choice.

Hiking
Extensive hiking trips into Alaska's back country differ significantly from backpacking trips in most of the rest of the US and any trip should begin with a stop at one of the state's four Public Lands Information Centers. Although there are extensive hiking trails in various regions of the state, treks often will be more of an overland-navigation experience, which can be extremely rewarding.

Hikers should take precautions to avoid unfriendly encounters with bears, particularly the Alaska brown/grizzly bears which thrive throughout much of the state. Make a noise as you walk, keep campsites clean, keep food away from sleeping areas, and always travel with one or more companions. Statistically, the larger the group, the lower the chances of encountering a hostile bear.

If attacked by a bear, experts agree that the victim should roll over onto their stomach and play dead. Trying to run from a bear may incite a charging reflex. The best bet is to give bears as wide a berth as possible. Alaska is their domain.

Those going on extensive hikes in the Alaskan wilderness should leave an itinerary with the Alaska State Troopers or,

Canoeing/Kayaking

There is no better way to explore the Alaskan outdoors than in a lightweight craft you paddle yourself. Most rivers are navigable by canoe, at least to some extent, and there are enough whitewater thrills available for kayakers to last a lifetime.

Anyone setting out on an extensive canoe/kayak trip in Alaska should leave a detailed itinerary with the nearest Alaska State Trooper office. People who don't come out of the woods when expected are certainly a lot easier to find if the rescue agencies have some idea of where to start looking.

A particularly good canoeing experience is the Swanson River system of canoe trails near Soldotna on the Kenai Peninsula. Weekend adventures or 2-week expeditions are possible in this region, just a 3-hour drive from Anchorage. Prince William Sound also offers endless paddling opportunities but be aware that the weather can often be overcast and rainy. For more details on the Swanson River system, contact: Kenai National Wildlife Refuge, P.O. Box 2139, Soldotna, AK 99669; tel: (907) 262-7021.

when appropriate, at the headquarters of a national park.

Cycling

Hundreds of cyclists make long-distance trips by pedal power along Alaska's road system every year. These trips are often as much a test of the ruggedness of the bikes and riders as they are a pleasurable journey. Cyclists should be warned that in many places bike shoulders are narrow, and it is a long way between cities, even on the road system.

Anchorage and Fairbanks have elaborate networks of bike paths/jogging trails. These often are splendid, safe paths set well off the road. In summer they are used for biking and walking, in winter for skiing.

Diving

Recreational diving in Alaska is not for the faint-hearted as the waters are quite cold. Local divers prefer dry suits to the older, more common wet suits. Currents in salt water are treacherous. Inquire locally before undertaking any dives.

Once underwater, the cold northern seas offer much. The water is clear, except near the mouths of major, silt-laden rivers. Seafood can be harvested while diving, to be enjoyed once you're on land.

Few recreational divers go diving in freshwater in Alaska. Major rivers, usually heavily laden with silt from headwater glaciers, should be avoided by divers.

Several companies have opened dive shops lately in Craig, Sitka, Ketchikan, Juneau, Kodiak, in the Prince William Sound area, and on the Kenai Peninsula. They offer guided dives, along with opportunities to dive with Stellar sea lions and to see fresh- and salt-water fish.

Fishing

The number of people who have long dreamed of fishing Alaska's pristine waters for massive king salmon, leaping trout, and wily northern pike must surely be in the millions. All those fish are there, and more. But they're not inclined to just leap in your boat. Prime fishing takes a little bit of planning and a few logistics.

Most roadside streams and lakes experience more fishing pressure than they can naturally stand. However, you don't always have to mount a major expedition to find good fishing.

Streams that cross the various roads in the state will be heavily fished near the highway. A short walk upstream, or down, should put you in all-but-unfished territory. The easiest way to calculate the necessary walking distance is to walk until there are no more footprints visible at stream side. There are exceptions to this rule, particularly in streams with heavy runs of salmon, but if trout or grayling are your quarry, hiking up or down a clear stream rarely fails.

Those wishing to catch a monstrous salmon or halibut would do well to enlist the services of a fishing guide. Guide services are located near most of the major fisheries. Rates typically are $100 a day or more per person but should provide more adventure than most anglers can imagine. Your best bet for salmon fishing with guides is on the Kenai River near Soldotna, in the Matanuska Valley or on a fly-out trip from Fairbanks or Anchorage to a remote lodge or camp. The king salmon and red salmon fisheries in the area are famed throughout the world.

Fishing licenses are available at almost all sporting goods stores, most variety stores and at several grocery stores. Anyone of 16 years or older must have a fishing license in their possession when angling on Alaskan waters.

Halibut fishermen flock to Homer and Seward every year for the opportunity to latch on to a bottom fish that can weigh 300 lbs (136 kg) or more. Several fish of 100–200 lbs (45–90 kg) are caught every year by charter boats operating from the Homer Spit. Again, about $100 buys a day's fishing per person.

Write Public Communications, Alaska Department of Fish & Game, Licensing Section, P.O. Box 25526, Juneau, Alaska 99802, tel: (907) 465-2376 for information.

In recent years, a rash of first-class fishing resorts has developed in many areas of the state. These are usually in remote areas, and involve flying in via floatplane. For those who have the $2,000 or more per person for a week's fishing, these offer an unforgettable experience.

Golf

While golf in Alaska may never be as popular a draw as it is for destinations such as Hawaii, there are a number of courses in Anchorage and Fairbanks, as well as ones in Wasilla, Palmer, Homer and Juneau.

The three most popular public courses are in Anchorage: Moose Run, the state's oldest course, owned by the Army; Eagleglen, considered by many to be the best in the state; and the Anchorage Golf Course.

Golf tournaments in Alaska range from the serious to the hilarious, such as Nome's Bering Sea Ice Golf Classic, an annual fund-raising event played in March on a 6-hole course on the frozen Bering Sea, or Kodiak's par-70, one-hole spring contest which is held on the side of 1,400-ft (430-meter) Pillar Mountain.

Hunting

Citizens of countries other than the United States must enlist the services of a licensed hunting guide for hunting any big game animal in the state. Guided hunts typically cost from $2,000 for a single-species hunt to $10,000 or more for

particular high-quality or multi-species hunts. A typical $2,000 hunt buys a few days of hunting caribou. The $10,000 might buy two to three weeks of hunting from several lodges or camps.

A complete list of registered and master guides is available for $5 from: Department of Commerce and Economic Development, Division of Occupational Licensing, Big Game Commercial Services Board, P.O. Box 11806, Juneau, AK 99811-0806, tel: (907) 465-2534.

US residents of states other than Alaska may hunt big game without a guide, except for brown/grizzly bear, mountain goat and Dall sheep. For these animals, non-Alaska residents and US citizens must engage a guide or be accompanied by a family member – only father, mother, sister, brother, son or daughter qualify – who is a resident of Alaska.

Regulations affecting hunting areas, bag limits, and methods and means are extremely complex and vary from region to region around Alaska. To get a license and copies of the hunting regulations write to: Alaska Department of Fish and Game, Licensing Section, P.O. Box 25525, Juneau, AK 99802, tel: (907) 465-2376.

Study the regulations carefully before hunting. If in doubt about any regulation, inquire locally with the Alaska Department of Fish and Game.

Licence & Tag Fees: tel: (907) 465-2376 for current charges.

Skiing

Both downhill and cross-country skiing are popular in Alaska from November through May. There are trails for cross-country skiing throughout the state and several areas have developed ski facilities, including Juneau, Anchorage, Palmer and Fairbanks.

The state's largest ski area is Alyeska, located 40 miles (65 km) southeast of Anchorage in Girdwood. The resort offers 2,500 vertical feet (762 meters) of skiing, including, on occasion, night skiing. The resort has added a high-speed aerial tram capable of carrying 60 passengers at a time, and the 307-room Westin Alyeska Prince Hotel, with a swimming pool, restaurants, exercise facilities and meeting rooms.

Closer to Anchorage is Alpenglow at Arctic Valley, which also offers downhill skiing. Several parks in the Anchorage area are also popular for cross-country skiing, including Russian Jack Springs, Kincaid Park, Far North Bicentennial Park, Hillside Park and Chugach State Park.

In Juneau, alpine skiers head for Eaglecrest Ski Area on Douglas Island, 12 miles (19 km) from downtown Juneau. Facilities include two chair lifts and a day lodge.

Fairbanks offers a few privately-owned downhill areas, including Cleary Summit and Skiland.

Popular cross-country trails in town include the Creamers Field trail near downtown, Birch Hill Recreation area and those on the University of Alaska campus. Not far away is Chena Hot Springs Resort, which has trails as well as after-ski relaxation.

Spectator Sports

For those who like to watch rather than participate, there are a variety of sporting events ranging from dog sled racing to hockey to college baseball.

Baseball

Alaska has one of the most impressive semi-pro baseball leagues in the country. The Fairbanks Gold Panners, the Anchorage Glacier Pilots, the Anchorage Bucs, and the Kenai Peninsula Oilers are comprised of college players lured north by the long days and opportunity to play ball. Games are played in modest stadiums with double headers played late into the evening – without artifical light.

Prices are cheap. A few dollars gets you into the bleachers (the wooden seating area). Be sure to carry insect repellent, especially to games in the Fairbanks area, as well as a light jacket for cool evenings.

A good bet is the Midnight Sun Game in Fairbanks, which starts late at night on June 21, without lights, in celebration of the summer solstice.

Basketball
Probably the most-watched spectator sport in Alaska is high school basketball. Every community with seven or more students has its own school and enough players to field a team. Regional tournaments abound in late winter, with the state championship played out in Anchorage in March. Pick-up games and adult city league games also are popular, especially in rural areas.

The Great Alaska Shoot-Out, held the fourth weekend in November in Anchorage, attracts top-rate college teams from across the United States.

Hockey
Hockey teams from the University of Alaska-Fairbanks (the Nanooks) and the University of Alaska-Anchorage (the Seawolves) play between October and March against college teams from the rest of the U S. Call UAF for information, tel: (907) 474-6805.

The West Coast Hockey League's Anchorage Aces also play during the fall and winter, drawing rowdy crowds that take their hockey seriously. For information, tel: (907) 258-2237.

Further Reading

General

Alaska A to Z, Vernon Publications, 1993.
Alaska's Southeast: Touring the Inside Passage, by Sarah Eppenbach. Globe Pequot Press, 1991.
Alaska: A History of the 49th State, by Claus M. Naske and Herman E Slotnick. University of Oklahoma Press, 1987.
Alaska: Reflections on Land and Spirit, edited by Robert Hedin and Gary Holthaus. University of Arizona Press, 1989.
Alaskan Eskimos, by Wendell H. Oswalt. Chandler and Sharp, 1967.
Alaskans: Life on the Last Frontier, by Ron Strickland. Stackpole Books, 1992.
Arctic Dreams: Imagination and Desire in a Northern Landscape, by Barry Lopez. Charles Scribner's Sons, 1986.
Arctic Schoolteacher: Kulukak, Alaska, 1931–1933, by Abbie Morgan Madenwald. University of Oklahoma Press, 1992.
Art and Eskimo Power: The Life and Times of Alaskan Howard Rock, by Lael Morgan. Epicenter Press, 1988.
As Far As You Can Go Without a Passport: The View from the End of the Road, by Tom Bodett. Addison-Wesley, 1985.
Burning the Iceberg: The Alaskan Fisherman's Novel, by Whit Deschner. Eddie Tern Press, 1991.
Coming into the Country, by John McPhee. Farrar, Straus and Giroux, 1976.
Degrees of Disaster: Prince William Sound: How Nature Reels and Rebounds, by Jeff Wheelwright. Simon and Schuster, 1994.
Eskimo Legends, by Lela Kiana

Oman. Alaska Methodist University Press, 1975.
Going to Extremes, by Joe McGinnis. New American Library, 1980.
Iditarod Classics: Tales of the Trail Told by the Men and Women Who Race Across Alaska, by Lew Freedman. Epicenter Press, 1992.
Ipani Eskimos: A Cycle of Life in Nature, by James K. Wells. Alaska Methodist University Press, 1974.
Klondike Women: True Tales of the 1897–1898 Gold Rush, by Melanie J Mayer. Swallow Press, 1989.
Kobuk River People, by J. L. Giddings. University of Alaska Press, 1961.
Midnight Wilderness: Journeys in Alaska's Arctic National Wildlife Refuge, by Debbie S. Miller. Sierra Club Books, 1990.
Northern Lights: Tales of Alaska's Lighthouses and Their Keepers, by Shannon Lowry and Jeff Schultz. Stackpole Books, 1992.
Shadows on the Koyukuk: An Alaskan Native's Life Along the River, by Sidney Huntington. Alaska Northwest Books, 1993.
Stalking the Ice Dragon: An Alaskan Journey, by Susan Zwinger. University of Arizona Press, 1991.
The Alaska Almanac, Alaska Northwest Books.
The Alaska Highway in World War II, by K. S. Coates and W. R. Morrison. University of Oklahoma Press, 1992.
The Alaska Highway: An Insider's Guide, by Ron Dalby. Fulcrum Publishing, 1991.
The Eskimo Storyteller: Folktales from Noatak, Alaska, by Edwin S Hall, Jr. University of Tennessee Press, 1975.
The Eskimos of Bering Strait, 1650–1898, by Dorothy Jean Ray. University of Washington Press, 1975.
The Great Bear: Contemporary Writings on the Grizzly, edited by John A Murray. Alaska

Northwest Books, 1992.
The Last Light Breaking, by Nick Jans. Alaska Northwest Books, 1993.
The Wake of the Unseen Object: Among the Native Cultures of Bush Alaska, by Tom Kizzia. Henry Holt and Company, 1992.
To the Top of Denali: Climbing Adventures on North America's Highest Peak, by Bill Sherwonit. Alaska Northwest Books, 1990.
Travels in Alaska, by John Muir. Houghton Mifflin, 1979.
Two in the Far North, by Margaret E Murie. Alaska Northwest Books, 1978.

Other Insight Guides

The 190-title Insight Guides series covers every continent, marrying high-quality text with stunning photography as in the present book. A complementary series of more than 100 Insight Pocket Guides provides timed itineraries and recommendations from local experts and are designed for the reader with limited time.

Among other Insight titles which cover this part of the world are:

Insight Guide: US National Parks West provides full coverage, including striking photography and comprehensive chapters on all the main national parks in the western part of the United States, including Alaska and Hawaii.

Insight Guide: Canada focuses on this vast country and gives a real insight into the dramatic changes now taking place, from the Pacific-oriented west coast to francophone Quebec.

Insight Guide: Vancouver captures every aspect of this young city, cut off from the rest of Canada by the Rocky Mountains. From its wonderful Victorian architecture to its appeal to movie makers, everything you need to know about fast-changing Vancouver is here.

Insight Pocket Guide: British Columbia combines a series of full-day and half-day itineraries with personal recommendations from the author to produce a rigorously practical guide for the visitor passing through.

ART & PHOTO CREDITS

Alaska Division of Tourism 69, 130/131, 166B
Alaska Division of Tourism/Al Clough 71
Alaska Division of Tourism/John Hyde 268B
Brian and Cherry Alexander spine center, front flap bottom, 1, 38, 43, 111, 114B, 136, 138B, 168B, 240/241, 277, 302/303, 307, 308
Roy Bailet 147, 174/175, 224/225
Bruce Bernstein Collection 18, 19, 24, 32, 33, 206, 267
Maxine Cass 143, 208BR, 296
Julie Collins 60, 61, 306
Alex Demyan 85, 112B, 139
Lee Forster 301
Hara 8/9, 132, 172
Kim Heacox 88/89, 100/101, 120B, 129, 220, 233B
Holland America Westours, Inc. 127
Kyle Lochalsh 92, 118, 188/189, 202/203, 300B
Gary Lok 42
Mary Evans Picture Library 148
James McCann spine top, 64/65, 66, 75, 234B, 243, 247, 262R
Rick McIntyre front flap top, 6/7, 76R, 78, 79, 83, 93, 126, 230R, 231, 237, 298
National Maritime Museum Picture Library 117
Allan Seiden 58, 116, 123, 135, 208BL, 211, 212, 236, 286, 309
Bill Sherwonit 12/13, 76L, 80/81, 87, 91, 95, 96/97,

109, 152/153, 167, 180/181, 182, 183, 185, 186, 187, 191, 193, 195, 196R, 198B, 199, 201, 218, 235, 282, 297, 299
Jeff Shultz back flap top & bottom, back cover right & top right, 14, 48, 63, 70, 74, 77, 90, 94, 98/99, 108, 115, 121, 124/125, 173, 179, 204, 216/217, 221, 226, 251, 261, 265, 272/273, 275, 278, 279, 288, 291
Mark Skok 44/45, 62, 196L, 258/259
Tony Stone Worldwide 52/53, 219, 274, 294/295
Topham Picture Point 16/17, 30/31, 35, 86, 162B, 207, 210
University of Washington Library 22, 23, 27, 29, 36, 39, 40, 178B
Vautier-de-Nanxe 20, 34, 41, 169, 190, 200B, 205, 209, 242, 266, 281, 283, 289, 304, 305
Harry M. Walker back cover left, 10/11, 46/47, 49, 50, 51, 54, 55, 56, 57, 59, 67, 68, 82, 84, 102, 106/107, 113, 119, 122B, 133, 137, 140/141, 142, 144B, 145, 146B, 149, 156, 157, 159, 160, 161, 163, 164, 165, 170/171, 176, 177, 184B, 192, 194B, 197, 213, 222/223, 227, 230L, 232, 238, 239, 244, 245, 246L, 246R, 248, 249, 250, 252B, 254B, 255, 260, 262L, 263, 264B, 269, 270, 271, 280, 287, 290B
Angela White 37

Picture Spreads

72–73: clockwise from bottom left-hand corner: Rick McIntyre, Bill Sherwonit, Rick McIntyre, Alex Demyan, Rick McIntyre, Bill Sherwonit, Rick McIntyre, Rick McIntyre.
150–151: clockwise from bottom left-hand corner: Corbis-Bettmann/UPI, Corbis-Bettmann, Archive Photos, Corbis-Bettmann, Archive Photos, Archive Photos, Archive Photos.
214–215: clockwise from bottom left-hand corner: Harry M Walker, Harry M Walker, Harry M Walker, Harry M Walker, Bill Sherwonit, Bill Sherwonit, Harry M Walker.
256–257: all pictures by Brian and Cherry Alexander.
292–293: all pictures by Harry M Walker, except bottom right-hand corner (totem pole) Bill Sherwonit.

Map Production Colin Earl
© 2001 Apa Publications GmbH & Co. Verlag KG (Singapore branch)

INSIGHT GUIDE
alaska

Cartographic Editor **Zoë Goodwin**
Production **Mohammed Dar**
Design Consultant **Klaus Geisler**
Picture Research **Hilary Genin**

Index

Numbers in italics refer to photographs

A
C
D
E
F
G
H
I
J
a
b
d
e
f
g
h
i
j
k
l